FREE FRENCH SPITFIRE HERO

*This book is respectfully dedicated to the inspirational memory and
sacrifice of
Commandant René Mouchotte – Free French Spitfire hero.*

FREE FRENCH
SPITFIRE HERO

The Diaries of and Search for René Mouchotte

René Mouchotte DFC, CdeG

With Dilip Sarkar MBE, FRHistS and Jan Leeming

AIR WORLD

AIR WORLD

FREE FRENCH SPITFIRE HERO
The Diaries of and Search for René Mouchotte

First published in Great Britain in 1956 by Staples Press Limited as *The Mouchotte Diaries 1940–1943*, and, having been translated from the French by Philip John Stead, was edited by André Dezarrois. Originally published in France under the title *Les Carnets de René Mouchotte*.

This extended edition was published in 2022 by
Air World Books,
An imprint of
Pen & Sword Books Ltd,
Yorkshire – Philadelphia

ISBN 978 1 39904 027 3

Typeset by SJmagic DESIGN SERVICES, India.

Printed and bound in the UK by CPI Group (UK) Ltd.

Pen & Sword Books Ltd incorporates the imprints of Pen & Sword Archaeology, Air World Books, Atlas, Aviation, Battleground, Discovery, Family History, History, Maritime, Military, Naval, Politics, Social History, Transport, True Crime, Claymore Press, Frontline Books, Praetorian Press, Seaforth Publishing and White Owl

For a complete list of Pen & Sword titles please contact:

PEN & SWORD BOOKS LTD
47 Church Street, Barnsley, South Yorkshire, S70 2AS, UK.
E-mail: enquiries@pen-and-sword.co.uk
Website: www.pen-and-sword.co.uk

Or

PEN AND SWORD BOOKS,
1950 Lawrence Road, Havertown, PA 19083, USA
E-mail: Uspen-and-sword@casematepublishers.com
Website: www.penandswordbooks.com

Contents

Foreword

by Lord Peter Ricketts GCVO, GCMG

In July 2012, the magnificent ballroom of the British Ambassador's Residence in Paris was the setting for a very special – indeed unprecedented – ceremony. As the Ambassador, it was my privilege from time to time to present honours on behalf of Her Majesty the Queen to French citizens who had given outstanding service to the cause of UK-French relations. But on that warm July evening, with the French windows open on to the immaculate lawn, I was honoured to host an occasion which paid a long overdue British tribute to one of the greatest of the Free French fighter pilots of the Second World War.

The hero concerned was Commandant René Mouchotte and his family had come to the Residence almost 70 years after his death in combat in 1943 to receive the gallantry medals which he had been awarded but which he had never received. By good fortune, the then Chief of the Air Staff, Air Chief Marshal Sir Stephen Dalton, was also in Paris that day, and was able to present the Mouchotte family with René's Distinguished Flying Cross (DFC) and the Battle of Britain Clasp to the 1939-45 Star, awarded only to those who had taken part in the Battle of Britain.

Sir Stephen was also able to present the medals won by Colonel Henri Lafont to his family. It was fitting that the two families should be together. Mouchotte and Lafont were both young airmen on a base in Oran in June 1940 when France capitulated. Determined to escape and join the RAF, the two comrades made a hair-raising illegal flight to Gibraltar, then served together in the Battle of Britain in 615 Squadron, and later in the Free French squadrons. Lafont survived the war and went on to a distinguished career in the post-war French Air Force.

I shall never forget the emotion of being able to express to the Mouchotte and Lafont families what a debt of gratitude our nation owed to the extraordinary courage and devotion to duty of the two young men whose bravery was finally being honoured that evening. And this moving occasion was made possible by one person, Jan Leeming, who had pride of place at our little ceremony in the Residence. Rightly so, since it was Jan's tireless research work, and great gift for human relationships, which rescued René's epic story from the obscurity into which it had fallen.

I am delighted to contribute a brief word to introduce this important book, which serves two purposes. First, it makes available to a new generation of readers the vivid diary which René Mouchotte kept throughout his RAF service. Second, it presents in the Epilogue the remarkable story of Jan Leeming's 'search for René'.

The diaries are a breath-taking read. They have all the drama of a thriller combined with the immediacy and freshness which only a diary written in the heat of the moment can bring. René was quite clearly an exceptional pilot, and one with the stamina and mental strength to survive three years under the constant stress of front-line flying involving almost daily dogfights. He lost many close friends, some shot down in front of him. But he was more than a great pilot. He was a born leader, overcoming his early feelings of loneliness and his status as an outsider in the RAF to rise from a Flight Sergeant to commanding a Free French squadron and at times leading an entire Wing into combat. On top of that, he was deeply patriotic, a thoughtful and sensitive man who missed his mother deeply and spent much of his scarce free time worrying about her.

Although the Mouchotte diaries were published in French and English after the war, they have long been out of print. We owe it to Jan Leeming's commitment and resourcefulness that the full human story of René's heroic life and tragic death can now be told. Her Epilogue is a deeply moving account of years of patient work and some incredible pieces of luck. Along the way, she had help from many people, as she recounts. One of those was Ian Reed, then the Director of the Allied Air Forces Museum and Yorkshire Air Museum. It was he who discovered that the medals due to Mouchotte and Lafont had never been awarded, and we were happy to have Ian with us on that special July evening when that long-standing injustice was finally put right.

Jan has therefore done a great service in bringing back to life the memory of a remarkable Frenchman who served valiantly and made the ultimate sacrifice in the cause of freedom. His story reminds us of the deep ties which bind Britain and France. As he was escaping from Oran in 1940, Mouchotte mused on the future:

> I foresaw my success everywhere, my return to a France delivered from the oppressor. Why not? Is not success a question of will-power … and a bit of luck?

René Mouchotte's luck eventually luck ran out and he did not live to see France delivered from the oppressor. But thanks to Jan Leeming and historian Dilip Sarkar, his words live on to inspire us.

Lord Peter Ricketts GCVO, GCMG
British Ambassador to France, 2012–16

Preface
by Dilip Sarkar

After months of high-tension, Hitler at last flung the full force of his mighty Wehrmacht against the West on 10 May 1940. In just six blood-stained weeks, the unthinkable came to pass. In quick succession, the Netherlands, Luxembourg and Belgium fell, the British Expeditionary Force was ignominiously evacuated from the beaches of Dunkirk, and, on 22 June 1940, the French were humiliated when forced to sign an armistice at Compiègne – in the very railway carriage Germany had signed the surrender document in 1918.

Thereafter, German forces became an army of occupation in northern France, whilst Marshal Phillipe Pétain established a collaborationist regime in Vichy. In London, however, the French General Charles de Gaulle, a member of the French cabinet during the Fall of France, established a French government in exile, rejecting both the armistice and Pétain's Vichy government. On 18 June 1940, when all appeared hopeless, de Gaulle appealed via the BBC for free French servicemen to join him and continue the fight.

One of those who joined the ranks of the Free French forces was pilot René Mouchotte. Few first-hand accounts from Free French airmen have been made available in English, which is one reason why the story of Free French airmen remains comparatively unknown – unlike, say, that of the Poles, which is now a well-trodden path. The fact that the bibliography in English is comparatively limited, also makes these diaries of René Mouchotte precious and vibrant primary source material indeed. The diaries are written with depth and feeling, providing a unique insight into one man's war to free his homeland, from the cockpit of a Spitfire many thousands of feet above enemy-occupied France, and in them his story, including how he came to England in 1940, is well-told. Although killed in action just six days after his twenty-ninth birthday, Commandant Mouchotte has done history, and his Free French airmen comrades, a great service indeed.

Born to a wealthy family on 21 August 1914, Mouchotte joined the French Air Force in 1935, completing his statutory military service, becoming a reservist and resuming civilian life in January 1939. Recalled at the outbreak of war, he found himself serving as a flying instructor and then converting to twin-engine aircraft at Oran, Algeria. As described in his diaries, after the Armistice he escaped to the UK together with Henry Lafont and joined the RAF, flying Hurricanes with 615 Squadron at Northolt, shortly before the Battle of Britain's end.

On 11 October 1940, René flew his first operational sortie, an uneventful patrol, thereby qualifying for the coveted Battle of Britain Clasp to the 1939-45 Star. In so doing, he joined the twelve other Free French pilots whose names can also be found amongst those of Churchill's Few.

During the Battle of Britain, Polish and Czech squadrons performed well, one exceptionally so, and afterwards the process continued to concentrate free airmen from the occupied lands into squadrons comprising airmen from their own countries. Amongst these was 341 'Alsace' (Free French) Squadron, which Mouchotte was promoted to form and command at Turnhouse in January 1943. In due course, he would take the squadron south to join the Biggin Hill Wing. It was as part of this Wing that Commandant Mouchotte led 341 Squadron with distinction until his death in action on 27 August 1943. His was a keenly felt loss indeed.

The Mouchotte diaries were originally published in 1946. In this new edition certain appendices from that original version have been deleted and superseded by those appearing in this volume, bringing the story of René Mouchotte up to date.

Uniquely, the former BBC broadcaster Jan Leeming – arguably a national treasure – provides a deeply moving account, in the Epilogue, of her personal journey, her 'Search for René', resulting in what amounts to what my good friend Professor Bernard-Marie Dupont, coincidentally also a Frenchman, once described as a 'posthumous friendship'. This is powerful. That the story of this Free French Spitfire pilot, killed long ago, has so touched the heart of and moved someone who never met him in life, is extraordinary.

This is a prime example of the sacrifices of these airmen still having currency and the ability to move and inspire. It is especially fitting that Jan's connection was with a Frenchman, because hopefully this book, which has arisen from it, will inspire further interest in the wartime exploits of these brave Free French pilots – who, at least in the English language, would then not be quite as forgotten or side-lined as perhaps once they were.

Salut!

Dilip Sarkar MBE, FRHistS,
April 2022.

Acknowledgements

The authors would firstly like to thank the family of Commandant René Mouchotte. In particular, they extend their appreciation to Jacqueline Quentin Mouchotte, for sharing her unique insight regarding her brother's life with Jan Leeming, at the time a complete stranger, and Hubert de Lisle for his invaluable support of Jan's research over the years.

Martin Mace at Pen & Sword was, as ever, a great support, and the production team, as always, a pleasure to work with.

Jan Leeming would especially like to place on record personal appreciation to the following:

Janet Tootal BEM, who randomly chose René's name for me to sponsor from amongst the thirteen Free Frenchmen commemorated on the Christopher Foxley-Norris Wall at the Memorial to The Few – and who unknowingly started this incredible journey.

Group Captain Patrick Tootal OBE, DL, RAF (Ret'd), Honorary Secretary of the Battle of Britain Memorial Trust and Battle of Britain Fighter Association.

Wing Commander Andy Simpson RAFVR(T), a Trustee of the Battle of Britain Memorial Trust and who accompanied me to Biggin Hill, gaining access to much documentation.

Mark Chapman, whose father was wartime aircrew and therefore able to add that perspective to my understanding of René's life and times.

Colonel John Powell, through whom the RAF HQ in Gibraltar was renamed 'Mouchotte Buildings'.

Owen and Mireille Leeming, who often gave me bed and board in Paris, and kindly translated for me.

Simon Vosters, Archivist, Middlekerke Town Hall, Belgium.

Ian Reed, former Director of The Yorkshire Air Museum.

ACKNOWLEDGEMENTS

James Murray, who introduced René's story to the BBC SE Commissioning Editor.

Matthew Wheeler, who produced and edited the Mouchotte documentary most sensitively.

Colonel Seb Pollington, who so willingly helped with the Mouchotte filming.

Dilip Sarkar MBE, without whom …

The Mouchotte Diaries
1940–1943

Introduction
by André Dezarrois

I knew René Mouchotte as the son of a family with whom I was friendly. Some years before the Second World War, I remember, he was present, one day, when I drew on my memories of days as a fighter pilot in Guynemer's Wing (the 'Cigognes') to talk about flying. How the boy's huge, shining eyes opened wide when I told him about this famous squadron! Later, when he was called up for his military service, he came to me for help to train as a pilot. I encouraged him warmly and intervened on his behalf with our Air Ministry. By the time he had completed his conscript service his dream had come true: he could fly.

His mother, admiring despite her natural fears, gave him a little sports plane, and one can well imagine how he spent the time he had off from the family manufacturing business in which he worked. Thus, he was readier than most when the Air Force recalled us in 1939. I soon had a letter from him, full of indignation, begging me to intervene at Air H.Q. where I then was. They were keeping him in the rear! There were not enough planes, especially fighters, for the reservists. But René Mouchotte had made up his mind to fly while he awaited the posting to the forward area for which he never stopped applying. He managed to get himself appointed as an instructor. He did the job so well that the grim military administration would not release him. He was an instructor in the rear and an instructor he must remain!

I did my best. I sought to interest one of my friends, the great roaster of fighter combat, in Mouchotte's fate. He made no secret to me of the fact that trained instructors were more useful to him in flying schools than in the fighting zone, where so little flying was done! There were new pilots to train by the hundred. But I had his promise: Mouchotte should see action.

May 1940 came with the speed of catastrophe; our training units were transferred to Algeria. I was glad. Mouchotte had been saved from the despairing massacre in which three-quarters of our fighter pilots were lost. The *Diaries* tell the story of what became of him then, and of what he became. Written from day to day, never revised (the author died too soon), full of sketches, drawings, etc., the small dark notebooks record how a Frenchman determined to fight when the Vichy Government laid down their arms.

Outlawed by this same government, he made his way to England from North Africa and became a fighter pilot with the Royal Air Force during the Battle of Britain. He was rapidly recognized as a daring and skilful pilot, developed impressive powers of leadership and became an outstanding tactician in the handling of masses of fighter aircraft. He commanded a British fighter squadron and was leading the Biggin Hill fighter wing when he fell. The official details of his citations, his death and the recovery of his body are given in the appendices to this book.

After God and his country, the big, handsome lad, so reserved, so likeable, had only one love, his mother. She always encouraged him to do his duty and never had greater dignity than when the enemy occupied our soil. Her son got a very few letters through to her, and to me, and I quickly guessed the fine way in which he had chosen to fight, though he let his mother believe he was safe in London in some Free French office under General de Gaulle.

The truth was kept from her until the Liberation, when Mouchotte's great leaders and his comrades in arms, General Valin and Colonel Dupérier, revealed the destiny which had been reserved for the son she worshipped. He had been posted missing for a long time when she came to me and said, 'I cannot doubt any longer. I shall never see my son again on earth.' She handed me the closely-written diaries, some sketches, photographs, press cuttings, ribbons, medals, citations and a flying-log. 'Here is all I have left of him. Will you read it? You understood his nature so well and always advised and encouraged him. Will you publish it? Surely there is a lesson here for the young men of the country for which he gave all he had.'

'Have we the *right* to publish it?' I asked, later. Mouchotte had not written for publication. 'These pages are intended to be read only by me in some years' time,' he had written in the margin, as if to excuse their frank and confidential nature. Colonel Heurtaux, Guynemer's best friend, the great Resistance leader under whom I had the honour to serve, who had just returned from Germany's prisons and torture camps, gave me my answer: 'The diaries are not "literature". They contain love of country, the heart of a fighter pilot, a leader's soul. The sons of France need the nourishment they have to give,' he said.

In this spirit and with those scruples, the *Diaries* were published in France in 1949. I am happy to send them forth now in an English version, to be read by the people among whom he spent his valiant exile. A people he learned to understand and esteem, a great nation which, by its stubborn, heroic battle in the London sky from summer to autumn in 1940, saved not only its own independence but also the honour of the free peoples. He regarded many of them as his friends and some of them, I know, remember 'Commandant René'.

A. Dezarrois

Chapter 1

Oran, June 1940

June 17th, 1940

I have just heard the incredible news of the Capitulation on the radio. The thing is so inconceivable that you boggle at it, shattered, imagining all manner of things – a nightmare, a mistake, enemy propaganda – to try and efface the horrible reality. The wretched radio completely shattered our over-strained nerves by sounding forth a ringing *Marseillaise*, the last call of a France that yesterday was free.

I cannot remember ever feeling anything so intense and sad. I wanted to run, to show everyone I still had the strength and energy to go on fighting. France must always be France. Her heart still beats in spite of those who want to kill her without letting her struggle. I was possessed by a huge disgust for the twenty years since 1918, when our politicians showed the world their squabbling and incapacity.

Today is the reckoning for them. Why did our elders fight if not for honour and peace? Yet from 1919 onwards steps were taken to see that the 'last-war soldiers' had no right to a voice in the councils of the nation. The embarrassing folk who had died a thousand deaths for four years to keep their native land free were thrust aside. How could they have foreseen such sabotage of their victory?

Four o'clock

It isn't possible. Our spirit is coming back. France can't be beaten like this, even if she has been the victim of saboteurs and traitors. Thank God there are *active* men who still have faith and courage. Many will arise to revive the spirits who fail at the sight of shameful examples …

North Africa will break away from metropolitan France. Armed, she will stand firm. What will be the terms of the Armistice they have announced? Who can we believe now? They seem to be using Marshal Pétain, that living legend, as a banner. He was appealed to when the situation was obviously desperate. Is what he is going to tell us to do what his French heart really implores him to say?

June 18th

France surrenders: her army, her navy, her air forces. General Noguès has just issued a rousing appeal to the troops in North Africa. A little hope. No other news. I haven't much faith. What will happen to England?

June 19th

I haven't been in action yet. Not because I haven't the skill; I have enough flying hours. Others with less have been fighting since September. Nor because I'm in love with being grounded; I've put in three applications to go, which resulted in my being posted – after five months of war – to the course of higher training for instructors. I've been an instructor. Impossible to get out of the toils. Yet I have got something out of it: *my pupils have taught me to fly.* Then Avord was bombed. Everything destroyed. We moved to a *château.* Night and day we hunted intangible parachutists.

Guérin and I received orders to go back to Algeria. At Marseille we learned that we were being posted to Algiers as instructors on twin-engined machines. The end of our hopes of going to the front on fighters. We were furious.

We decided to risk it. After all, there was a war on. The only fighter-instruction unit in North Africa was at Oran, the fighter springboard. We had to pass out there to make our dream come true. Without tampering too much with our posting orders (we could use our colonel's name: Avord was no more), after many verbal assertions, the Marseille area commander sent us off to Oran. What a day that was! We were no longer instructors. But what sort of a welcome awaited us in Oran where we were not expected? For once the breakdown of the French staff was on our side. Not only did Oran accept us when we landed as fighter pilots in training but Algiers never claimed us.

Yet it was written that we should not fly.

June 20th

So North Africa is not putting up a fight. But why do so many planes from France crowd our aerodrome? There are a thousand today, jammed wing to wing. Some take off for the south, others land direct from France, some vainglorious, some damaged, to take shelter. Or have they had orders to go far away to Southern Tunisia to be put out of action?

Our squadron leader has just sent for us to appeal to our sense of discipline and resignation. How very wretched the man was! It was hard for him to find words to express what he didn't believe. We sensed an appeal in his eyes, like hope. Perhaps I am not the only one who is thinking of a different future than the one they are preparing for us.

I mean to go to England. Since my country has rejected me as a combatant, I will fight for her in spite of her and without her.

I have just been to see Colonel de Fond-Lamotte. He is a tough last-war veteran with thirty-two wounds, twenty-seven of which could have killed him. 'Steel-all-through' is his nickname, because of the platinum 'extras' skilful surgeons have fitted into his body to replace broken bones. He always volunteers for dangerous missions and still flies, despite his age.

I was sure he would see me and understand. I found him in front of a hangar.

'We must clear out, my boy, and I'm taking those with guts.'

'But where to, Colonel?'

'Come and look at the map with me.'

I was unlucky; two majors came up to talk to him. The three of them went away, leaving me alone and disappointed.

Charles Guérin came to me, too, to confide that he wanted to go. I am glad he shares my feelings. Damn you, Charley, you and I were born to follow one another. We swore not to escape without each other.

A succession of news items from France, each more worrying than the last. And my poor dear little mother, always so uneasy about your son, what dreadful ordeals are you going through at such a time? Should I succeed if I tried to rejoin her? Won't France become a second Czecho-Slovakia, her young people mobilized to work in German camps and factories? What a dilemma.

My poor little mother, how I hate these savages. The thought that they might touch a hair of your head makes my blood boil. I have a calm, mild nature but I have not been myself for over a week. I dream only of fighting, of shooting down some of these Boche vermin. *I see red*, as they say; my life no longer matters to me. Only on the day when I kill my first Boche shall I be able to congratulate myself that I have followed my destiny.

I have made up my mind. I am going to England, or Malta, or Egypt; I don't know when, where or how, but I shall never contemplate remaining under the orders of Franco-Boche authority. Maybe in the future we shall know the truth about these painful days we live in. I want to be one of those who will chastise the men responsible for this war, for justice will inevitably be done. That same harsh justice will punish those who have now surrendered France while she could still fight, who abase themselves before the invader, and hand over, despite itself, the nation which was entrusted to them. The propaganda is filtering through even here; many are already turning their backs on England, their former ally, to blame her for the catastrophe. That is enough about that. It hurts too much. *I've got to get away*.

When I woke this morning, I learned of a plane escaping with three men on board. Yesterday two succeeded in getting away. The Commanding Officer at Oran has decided to stop any further attempts. A Germano-Italian Commission is arriving in a few days. The clauses of the Armistice will have to be respected. The Government has given strict orders that no unit of the naval and air fleets shall go to England. Fear of responsibility? Fear of reprisals? Confusion? Whatever the reason, nothing will excuse the draconian measures that are being taken to prevent Frenchmen avenging their country. I have been back to see Colonel de Fond-Lamotte. He is no longer in command of the station. Significant. Colonel Rougevin-Baville has replaced him. He seems even more respectful towards orders received.

I met old 'Steel-all-through' in the corridor.

'Excuse me, Colonel – '

He took a good look at me, then, without a word, turned his back on me and went into his office. It was enough. I understood. Poor man.

June 28th

One day after another. We do nothing. Flying is forbidden. I feel myself more and more a prisoner. The multitude of ultra-modern aircraft spread over the aerodrome looks more like theatrical scenery than the real thing. Charles and I wander about on our own looking for the slightest loophole. There was an unsuccessful attempt this morning: a Bloch 174 bomber, piloted by two youngsters, unluckily crashed while taking off. The imprudent ones were unhurt. It was the first time they had flown that type of aircraft. The Commanding Officer has gone crazy. He is having the petrol tanks drained, the magnetos removed and the planes locked wing to wing. The ones who escape now will be pretty crafty characters.

Chapter 2

The Flight of the Goéland

June 29th, 1940

Things are happening fast. Charles and I have decided to go today or tomorrow, for the mechanics are busy draining the petrol from the tanks. We have considered several plans. It would be possible to get to Dakar either by stealing a car or by train. Poles are leaving there for England and it would not be difficult, with their complicity, to get Polish uniform. We settled on another scheme: to escape by plane to Gibraltar or Egypt. An inoffensive Goéland, perfectly camouflaged, bang in the middle of the landing-ground, seems to be inviting us to escape.

Guérin knows several pilots who also want to get away. I am afraid that if there are too many of us, we shall be risking failure. Our plan is beginning to get even more delicate because I have brought two new recruits to our little group. We have therefore decided, working together, to go in two Goélands, each carrying six men.

Every hour that passes brings new problems. Our objective is settled: Gibraltar. It is the nearest point (about 475 kilometres). We shall have to economize fuel, not being sure of finding full tanks, and we shall consider ourselves lucky if we have enough to reach the Rock (the range of our plane is about 1,200 kilometres).

Will there be an aerodrome to receive us? A transport plane can't land on a pocket handkerchief. But we have resolved to come down in the sea if necessary; that won't stop us. The awkward bit is undoubtedly our getting away from Oran.

The aerodrome looks as if it is under siege. Each plane is guarded by day by an armed sentry. Mechanics are busy draining petrol. Others are working on the batteries and even dismantling propellers. The landing-ground and the camp have been invaded by armed men. Finally, they have taken care to barricade the armoury windows.

How slowly the hours of this June 29th, 1940, are flying! 11 a.m. Shall we be gone tonight? I never cease mingling the thought of my mother with the act I am about to perform. I do not intend making the slightest modification of what I believe to be my duty but I cannot help thinking that my decision will cause many a tear to the mother I shall not see for months, perhaps for years. My other comrades will be demobilized; soon they will return to France. They will help their families to bear the sufferings of the Occupation.

What is my duty? To give moral and material help to those I love or attempt a dubious adventure to satisfy an idea of vengeance? Should I be of more use with them or in a fighter? I am not ignorant of my mother's poor health and weak heart. I close my eyes in despair. What would she advise me to do? Would she speak to me as a mother or as a Frenchwoman, if she were at my side? Once I am over there, I shall not even be able to write to her ... When she no longer has news of me, will she think I am a prisoner, or sick, or dead, perhaps? Poor mother, I'm trying to think how I can let you know. A good friend I knew at Istres, in whom I have great faith, has promised me that when he returns to France, he will write to you.

I simply cannot understand our leaders' mentality. We see some dumbfounding things here: it is a question whether the men who command us today still deserve the name of French officers.

A meeting at one o'clock of those who have agreed to escape with Charles and me. My room looks like a headquarters. On the table I have spread a map. We count up and there are fourteen of us! We do not conceal from ourselves that our attempt is a pretty risky one. If we have the luck to get away, we shall be the only ones who have done so. Yesterday's two unfortunates are in prison at this moment, waiting to be sentenced by court-martial for stealing an aircraft and desertion. Shall we be luckier? Whatever happens we must try, cost what it may, and not let ourselves be influenced by the obstacles that are bound to stand in our way.

We have decided to take two Goélands and a little Simoun. Charley will pilot one Goéland and I the other. We are allotting five passengers to each. Later we will consider the possibility of flying together but it is settled that each crew shall form a unit independent of the other; thus, if one party is caught, the chances of the other will not be prejudiced.

Fayolle will pilot the Simoun, with Sturm. An admiral's son, he is also the grandson of the famous General Fayolle. In my plane I am taking two sous-lieutenants, an infantryman and a cavalryman, deserters some days old who escaped from France in the bunkers of a collier after dodging endless pursuits and stealing a car to reach a port. In his, Guérin will have comrades who are already in his own squadron, whom he has incited to escape with him.

When shall we go? Another meeting at five o'clock.

Each of us has an individual task to fulfil both on his own account and for the team: to see which way the wind is, to find out what the latest measures against escapes are, to be sure of the help of trustworthy friends. As pilot, I have to see to the plane, its position, its working condition, how much fuel it has. One point worries me: starting the engine. A transport plane doesn't start as quickly or as easily as a passenger plane; it is essential to warm up the engines for at least ten minutes before taking off. But there is no question of us doing that. We shall press on. I therefore had to find out as much as I could about starting the engines. Not much success; the mechanics I asked, fighter specialists, did not know the Goéland engine. Impossible to go near the one selected for me. How can I find out if it has petrol?

One of my friends confesses that he has been to see the British Consul in Oran this week. He came back completely discouraged. Far from approving, they painted a grim picture of the existence awaiting him if he succeeded in reaching England. The poor fellow therefore has no further desire to desert. He nevertheless thought it might be useful to let me know that England may not be in the least what we imagine and that it is very likely we may be sent back to France. As deserters our fate would be sealed. Unless they kept us in a prison camp, another charming prospect. It is probable that if we are accepted, we shall be left penniless, that we shall not be employed as pilots but used as infantry, etc. ...

On the other hand, he thought that by staying here he would soon be demobilized. I turned my back on him, not wanting to waste any more valuable time. What good could his suppositions do me? Haven't I decided to go? Besides, I feel I shall succeed. I must succeed.

I have just heard that our Colonel is calling all the squadrons together at 4.30 to talk to them. I cannot help seeing a connection between this speech and yesterday's abortive escape. Is he going to threaten us and tell us of the latest measures against these untimely flights? A fine time for us ...

I met Guérin looking dejected. His Goéland had been moved. They have towed it across the landing-ground into a hangar and shut it in. So, everything is going against us. How shall we manage to overcome these obstacles? It is lucky, though, that the police have not yet invaded the aerodrome, as an officer gave us to expect yesterday. I went with Charles to look at *my* Goéland. It is still slumbering peacefully there in the middle of the landing-ground. As long as it has petrol … How can I find out?

I have decided to take Guérin with me. One of our comrades will give up his place to him. After all, it was we who took the initiative in the escape. It is only fair that he should be in on it. As for the little Simoun, Fayolle has contrived to approach it without being noticed and is radiant with joy. The plane has a full supply of petrol and oil; it asks for nothing better than to leave this unhospitable land.

I have just learned that the training unit is being disbanded in a few days' time. The pilots are being sent to the mountainous region in the south to form youth camps. The Hitler regime is beginning. I must get away, the sooner the better.

We have to go and hear the Colonel's speech. Surely it will be about the last untimely departures of planes from Oran. We shall see. We are somewhat uneasy. Have they taken new measures to prevent any attempt at escape? Or are they, on the other hand, trying to appeal to our emotions? The sudden *contretemps* is holding up our preparations. Have our superiors got wind of our project? Why did they move the first Goéland from the landing-ground? I am going to have a look at the other. It is still in the same place.

Four o'clock. I have been noting down on paper all the information, fugitive as it is, about the engines and how to start them, details obtained for me by an excellent mechanic whose silence has been assured. As for the state of the fuel, I shall try and get to the Goéland at nightfall. There is no question (on account of the speech) of leaving tonight. Tomorrow morning, which gives us more time to prepare.

The Colonel, as we expected, began by talking discipline and good example. Without excessively bemoaning the ordeal of France, he tried to give us a glimpse of the France of tomorrow, built by the resigned youth of the nation, full of prudent courage: work, discipline! He made a savage attack on stupid 'quixotry', the lamentable and cowardly attempts to escape, the work of idle adventurers seeking to avoid the hard work before them. They will go before a court martial charged with stealing military material and with desertion... They will return to France only to be shot; their families and their descendants will suffer the shame of one of their kin being a traitor to his native land, etc. …

Will all this discourage certain of our comrades? I suspect some of them of joining our group in an imitative spirit or to boast about having done so, being sure that the attempt will not come off. I admit that so far everything is against us and only boldness can help. The test is hard, our plan flimsy, our chances slender ... Guérin met me as I was getting ready to go and examine the tanks of my Goéland. He had come from it and, according to him, had not been seen. He was radiant. It is full up with petrol and oil. Nothing to fear in that respect.

11 p.m. The time for action is near. Fifteen of us gathered in my very small room, talking in low voices by candle-light. We looked like real conspirators. We were divided into three teams: the Goéland team, six; the Simoun team, two. The rest are going to try and get away in an American bomber which is not far from our Goéland. The question before us was whether we should embark tonight or tomorrow morning. Nearly everyone chose tomorrow. I succeeded in convincing my team that it would be wiser to make the attempt tonight. Guérin agrees with me. We are getting ready.

I wrote a letter to a good friend who is staying behind. I charged him to look after my baggage and reminded him once more of his promise to reassure my mother. Poor mother ...

We have the password, the position of all the sentries, the time of the rounds, etc. On the landing-ground two cars with headlights are plying to and fro in front of the hangars. It will have to be done quickly. We have three revolvers; one never knows, and we are resolved on doing everything to succeed. The die is cast. We count up for the last time. We are off ...

The darkness was far from complete. A very light sky. We went forward cautiously, in Indian file, avoiding stones. Five minutes later we entered a danger zone. No more trees, nothing to hide behind, sentries near. We had to cross the embankment of a railway which ran through the camp; this was the difficult bit. Having conferred in undertones, we decided to cross it as quickly and as quietly as possible. The first man went, then the second. My turn. What a racket! The stones clattered noisily; we must have been heard within a 200-metre radius. The moon was shining.

Damnation! A sentry's 'Who goes there?' burst forth less than 20 metres from us. We were flat on our stomachs, behind a bush. One of us, still on the slope, sent stones cascading. We held our breath ... The sentry was a native; I gathered that from his accent. We remained there, motionless. The sentry kept equally still. He must have been more scared than we were. Would it be better to spring on him and disarm him, or try to hold him in parley? Five mortal minutes passed. Suddenly more pebbles fell. A metallic noise accompanied them. The sentry had drawn back the bolt of his rifle. We could not stay where we were; he was quite capable of opening fire on us. Just as I was getting to my feet, I heard 'Paris!' – the password, spoken by Guérin as he advanced.

'Well, everything all right in this sector? Nothing to report? This is the security patrol. Fine, you're doing a good job.'

His voice may have trembled a little with the recent excitement. During this time, in twos and in step, we passed behind them and made for the hangars.

'Now go and keep a lookout at the other end; there's no sentry down there. Goodnight!'

The trick worked. Revolver still in hand, Guérin rejoined our little group, hidden in the shelter of a hangar. We were still nervous; there were officers on rounds everywhere tonight and the man might tell them his story.

The light vehicles came and went quietly on the landing-ground. From time to time the headlights swept the vast field with its hundreds of sleeping planes. Then we heard the sound of the engines die away while from the opposite direction the sound of engines grew louder.

We had to cross this zone and get to our Goéland. We waited for another car to pass and then moved, praying that no sentry might spot us. We were walking exposed and no one could doubt our intentions. We went fast; despite our care the cement rang under our feet. At last, there was earth and the first planes' shadows. We went on. The car behind us appeared again, advancing slowly … Should we find our plane easily in the dark? At last, we had it before us. Incredibly happy, we climbed in and hastily drew the curtains over all the windows and locked the door. Each in a seat, we tried to get some sleep; unsuccessfully because we all felt too nervous.

Only a quarter of an hour after our arrival came the first alarm. The sound of footsteps. We all lay down flat and held our breath. The sounds came closer. This was it. Voices whispering breathlessly. Our hearts beat an extra pulse. The door was roughly and insistently shaken. Then there was calm again; the footsteps went away. I peeped out and saw three shadows disappearing, carrying suitcases … We were not the only ones intending to depart. Half an hour later and *we* should have found the door locked.

We settled down once more. I shut my eyes. Where should I be tomorrow at this time? Too late to draw back now. Anyway, I didn't want to draw back. Each minute that passed brought me nearer to my departure into exile, a departure considered and willed, the consequences of which I had taken into account. Tomorrow I should be on English soil or I should be dead.

The quarter hours passed slowly. We had fixed the time of departure at 4.30 and it was now 1.0, I wanted to sleep. I could still hear the car engines on the landing-ground. From time to time one of them came into the midst of the planes; the headlights swept our machine, lingered an instant, then went to seek elsewhere. I could not stop myself mentally retracing the events, as rapid as they were tragic, which had thrown into confusion and annihilated thousands of lives in the space of a few days. What I was about to attempt this morning, how many other rational beings were not attempting or dreaming of attempting? If I had stayed behind, should I have been able to stand the incessant vexations, obeying each day the orders the Boche gave to humiliate us, witness to the shame and cowardice of a government continually flaunting its arrogance?

Eventually seeing France being engulfed little by little beneath the Nazi dust, and watching all this while trying not to react? I could not have done it. The concentration camp awaited me. God, how I should have loved to go to sleep and not wake up till I was in Gibraltar! I felt absurdly apprehensive. I should soon have need of all my resources. Five lives and mine as well to transport far away. As in the dentist's waiting-room, I longed for the door to open quickly and be done with it. I looked at my watch every two minutes. Once more the car left the hangars and came close. Once more we came out of our torpor to fling ourselves face down while one stayed by the door with his revolver and I knelt down between two seats to watch, lifting the corner of a curtain. This time the alarm looked more serious, for after sweeping us with its headlights the car drew up barely 30 metres away. Two shadowy figures got out and same towards us. I gave the alarm. All were stiller than stones. I could not stop my heart dancing a mad saraband; I felt its beating must be audible. The shadows were certainly heading for us. There was no doubt about it. We were caught.

Our plan had been discovered. Flight? Too late. Defend ourselves? Six against two, we should easily overcome them and then take off in the darkness … Now they were at the door. They knocked. As long as they didn't think of climbing on the wings; the emergency door beside me was not fastened. They shook the door, but it would not open.

'Open up in there!'

We held our breath. Suddenly the beam of an electric torch lit up the interior of the Goéland, through the uncurtained window of the entry. Catastrophe … Overlooking the scene, I saw the beam stop on Sorret's arm and wristwatch. This time the door was shaken roughly and – blessing! – we heard: 'Open up. It's Georges.' It was the friend who had given us the password. He had changed the sentries and had come to give us the latest tips. We could have embraced him in our joy. Delightful to stretch one's legs and jump down to the ground for a few moments. Five minutes later we got in again and shot the bolts of our prison. In an hour it would be nearly time to take off. We should need good visibility; fifty planes were drawn up in no particular order around us and it would be preferable not to run foul of them. In case of accident, we had planned to make for the other end of the aerodrome, where one of our friends was in command of the guard.

Four o'clock. I got out my bit of paper and, with my fingers over the torch, let through just enough light to spell out what I should soon have to do. The car continued its tireless exercise; twice more it came dangerously near our machine. ... One of us managed to get to sleep and his regular snores created a sense of security in the cabin. Idiotic!

4.30. The day had not yet broken. A faint light was barely outlined down in the east. Impossible to go yet; it would be stupid to risk an accident by being over-precipitate. We must, however, be off about five o'clock, the hour at which the patrols were relieved and the watch on the landing-ground became extremely strict. We had no intention of finishing the war in prison. We would leave at 5.5, but we must be able to see to take off. Behind me they were protesting that the time had been fixed for 4.30, the sooner the better. We settled on 4.45, time to get the engines going, which would be perfect. I noticed that as the line of the horizon grew lighter the hangars, which had stood out clearly in the darkness, seemed to be becoming indistinct, so that the contours were barely visible. Mist. We really were in luck. What did it matter how we did it, the great thing was to get away. That was our sole immediate objective. Afterwards, we would see. I got into the pilot's seat. Guérin sat beside me. Off we go!

We thought for a moment. Two engines had to be started. If one were recalcitrant, we were lost. Ah, how gratefully I pay homage to Renault Motors! Petrol, switches, magneto. ... The starboard engine started. I opened the throttle in order to pull up the flaps, while Guérin braked the port wheel to swing the plane towards the take-off. During this time the port engine started. The terrible noise must have been ear-splitting in the darkness. We learned later that the aerodrome car rushed towards us. The navigation lights blinded us.

Without a second's delay I opened the throttles and started the take-off, my two hands clasped round the stick. The engines had to be warmed up for a quarter of an hour before taking off. Too bad. We should see. Fifteen seconds had been enough to start them. Alas! Guérin had braked too much to the left ... A bad direction. The speed increased. I saw the shapes of several bombers in front of us, a little to the left, we just scraped past. And the plane was still moving. How long it took! In the dark it is hard to judge. Even so, the engines did not seem to be pulling. What was the matter?

The landing-ground was enormous but I had the impression we were already at the other end. I pulled the stick back timidly; the plane lifted but fell heavily. Yet it had to be done. I helped it again; we took off. Coming down again, the port wing tip touched down. What now? This was a calamity. I strove desperately with rudder-bar and stick, trying to relieve her. We were skirting the great salt lake of the Sebkra. She returned to the horizontal, but with great difficulty. Over my shoulder, Lafont caught the lever of the undercarriage and retracted it. That lightened the Goéland a little. I looked at the rate-of-climb indicator.

Hurrah! We were climbing. But what a take-off! I was sweating all over. I coarsened the pitch of my propellers. No change, or only a hundred revolutions less on the rev. counter. The plane gained altitude painfully. We circled over the Sebkra in the hope of seeing Fayolle's little Simoun appear. If only they could manage it! Then we headed for the sea. I had great difficulty in gaining altitude; each time my rate-of-climb indicator showed plus one or plus two, my air-speed indicator immediately dropped to 120. I got it up to 130, 135, but to do so I had to put the rate of climb at zero or minus a half. What was not working? The engines were going well. I tested the propeller pitch control. They answered well, but each time without much change on the rev. counter.

Suddenly I understood. Our plane had been visited by the gentry. Instead of emptying the petrol tanks, they had simply *put the propellers out of order*. This criminal act nearly cost us our lives. Our Goéland, loaded with six passengers, had taken off at coarse pitch when at fine pitch it would already have been a near thing. It was as if one had expected an overloaded car to start in top gear. How had we done it? A miracle! The darkness was less thick. Behind us the day was breaking slowly. Many little efforts got the plane up to 800 metres. A heavy mist hid the ground details. But we preferred to fly over the sea, the anti-aircraft batteries on the coast being wicked and numerous. Were we not deserters now? Deserters! That would have made me want to laugh, if my nerves had not been so strained. I went on gaining height, still very painfully. The cruising speed of the Goéland was 220 kilometres an hour. We were doing 120. Slower than a tourist machine. Anyway, the great thing was to reach Gibraltar.

My right hand went instinctively to the propeller pitch control. I came to the conclusion that the propellers were nearly fully feathered, that is to say, in the position of propellers turning at engine speed but without producing a useful effort: the plane became a glider. I could not bless Providence enough. How did we escape being smashed at the take-off? How did the machine, overloaded as it was, contrive to stay in the air when I had torn her off the ground at such impossibly low speed?

It really was a miracle. I tremble when I think of the frightful second when the wheels had left the ground and I felt the plane sink after the determined lift and then, despite my efforts, drag to port while I was tensely holding my stick and rudder-bar to starboard. The darkness made the thing more dramatic. I distinctly remember having a vision of crashing. Luckily, I had told little Lafont to stand behind us; his weight in the tail of the machine might have been fatal.

What a strange sensation that ascent into the night was! The sky was full of stars, in which we seemed to swim in unreality. My shirt was soaked, I was dazzled by the instrument panel light, with only my instruments to guide me: I acted more or less as an automaton, only my reflexes working for me. Then suddenly I roused out of my torpor. I saw the end of the immense salt lake of the Sebkra. Here was the sea. Our joy burst out at last and we all sang in chorus, howling as loud as we could, almost breaking our voices: 'Four o'clock in the morning, tomorrow already and the day is breaking!' If old Lyne Clevers had heard us singing one of her hits! Sorret told us that just as we left, he had seen through the window the aerodrome car coming full speed at us, headlights fixed fiercely on the fleeing bird. They saw a lovely take-off. …

As long as they hadn't sent any planes in pursuit. At the speed at which we were going they would soon have caught up with us. I would rather have landed in Spanish Morocco than have gone back. I looked at Guérin out of the corner of my eyes, seated next to me; he had his eyes closed, exhausted. I sent him to go and sleep in a seat at the back. I looked at the map. Heavens, how slowly the coast was passing! We were about 30 kilometres out to sea.

I preferred to take the short cut and leave the coast of Spanish Morocco well to port. The altimeter rose painfully. A layer of transparent mist covered the sea and the shore. I dared not think of fog. It would surely vanish when the sun was up.

I had the impression of living in a dream, a wonderful dream. So, destiny was on our side: all those obstacles overcome, that mad departure. We should soon be in Gibraltar. We should land without accident. I visualized our arrival in England, my battles as a fighter pilot. I foresaw my success everywhere, my return to a France delivered from the oppressor. Why not? Is not success a question of will-power … and a bit of luck? The take-off and the flight had proved that luck was with me; it would not abandon me. Nothing would stop me accomplishing what I had marked out for myself.

The sun was on the point of rising. To port we saw the great Tres Forcas peninsula.

Lafont wanted to take photographs. He asked Guérin to return to my side. Now the sun was rising. 'Smile please, gentlemen!' We turned round. Click! The snapshot was taken. After the crew, the passengers, then Spanish Morocco. What a souvenir, if the negatives were all right!

We had now been flying for over an hour. We flew horizontally, which gave me a speed of 130 kilometres, according to our air-speed indicator. Not much, but we were in no hurry. No one was expecting us! I was dreadfully hungry. We had climbed to 2,000 metres. I considered it useless to reach a higher ceiling. It had taken fifty laborious minutes to attain that altitude. Well, there we were, but alas I had other things to worry me. Far from vanishing, the mist had grown thick enough to hide the sea and the coasts of Africa beneath us altogether. I therefore kept faithfully to my course.

Only the Balearic Isles, very far to the north, were visible. It was a problem to know whether this thick compact white cloud went down to ground-level or whether, once we were down through it, we should have enough altitude to navigate. At present only the Balearics and a faint shadow of the Spanish coast served as landmarks. Never mind. We should see.

Another thing was rather alarming, too. My petrol gauges, instead of showing less, showed more! There even came a moment when the needle on the dial passed the 'full' and went back to 'empty'. Gauges out of order. At any moment I expected to hear the fatal splutter of the engines, then the silent descent, down through that accursed cotton cloud. … Then the open sea. … I smiled, not seeing myself swimming dozens of kilometres. What a grand splash we should make for the entertainment of the Spaniards! … 'The six French deserters, avid for heroic adventure, ended their epic wretchedly in a Spanish gaol.' But the engines were still going full blast.

My passengers were quiet enough. They did not guess the bizarre thoughts passing through my head. Perhaps they thought themselves on a regular Air France flight. I was thinking of my mother. If only she were aboard with me. I should be so much reassured then than by knowing she was in that hostile country. But I do not know that she would feel very reassured up here with me. …

We could not be far from Gibraltar now. I never stopped looking at the map. The Balearics were unmistakably north-north-east of us; ahead was mist. The same to port. If it had been clear we should have had the famous

Rock in sight long ago. In flying through the mist, we must not crash on it. Ten more minutes went by and suddenly I thought I could pick out, just ahead, cloud of a different kind. It no longer had that uniform, cottonish consistency but revealed deeper crevasses of less regular and darker colour. It might be that the sea stopped here. It could be the North African point of the Straits of Gibraltar. I had to make up my mind: the invisible Rock inspired mistrust. I turned about fifty degrees to starboard and we were on our way down. The delicate moment had come. If only I had made no error in my navigation! The cloud drew close. We were at only 900 metres. I slowed down the engines a little. An instinctive and useless action, but it would not do to neglect anything.

Six hundred metres … 500 … 450. We were in the cloud now. The bank was not too thick. But oh, miracle! Gibraltar, the magnificent Rock, rose up there before us, five or six kilometres away. It was planted there, its summit hidden in the clouds. We should have shouted 'Alleluia'.

The end was attained. Emotion choked me. We wanted to throw ourselves into each other's arms. But the surprise had been too sudden; our reaction was numbed. We were flying at about 250 metres above the waves. We were going in. To port I saw a destroyer, across whose course we were cutting. I thought it wise to show our friendly feelings by putting down my undercarriage and waggling my wings a little. Then, for greater security, I swung away slightly and left the ship well to port.

Only too clearly, I recalled the anti-British propaganda which had broken out in the Germano-French press as soon as the Armistice was signed. That campaign is still going on, incidentally, so much so that some people envisage the possibility of war between France and Great Britain. My measures of caution, if taken in a somewhat ironic spirit, were none the less excusable. I accentuated the waggling of my wings to show my markings clearly, for the Rock was getting close. We were less than 100 metres above sea level. I raised the engine speed to the maximum, which gave me 150 kilometres an hour. I was looking greedily at the celebrated and menacing Rock, for I knew its reputation for formidable defences.

We were very close now. We soon passed its huge spur. I had little time to examine it, which I regret. We flew parallel with the east flanks of the Rock. Huge cemented walls, almost vertical, sank into the sea, probably to make access on this side more difficult. We flew along the vast fortress at less than 100 metres. Suddenly it broke, as if split by a sword, and gave place to a level shore. This part of the peninsula is flat and only a few metres above sea level. I knew the Spanish frontier was close. Once over the wall, the frontier of the two countries was the first thing I looked for. I soon spotted it. It took the form of a line of barbed wire. To avoid it I had to turn steeply, and my sick Goéland was very heavy. I had not the slightest desire to die from a Spanish bullet.

So far, the English had given no indication that they were aggressive and I could disregard Spanish hostility. I turned timidly, but I felt a heavy, heavy machine. We were perhaps overloaded. However, the turn to port was made, steeply enough, and we passed just above the top of the wire. All was well, or at least so I thought, but Jimmy told me later that he had clearly heard machine-gun fire. Joy! Flying along the diabolical wire I saw a splendid racecourse with – stupefying! – a huge white 'T' indicating the direction of the wind and an immense white circle in the middle. Had they turned their race-course into an aerodrome just for our benefit? What a good augury! We did not hide our delight.

We continued the turn, hesitant and very timid, making a wide circle above the roads. I noticed I was losing more and more height and we scraped over the masts of a multitude of ships. My kite was not one of the most reassuring and I was not to be at my ease until shortly afterwards, when I had a good hot cup of tea in front of me. My wide turn had taken me well out and gave me time to regain 50 metres on the new direct course. If I fluffed the landing, should I have enough power to take off again? I approached the race-course, and from where I was it looked terribly tiny. I concentrated hard. I put my flaps down rather soon; I prefer it that way. But it made me lose altitude too fast.

A big burst from the engine; the plane was dragging; I was getting near the limit. I cut down the speed. In spite of my concentration on the landing, which went off very well, I noticed hundreds of English soldiers to right and left, running and waving wildly. But our eyes were also drawn to three or four French planes whose tricolour markings rejoiced our hearts. So, others had preceded us? There were people here to expect us and greet us. Our nerves relaxed. Cries of joy filled the plane, all the louder because the engines were running quietly. Once we touched down, I braked lightly at first, then increasing the pressure. The plane stopped in the white circle in the middle of the landing-ground. There is no doubt about it: the Goéland is a marvellous aircraft. M. Renault and his engineers are entitled to my eternal gratitude.

From habit, I turned to port. They were waving a little red flag there. As I taxi'd along I could not help being delighted by the exquisite sensation of being bounced by the slight shock of the wheels on the grass. Guérin pointed out a French airman on my right. I opened a panel. There were welcoming shouts of 'Cheerio!' coming towards us. I manoeuvred the plane into position and then, once the propellers had stopped, there was a rush to the door to see who would be first to set foot on the soil of Gibraltar. It made me forget to turn off the petrol, to turn off the switches, magnetos and main switch, to turn off the navigation lights, to close the circuits, to lock the controls; my flaps were left down. I rushed like my pals but, being the furthest forward, I was last out.

A crowd of soldiers surrounded us. There were handshakes, great smacks on the back. What big, kind fellows they were! They fought to offer us the first cigarette. There must have been fifty of them at least. One came forward with a notebook to write down our names. Another collected cameras. A third asked for our guns. They could not help smiling at the sight of the positive arsenal we pulled out of our pockets: revolvers of all types, pistols of every calibre, and I had a retrospective thought of the lovely scrap there would have been if anyone had caught us in Oran. We had all been resolved to sell our lives dearly rather than let ourselves be stupidly ensnared into finishing the war in a cell or in front of a firing squad.

Chapter 3

Gibraltar

July 3rd, 1940

Here we are, aboard a small ship which might at first sight pass for some sturdy, inoffensive cargo steamer but which, to us who are in her, turns out to be almost as heavily armed as a naval patrol vessel. Crammed with mines, it has six machine guns, two guns, and its hold is stuffed with ammunition. This is comforting when one considers the value of the bait the convoy offers to the enemy's unholy desires. We are sailing in a convoy of twenty-one ships which ours, the *Président Houduce*, is escorting, together with an English destroyer.

What a feeling of well-being I have as I lean on the poop-rail, fascinated by the water sliding along the hull! My heart is prey to uneasiness about the dark and uncertain future, but my body is relaxing lazily from an over-powerful effort. I am remembering. …

Once the formalities were over, our first need was breakfast. Kindly Tommies took us to the officers' mess, where we had a royal reception. We were so hungry that we postponed the indispensable wash. Our exhaustion and our plans were forgotten; we were nothing but poor creatures fascinated by the lavishly loaded table. Ah! We did not have to wait to satisfy our desires. Soft-boiled eggs, fried eggs, bacon, toast, jam, all in abundance. Never have I found these simple dishes so attractive.

One thing struck us, though it did not astonish us: the difference between the country we had just left and this one. In the former there was quietude akin to indifference, then the surprise of alarm, and lastly bewilderment, dejection and degrading submission. Here there were young men with open, smiling faces, sure of their strength, with confidence in their leaders, ardent, and able to find words of comfort for the friends who had sought them out.

The Mess President was quite young. He spoke a little French; our flight had aroused his enthusiasm. A car came for us. Destination? The Admiralty.

Our drive through the town attracted the attention of swarms of people. News of the arrival of a French aircraft had travelled as fast as a lighted train of gunpowder. Arms waved. We had to salute, smile back. France, after all, was still France.

If the population was curious to see us, we were no less so to admire the town, seven-tenths of the population of which are Spanish, the rest English: soldiers, sailors and officials. Fortification walls everywhere, blocks of concrete crowned with iron teeth. On all sides a tangle of barbed wire, deep trenches crossed by frail footbridges. Tank traps here. A concentration of anti-aircraft guns there. New discoveries every moment, but we never tired of admiring the rigid discipline of the troops, grimly devoted to their orders. It is this respect for law and order, this love of tradition, this confidence in her own strength that multiplies Great Britain's power tenfold. The Rock, in a way, is the symbol of English unity. Each man seems to be doing his duty, and more. A lorry full of soldiers came towards us; hands waved. '*Vive la France!*'

Three times we were stopped and each time a secret password cleared our way. A formidable studded door halted us for some minutes. This was the sanctuary of the Admiralty. Docks and courtyards flanked by severe buildings, a quay. The roads appeared. I had more time to admire them now than from my Goéland. Packed with naval units. There was an aircraft carrier. I learned it was the famous *Ark Royal*, supposed to have been sunk by the Boche!

We were in the corridors of the Admiralty. Vague uneasiness. What sort of reception would they give us? I remembered the words of the British Consul in Oran: concentration camp, return to France, etc. Who could prove we came in good faith? One thing tormented me: had the French Consul in Gibraltar enough influence to cause French pilots who landed here to be handed over to him? If so, I would escape to Portugal. One more escape, more or less.

All the corridors in the world are designed to keep wretched visitors waiting for long hours. This one kept up the tradition. No sound in the building. Officers in shorts and shirts passed, silent as shadows. The sun had come out. It must have waited for us to land, confound it! It was almost too warm. At last, a door opened. We went in. To our stupefaction, two French officers rose as we entered. A captain and a commandant. The latter took the initiative in questioning us.

Hair cut short, rectangular head, eyes that seemed to shoot at us, so hard they were. On his feet, he seemed immense. A curt, harsh voice. He wasted no words. Hands behind his back, his rapid questions exacted rapid answers. Where do you come from? How many of you are there? Who took the initiative in escaping? The captain wrote swiftly. I looked at Charles. Like me, he had been seized by a terrible doubt: had we fallen out of the frying pan into the fire? Sweat damped my forehead. Stupor possessed us, making our answers awkward and often incoherent.

Now he was taking our names, our papers; now he set about each of us individually. All the agony and despair of the last twenty-four hours were laid bare before this man, not a muscle of whose face showed his feelings. Not a word came from his mouth that might enable us to guess what fate awaited us. He let us talk, his eyes boring into us. Finally, when Jimmy, who was last, had ended his story, which, like the rest of us, he had tried to cut as short as possible, an amazing and unforeseeable miracle took place. The commandant's face lost its savage look, his eyes softened and a smile lighted up the severe prosecutor's face.

'Boys,' he said, 'what you have done is all the better for being difficult and dangerous. You were on the horns of a tragic dilemma. Your affections, your families, the interests, perhaps, of a whole life, opposed themselves to your duty. You made the choice. ...'

His voice was rapid, abrupt, but the tone was fatherly. He himself had deserted a few days before. He was going to join General de Gaulle in England. *This was the first time we heard General de Gaulle mentioned.* We knew vaguely that he existed and what he had done, so we were eager to know what he was like. At every sentence he spoke, multitudes of questions were on our lips, and little by little, patiently, he slaked our thirst. Now we knew under what leader we were to be the first legionaries.

Suddenly there was a droning in the air. A plane ... French, perhaps? Then we thought of our comrades in Oran, those in the little Simoun, de Joffre and Fayolle, whose absence was worrying us. Then there was silence again and once more our questions poured forth. Others had landed before us. Some young pilots with barely thirty flying hours had escaped in a Morane 230. Others, under the fire of the police, had dived into the water and boarded a Polish ship as it sailed.

A sergeant-major, revolver in hand, with a few men, had seized a military vehicle and, after endless wanderings in Southern France, succeeded by a miracle of boldness in getting aboard a tiny collier. Two pilots, flying to Gibraltar in a grounded plane, had come down in the harbour, not having seen the racecourse. What emotion when they found themselves received by two French officers! Like us, they had thought they were in the snare.

25

How many heroic acts there had been, performed by many who fell, but the survivors knew the joy of having fought to remain free and French.

One question burned on my lips.

'Can we hope to fly with our English comrades in the R.A.F.?'

The reply was reassuring. We were expected in England, where everything was ready for our rapid training on English planes. Our delight turned into enthusiasm when, after a bustle in the corridor, we saw our two friends Fayolle and Sturm come in. We surrounded them and bombarded them with questions. The commandant had hard work to restore calm. Something rather amusing had happened to them. They had first intended to escape in a Glenn Martin, a difficult business, for it is a ticklish aircraft to handle, especially for people who know nothing about it. But the luck of the draw had decided it so, just as it had decided that two of our other comrades should take off in the Simoun at the same time as ourselves. The fact is that the latter two, whose names I have no desire to remember, although they had contrived, like us, the previous evening to reach their little plane and spend the night on board, experienced such fear of the act and its consequences when they heard us take off that at the very moment when they should have set off, when they had everything on their side, abandoned it like cowards and went wretchedly back to their quarters. I doubt whether they would have made very excellent fighters if they had reached Gibraltar. You can't be lukewarm in this business.

Our take-off had awakened little Fayolle. The time we took to get off the ground made him shiver in his shoes but his fears soon gave way to joy when he saw us succeed. After losing no end of time, he and Sturm managed to get to the aircraft, which was fortunately by a hangar a good distance from the middle. They took off without trouble and reached Gibraltar as if on a pleasure flight. To describe the emotion which gripped us is difficult. We met like brothers after years of separation.

When we left the Admiralty, we each had a book in our pockets. Our brotherhood in arms began. We were like children, astonished by everything. A French officer caught up with us. Two of us were invited aboard the aircraft carrier *Ark Royal* to drink a welcoming glass. I felt too dirty to accept. Unshaven, capless, one of us in sandals, we looked an original lot but quite devoid of military uniformity.

At all costs we had to dispense with the duty of courtesy. But many other courtesies awaited us, and it was only after acceding to the wishes of some and the supplications of others, after a whisky here and strange drinks there, after answering the innumerable questions asked by everyone who had the least smattering of French, after a luxurious meal in the best hotel in the town, for which it was naturally impossible for us to pay, when we met at about two o'clock in Commandant Pigeaud's office at the Admiralty, that exhaustion overcame Charles and me and knocked us out. I heard the Commandant beginning to speak; it was very hot, the sun was dazzling, as I sat at a table everything suddenly appeared so strange and faraway. ... His voice seemed to buzz in my head. Before I collapsed, I heard the last echo of the Commandant's voice, saying, 'Let the poor lads sleep.' Later, they woke us. We were led out, half carried, like sleepwalkers, to a car. Half an hour later, fully dressed; we sank on our beds. How many hours did I sleep? I was drunk with slumber. They woke us several times. In the end a comforting bath put me right back on my feet.

We went into the town, Charles and I; my uniform was not very clean and I was a little ashamed, for everyone stared at us. We crossed Gibraltar, the narrow town leaning on the Rock. The population was an odd mixture of English and 'natives'. But the aboriginal Spaniards of Gibraltar profess an insolent contempt for 'Spaniards from the other side of the barbed wire'. *They* are 'British subjects'; the worst insult, the deepest offence, is to say to them, 'You Spaniards.' Many real Spaniards cross the frontier daily to work. In the evening they go home. These two peoples of one race ignore each other to the point of not speaking.

This morning the Rock newspapers, printed in Spanish and English, are full of the details of our escape and landing. They naturally do not give our names. They also report a sad accident which happened while we were asleep yesterday. Two bombers, piloted by French officers who had escaped from Casablanca, arrived at midday and, like us, tried to land on the race-course. The first overturned after landing, happily without casualties. The second served as a target for the Spanish artillerymen, having flown a little too close to the barbed wire. I have since learned that English soldiers immediately opened fire on the gunners and succeeded in killing some of them. But that cannot make up for the deaths of four young Frenchmen.

We could not pass a cafe without hearing shouts of invitation in our honour. It was dark. The streets were full of singing sailors, all half drunk. On two or three occasions it was impossible to refuse to go in and the general uproar when we appeared became a din the music could not drown. Glasses accumulated in front of us and our table became a rallying point, swaying with the crowd that pressed upon us. We had to drink. The cries and laughter there were at our grimaces! The *Marseillaise* was played.

The proprietor, a jovial fat man, after standing us a drink, had been to the orchestra to ask for our anthem.

Everyone, standing, roared with all their hearts. It was at once picturesque and moving, puerile and sincere. But the oddest thing was the orchestra, composed of attractive Spanish women, who had eyes only for us and seemed to be having a competition for which should give us most glances during *God Save the King*, which added something a little unusual to the majestic English anthem. Then there was a rush to shake hands with us. I do not know by what miracle the proprietor managed to insinuate himself among us but he was proud of the four words of French he contrived to yell at us and he protected us with his broad shoulders while we sought to escape, having given a firm promise to come back tomorrow.

The number of drunken sailors to be found in the streets was incredible. Numerous patrols were on the move, carrying rubber truncheons. They approached their victim quietly and without a word, in one grave methodical movement, the service-police knocked the scandalous object on the head, and he immediately collapsed into the arms of two sailors who were following to gather in the harvest. And the patrol went on, at the same measured pace.

So did we. On all sides there was the noise of orchestras, laughter, couples in the shadows – and the shadows were not few, for the black-out was observed. Another imprudence: a glance towards a half-open door and there we were, pushed, dragged, grappled with, among a surge of yelling heads in a thick atmosphere. All was still as if by magic; there was the *Marseillaise* again. Ah, these people did not need to search their consciences to know who their allies were! Some told me they did not believe in the Armistice, that it was a trick of the politicians, that North Africa would wake up.

Everywhere we found the same blind faith in the invincibility of the British Navy, in English method and tenacity. At the hotel, later, an old Englishwoman who spoke admirable French said to me, 'The bulldog is not our symbol for nothing. He takes a long time to make up his mind to bite, but once he has his prey he does not let go.' Everywhere we found the certainty which, in spite of the seriousness of the time, was to be read on all faces. Their strength to some extent lies in the impassiveness which makes them conceal every kind of emotion. And work goes on, where and when it is necessary that it should. How far we were from the waves of uneasiness which upset and then paralysed the provinces when our poor France was invaded! All this optimism gave a little warmth to our lacerated hearts.

This morning I met two Frenchwomen. What are they doing here? The prettier of them is the manageress of the Grand-Guignol in Paris. She told me she had put on a play in which Hitler was the hero and had displayed posters all over Paris showing his face green and bloodstained. She had received threatening letters, and when the Armistice came, she thought it prudent to escape. A small collier had brought her here with her friend; they were transformed into negresses by the time they arrived.

We had great difficulty in changing our money. The Admiralty would only change 176 francs for us: one pound. It is as if we had 50 francs in our pocket! With our one note burning there we all gazed at the thousand things we needed urgently without being able to satisfy our desire to buy them. Even so, we were staying at the best hotel in the town, where French was spoken. At luncheon an old lady, much moved, held an embarrassed conversation with us; she came over to our table, her admiration for us overcoming her reserve. She asked to be forgiven for her gesture, even before we knew what it was. Ours, so spontaneous and sincere, made her so upset emotionally that in spite of her husband's hesitation – he was afraid we should refuse – she had not been able to restrain herself from coming to offer each of us 1,000 francs. We were not to give her our answer until after the meal. She made her escape, hiding her tears, leaving us very confused and doubtful as to what to say. Alas, despite our desire to please her, we all agreed to decline her offer. One of us went to give her the embarrassing reply.

This afternoon the burial of the unlucky Frenchmen who fell into the harbour of Gibraltar took place. It was at two o'clock. There was a service; the church was full. Hundreds of women in mantillas sobbed. I was struck by the emotional nature of the Spanish women. Previously, in the street, nearly all the women in the crowd lining the pavements were wiping their eyes. The ceremony was extremely moving. The handful of young Frenchmen standing motionless round the coffins had just risked death or imprisonment if they had failed. How many of those who stood there will see their sweet France again? Their uniforms were old and dirty. They came from all branches of the services, but the Air Forces predominated. They, too, seemed to sense the poignancy of the moment, if one can judge by the discomposure some of them had little success in keeping from their faces.

We left the church, flanking the four coffins of four young men who believed in their star and who fell in the moment of success. They are the first heroes of the Free France which means to fight. The organ music accompanied us into the street. The heat was torrid. We walked a kilometre to the cemetery. The ceremony concluded very simply, while the trumpets preceding the salvoes sent forth their clear, sad notes.

I could not resist going to cast a grateful glance at my plane, which is resting a few hundred metres away. There it was, my good Goéland, guarded by two English soldiers with fixed bayonets. Inquisitive people's cars had stopped by the roadside. We had difficulty in explaining what we wanted. In the end they let us get in.

I could admire it at my leisure, the plane that had been the tool of my destiny. It was brand new, as clean as if on show at an exhibition. But for those out-of-order propellers, our flight would have been as uneventful as a pleasure trip. That take-off! The mere memory of it still makes me shiver.

With a supplementary tank, I should feel capable of flying to England … provided the famous propellers were fixed. But who could undertake to do that? The commandant asked me this morning what possibility there was of setting out on such a flight. I asked him in my turn if he could provide the mechanics and electricians, making it clear that without the supplementary tank I should refuse to take the risk. Poor old Goéland, will you be condemned to finish your career on this windy race-course, eaten away by time, sad relic of a glorious memory?

My eyes lingered on the harmonious lines, the long, tapering wings. I went on board and took the stick for the last time, the stick round which, the day before yesterday, my hands were clenched with the energy of despair. Lovingly I closed a contact which had been left open, set the pitch of those accursed propellers. The two Englishmen watched me; they looked too hot to understand. I got out sorrowfully, feeling that I should never see this friend of a night again. Of what kind of fate has it been the instrument? What future, with all its train of agony, mental conflict, effort and courage? Shall I survive the crossing? And when shall I see my poor France again, my dear mother whom I am overwhelming with pain? Shall I see my kinsfolk, my friends, my home again?

In spite of those who seek to stop me fighting for my country, in spite of my country herself, I am now committed to the crusade until victory or death. I regret nothing and I shall fight convinced of the greatness of the end I seek. Nothing shall change my mind, no enemy propaganda, not even my family, if they succeed in writing to me (I am ashamed of such a supposition). And if fate allows me only a brief fighting career, I shall thank Heaven for having been able to give my life for the liberation of France, struggling to the end, preferring death in the open sky to a life of humiliation.

Alea jacta est. This morning at ten o'clock we came on board the *Président Houduce*. It is four o'clock now and we are still at anchor in the harbour. Suddenly I thought I saw the heavy outline of *Ark Royal* moving. It was no error; she is gliding slowly out of the harbour, followed by a whole fleet. On what adventure is she going? What majesty, what a sense of power emanates from her! We are still in the roads while the English ships recede eastwards below the horizon.

The blast of a siren; we raise the anchor, while a destroyer turns broadside to us, gliding gently a few hundred metres away. The noise of chains resounds. The heavy engines vibrate. We are stopping at the harbour mouth. There are several wrecked ships around us. A convoy of twenty ships goes past; we are to form the rear-guard. The sun is going down; we skirt the huge Rock in the direction opposite to that in which we arrived three days ago, shaving the water. Clouds form on the crest and are detached from it, swept off by a north wind. I never tire of watching this phenomenon, while I also try to make out the African coast in the light of the setting sun. The ships, from big ones of 20-30,000 tons to tiny yachts of 100 or 200 tons, are formed up in two great lines, each ship preceding the next by 200 or 300 metres. The three mailboats are in the middle, the destroyer ahead, and ourselves in the rear, sailing up and down, to and fro, just like watchdogs.

Still lost in my dreams, I watch the sea darkening. I am thinking of my first sea voyage, when I was a child, and we had been on a visit to Corsica. I am thinking of France and this shameful Armistice. I am thinking of my mother and her patriot's heart, which must be bleeding; of her mother's heart, which is going to suffer. How will she know? When will she know? I met some sailors in Gibraltar who had been brought there by force and who are to be repatriated. I scribbled a few words to her address. ... Will Mayrand, in Oran, carry out his commission? Will the sergeant-major who lives at Bergerac go to Couze?

The African coast, chalk-walled, turns pink at the kiss of the setting sun. The water slides peacefully along the hull. Gibraltar's harbour grows small. The warm air is so peaceful! Destiny, destiny, how many times shall I question you during this voyage into exile? How much youthful energy of mind in all these ships heavily laden with war material is turning in upon itself in a last examination of its conscience before tomorrow's battles? The convoy is transformed into shadows. No lights are visible; Gibraltar is only a memory. The water alone remains to mirror my thoughts. A thousand spangles leap round the undulating foam of the wake. The sea, phosphorescent now, takes on emerald tones in places. I am trying not to think any more.

The *Président Houduce* escaped from Marseille, under the command of a determined skipper. Manned with a miscellaneous crew composed of elements brought together at the last moment, it was primarily chosen because its position in the harbour allowed it to be easily boarded, also because it is very well armed. It also contained hand grenades, torpedoes and a hold filled to bursting with ammunition. When some of the crew resisted, the sailors took the energetic course: 'There's a war on and he who isn't with us is against us.'

Among them were fellows who would have made an ideal crew of pirates and outlaws three hundred years ago. One of them, a quartermaster, was very proud to show me an arsenal of pistols and revolvers of all calibres in his cabin. He told me that one of the sailors had knocked out a German officer to get hold of the pistol he was showing me, but I suspect that he himself was the author of the deed. It was he, too, who informed me about the amiable company which was working the ship. 'A rough lot, for sure,' he said, 'the war's got prospects for them that it hasn't for the combatants on either side. …'

Once it was declared they all sought to satisfy their lust for adventure and easy gain. They think they have found the means to do so on board this old tub. The master first: he left the other skipper lying on the quay when the latter said that as he was a married man he wasn't going, after the other had asked him to. He is tough, surly too. His dream is to sail where he likes and board unescorted enemy ships. Armed as we are, he can then do as he will. If the Admiralty makes trouble, he will make himself scarce and go over to the Boche. A slave-trader's mentality.

The first night I only slept for a few hours. We all take our turn on watch against submarines. Mine, eight out of twenty-four hours, is from 1 to 5 p.m. and 9 p.m. to 1 a.m. Then one's sight gets lost in the darkness, taking each cap of foam for a periscope. The slightly darker waves look suspect at once. Towards midnight weariness overcomes one, the eyes suffer from being forced to concentrate, stinging with salt, heavy with monotony and the need for sleep.

Chapter 4

In the R.A.F.

July 25th, 1940

This morning we learned of our departure for St. Athan, a large station near Cardiff. So perhaps we shall soon be flying. A hope which still seems pretty remote. Parade at ten o'clock. It is now 9.30; we are gossiping in little groups in the immense entrance of the Empress Hall. Admiral Muselier has just arrived, alone, very informally. No one noticed him. … It is the first time I have seen him. Very young, very erect, he compels recognition by his piercing, strong-willed glance; he seems very good.

I was with two comrades. We are only sergeants. He came straight to us to shake hands; I was touched by such affability. He said a few words of welcome to us. We gave him our story, briefly. 'That's excellent, boys.' His face lit up with a broad smile, behind which we felt how well he understood. He himself has left everything and, like us, is condemned to death by his own country, which he has served all his life.

He talked to us about his plans, which we found far from displeasing, since our little group of pilots will be the first to leave. We shall go separately into an R.A.F. squadron until the day when the French are numerous enough to form their own unit. A few more weeks of patience and then a time of intense fighting and hope will open out before us. When I left Oran, I abandoned all hope of seeing my poor mother for a long time, of being of mental and material help to her in the terrible time she is going through. Since then, I have each day felt my heart a little fuller than the day before and the desire to pitch into the Boche racks me like an obsession.

Admiral Muselier came to say a few words to our little group of pilots. Symbolic encouragement. We shall have to uphold the good name of the French Air Forces in England. He also came to greet Lady Sinclair, the Air Minister's wife, who wished likewise to make a short farewell speech to us.

I was greatly honoured, also Charley. Before addressing us, Lady Sinclair wanted to meet two or three of our number. Who gave our names rather than others? I don't know. All our comrades, in having come here either by ship or plane, have deserved as well as we. ... We shall end by taking ourselves for heroes. ... Poor heroes, obliged to flee a country which refuses to defend itself and now disclaims them. ...

We went down to the lecture room where, it appeared, Lady Sinclair was waiting for us. A charming and most kindly woman greeted us, speaking impeccable French despite a very strong accent. I was struck by the plainness of her dress: a modest white straw hat with a wide brim and a gown that could not have been simpler, like a beach-dress. We had to tell her our story while one of her friends took notes and asked for full details. She was far from being intimidating, that charming lady, but why were her eyes wet with tears? What we did was only natural. How many others would have done the same if they had had the chance. We brought up a question we had thought about a lot since our escape: why should not some of us, each with knowledge of a part of North Africa, try to return there in a ship flying a neutral flag? We would bring back pilots and win over the undecided. The question seemed to interest her very much; she promised us she would mention it to her husband and, once again, she had our names noted down.

Cakes, coffee, and the conversation ended in an outburst of praise and good wishes for our two great nations. As she left us, she made us promise that we would write to her if we needed the least thing and come and see her if we were passing through London. She assured us, to our great joy, that we should not be inactive much longer.

We assembled in the great hall of the building. Some 200 men stood there in silence; each one of them had fled from conquered France. They were all survivors of more or less heroic adventures. Their hearts had all for a moment been prey to the same inner tragedy: 'Where does my duty lie?' Lady Sinclair came forward. Everything about her was kind, from her informality to the charming way in which she addressed us. She expressed her feelings for France in almost academic terms. She seemed much moved; her words seemed to come from her heart. She ended her little speech with a rousing '*Vive la France!*'

July 27th

We have been living here for the past two days like fighting cocks. The most diverse news is circulating on the subject of our departure to the front, leaving us alternately hopeful and despairing. I cheated a little over my flying hours this morning when an English flight lieutenant asked me how many I had. If only I have the luck to get away soon!

I feel it won't be long for Charles and me, judging by the interest shown in us in the different offices. I admire the English authorities' rapidity of decision where we are concerned.

July 28th

English comfort is no legend. The camp at St Athan, one of Great Britain's pilot-training centres, comparable with Istres, Avord or Rochefort in France, has sufficient amusements to keep its occupants in an excellent state of physical and mental health. A grand gymnasium, equipped with the most modern apparatus, a swimming bath comparable with the finest in Paris, tennis courts, a boxing ring, etc., a magnificent modern cinema, seating about two hundred, daily (always open) gratifies the young warriors with the latest films, which are changed every two days. …

The cleanliness of the buildings, the roads and the personnel surprises us. Everything seems to work perfectly, without a murmur and without the disagreeable and fastidious discipline ensured by the French sergeant-major. The Englishman has a sense of the duty to be done, from the commander who knows how to bear his responsibilities down to the private soldier who is sometimes obliged to carry out mean or tedious tasks, which he does without evincing surprise, his sole care being to do them well. Silence and obedience. A hive, a sanctuary.

July 29th

Orders have just arrived; we are moving house again; this time we leave for an R.A.F. squadron to be tried out, judged and then sent into combat. I prefer it. People have talked to me so often about the formation of a French squadron that I now dread the confusion, the interminable discussions between the French and English authorities and the jealousies. In such a case, it is obvious that the best material and the best missions would not be for us. There are only twelve of us going, twelve fighter pilots. The others are either bomber pilots or observers. Many of our young pilots are unemployable for the time being. Others are getting office jobs. I would rather not enlarge on the latter subject.

So now I am on the threshold of realizing a hope I formed at the beginning of the war without ever being able to realize it. Ten months in France, three vain applications to be sent to the front, one desertion: nothing worked. The last wile would have attained my end but the Armistice broke out. Obliged to desert a second time. … In England it has not taken more than a fortnight to decide my fate. Loss of time, bad employment of skilled men, administrative red tape are among the causes of the French collapse.

Women soldiers are extremely numerous in England and form a little army of their own, auxiliary to and in support of the big one in functions, uniform, ranks and communal life. In France one could not imagine the existence of such an army, probably because of the fear of ridicule. The spirit is so different here. These little soldiers each do their work with the utmost seriousness and astonishing conscientiousness. The first time I was saluted in the street in London was by a charming little blonde in uniform and nothing could have been more comical than to see her give the convulsive, snappy salute in the English style, turning her head towards me with imperturbable composure.

We have just arrived at Old Sarum, three miles from Salisbury (my nerves are on edge with being unable to pronounce 'Sools-beurré'). It is a pretty little spot in the English countryside, which is not in the least like ours, rich in wide, cultivated fields! Here there is only a succession of meadows in which innumerable cows graze. The city itself is typically English and would not be distinguished from its sisters if it did not possess the marvellous cathedral for which it is famous; its spire, the highest in England, is 150 metres in height and leans dangerously to one side.

We got here last night, and as from this morning we fly. It hasn't taken long. I was overjoyed to renew my acquaintance with the stick but the infernal throttle gives me endless trouble. The English, of course, do nothing like other people; on the road, they drive on the left; in aviation, they reverse the direction of the throttle so that in order to take off, instead of pulling it towards you, you have to push it forward. I always make mistakes with it in aerobatics. Re-education of the reflexes. It will be done.

July 31st

We read the following news in the papers this morning: 'All military personnel declared rebels, who have joined a foreign army to continue fighting, will be sentenced to death if they have not returned to France by 15th August.'

What are the real French of France thinking? Do they, perhaps, reject us too? Where are the real guardians of the truth? We others all have a sense of having done our duty, and no information from France, no propaganda whatever, will be able to deflect us from our line of conduct. A week ago, we learned we had been deprived of French citizenship. What does that matter? Will our country not receive us with open arms when we have contributed, after victory, to ridding her of the vermin who are laying her waste? *After victory*, what far-off sweetness there is to intoxicate one in those two words!

Today the 'death sentence' fills us with a feeling of great sadness and loneliness; the evidence of the irresponsibility of our miserable government is palpable in such a sentence. We are in a friendly country which has received us better than we could have dared to hope. But alas, today I realize only too well that we are alone and far from what we love.

August 1st

We fly every day, morning and evening, and waste no time. I am beginning to get used to the reversed throttle. Training goes on steadily; we have passed today from the little Tiger Moth to the big Hector. We are working at aerobatics on the latter machine. We shall soon have to give proof of our flexibility and virtuosity. So far, we have seen no English equivalent of our acrobatic Morane 230. Perhaps the fast planes we shall soon be given will prove very manageable.

August 5th

Charles and I have just been invited to a neighbouring lady's country home. A great reception was given in honour of the two Frenchmen. The two young daughters of the house did the honours. Introductions. All the fine flower of the district, girls in uniform and not in uniform, miniatures and caricatures, they all made inordinate efforts to give us the benefit of their three words of French, which they tore off at us with much laughter. Never, in so short a time, have I had to tell our story so often. In the end I knew the English sentences by heart, repeating the same words every time. But like a man who always tells the same joke, our adventure, which has an epic turn to some, now seems to me to be unworthily tame.

My friend Charles has been getting by manfully during his month here. His vocabulary increases on the average by a word and a half a week. I can make a faultless inventory of it: 'Yes. No. Darling. Very nice. I love you.' That is all.

We left that most hospitable house under an avalanche of enough 'Good luck' to make our boldest missions certain of success.

August 10th

Our training on the Hawker Hector ended today; we are packing our bags once more, this time for Odiham, where we shall find all our comrades from the French Air Forces.

August 12th

Little Odiham is the most ravishing specimen of the English countryside. Therefore, so as not to conflict with such a scene by constructing a military camp, a kind of village has been built in which each house represents mess, canteen, shop, postal section, etc.

The village has its streets, squares, lawns and tennis courts. The aerodrome is admirably camouflaged. Artificial hedges and thickets break it up and disguise it to such an extent that at 300 metres up it is hard to distinguish it from the rest of the country. I have even seen English aerodromes on which the hangars, for better concealment, were entirely covered with turf.

Our little group, and it alone, is to stay in England. We shall fly in an English squadron. I confess this is good news for us. We are certain to be fighting soon. I am dreaming of nothing but combinations for attack and defence in aerial combat.

August 14th

Hitler has announced his grand attack on England for this month. And, indeed, for the last ten days, the air raids have been more accurate and intense in all areas. The English victories increase equally; each day augments the number of victims. Yesterday, the record day, there were 172. We are the witnesses of the greatest aerial battle of all time. Shall we one day be taking part in it?

Each day several alerts collect us to watch, impotent, the passage over our heads of the German heavy bombers. But patience, my dream is coming true.

Today we are giving a ball in London: the Ball of Those Sentenced to Death. It is today, in fact, that the Germano-French Government is to sentence us to capital punishment if we have not returned to France. The highest London society will be present and it cannot fail to be a great success and very gay. ... We, the condemned, are in good form.

August 15th

We are doing nothing here in Odiham; the camp is a long way from anywhere. What a waste of time! Can it be the traditional slowness of the French administration General de Gaulle is said to have brought over? We spend our time wandering round the aircraft, listening to the news, learning English and eating. In England people eat very often but very little at a time, and I maintain that at the end of the day it hasn't worked because we are racked with hunger. The staple food is bread, butter and jam, all washed down with tea. At midday only, one is regaled with a slice of meat flanked by a boiled potato. Dinner consists of a sandwich. The beer is hard for a Frenchman to drink, it is so bitter.

We are off at last. They are sending us to the centre of England, to Sutton Bridge. There we shall handle the famous Hurricane, the English fighter; after that, posting to our squadron. I am really sorry to be separated from my best friends, especially from Guérin, whom I have been with since the beginning of the war and who has shared happiness and disappointments with me; and we lived through the agonizing hours of the escape from Oran together.

I cannot get used to the idea of fighting without him. I attach a ridiculous and perhaps slightly superstitious importance to this. Guérin was my only link with France and what I had loved there. We had so many memories in common that we used to take pleasure in recalling them, especially here. Many a time, in France, we went on leave together. We were almost brothers; we were going to be brothers in arms. … Tomorrow I shall feel terribly alone.

August 19th

Guérin has gone, with Labouchère and Fayolle. Now I am separated by the whole breadth of England from my three best friends. I caught the train this morning for Sutton Bridge, at two o'clock, north of London. I am with four very decent fellows I have known since I came to England. Then again, we have been split up in the squadron so that I have only one of them with me in my flight.

August 21st

Little Princess Margaret is celebrating her birthday today: ten years old. I am twenty-six. My little mother must be thinking more deeply about me today. I feel as if I were going through a nightmare.

Some of my comrades, unable to stand it any longer, have written to Unoccupied France. So far, we have been advised not to do that. I am haunted by the fear of reprisals against my mother, as against the families of the unhappy Czechs who were fighting in France at the beginning of the war. We French of Free France have two enemies who curse us: our own government and the Germans. I think Bergerac, where my mother must still be living, is in the Unoccupied Zone, but the danger is the same.

Our first walk on the aerodrome at Sutton Bridge was disturbed by an accident. A plane which had engine trouble at the take-off crashed a little distance away in a field. It was explained to us in a most matter-of-fact way that people no longer get excited about this, that the same thing happens every day, as the engines are defective. I confess that the impression was not a very agreeable one, these ultra-fast planes not being particularly amenable to forced landings.

We also learned that during the past month the authorities at the camp have recorded *a death a day*. The fact that as from next week I shall be flying a Hurricane regularly is far from reassuring. We hid our concern by vaguely carefree laughter.

I shall see many more of these, after all, and my feelings are of another quality. Have I not come to England to do a job which needs a cool head and sound nerves? Must not get soft, must get used to everything, must be astonished at nothing.

We have just been learning the Hurricane cockpit and nosing into a little of everything on the plane we shall shortly have to fly into battle and, I hope, to victory. Bigger than our Morane 406, better armed – it has eight machine guns which let fly at the same time. You let hell loose by pressing the firing button. It is much faster; it can do 330 miles an hour, which is about 480 kilometres an hour. But it is also much more complicated, especially for a Frenchman. To get used to our instrument panel means a total re-education of the reflexes. So many new dials, so many actions to perform before flying, when taking off, when landing. If I don't get it all by heart, I shall always be afraid of forgetting something and the least forget-fulness would be fatal.

The pilot must concentrate all the time; in this little factory transformed into a meteor he is at once radio operator, navigator, engineer and fighter. He subjects himself to terrifying acceleration, tremendous pressure, enormous differences in altitude, in a few minutes. Alone in his plane, he puts his nerves to a grim test. His health must be perfect. So, a fortnight ago, I decided not to smoke any more. I have succeeded and it has been tough, especially at first. During the first few days my comrades made a point of offering me cigarettes the whole day long, even going so far as to puff smoke in my face. What torture!

I did my first flight in a Harvard yesterday; very fast, I was sent up alone. But this morning, when I arrived at the squadron, I was told I was going to fly a Hurricane. Greatly excited, but above all very happy. Here at last was my moment to become a real fighter pilot. I settled myself in feverishly and they fastened me into the little meteor which was to tear me off the earth in the immediate future, mentally running through the *fourteen things* to do before taking off. I had taken care to learn them by heart, upon which I congratulate myself, for I am somewhat at sea among all these dials and levers, and the least forgetfulness, 'All clear?'

I opened the throttle. Difficult to describe my impressions. I had something of a feeling of entering into the unreal. I had suddenly become so puny and insignificant in the midst of this thunder that I did not feel myself to be responsible for the machine; it was carrying me away of its own accord. But the further I got from the ground, the more I recovered my sense and control of the plane. I made a good landing. I put down my undercarriage and flaps, set my propeller pitch, etc. The ground went past very rapidly. ... I was as happy as a schoolboy let out for the first time. So, this was the machine in which, in a fortnight, I think, I shall have to attempt the subtleties of aerial combat.

The French in London publish a daily paper called *France*. I have just received my first copy; it informs me that I shall soon be able to correspond with my family without fear. Eve Curie is in England and is writing for the paper. I saw her the day we arrived in Salisbury; she was glad to see Frenchmen.

Bombing is less frequent in England; the defence is good. Either they do not reach their target, or the bombing is ineffective. But it is accompanied by an intensive bombardment of phoney news in France. Thus, last week, while I was peacefully at Odiham, I heard on the Germano-French Radio Paris that the Boche squadrons had completely wiped out Odiham Aerodrome. ... Many of the bombs they drop do not explode. Unexploded bombs have often been discovered in England and in France, too, it seems; when dismantled, they contained a message of friendship from Austrian workers to their French or English comrades.

After ten hours' flying in a Hurricane, I am beginning to get quite used to handling the kite. Have made several dives from a pretty high altitude just to get that terrifying impression of speed. The shock near the ground squashes you down in your seat. Many hundred kilos press on your shoulders; you have a queer pain when you turn your head: an unmistakable pain stings the ear drums and makes you keep swallowing to stop it becoming an agony. The ground passes under the wings with terrifying swiftness. If you pull back the stick at that moment the plane shoots skyward like an arrow without losing speed, and a few seconds later you're 1,500 metres up. You can't amuse yourself in this plane by putting your arm out. The air pressure is so fierce it would be bent back and broken.

I have just been on a combat exercise with another Hurricane piloted by a Czech who has already had six victories in France. In my first combat I certainly bought it; the game consists of getting the enemy plane as often and as long as possible on your sights, i.e. on your own axis. You take off back to back, as in a duel, and each must compete in manoeuvre and cunning to elude and defeat the other. You put yourself unconsciously in the unlikeliest positions and if you don't succeed in keeping behind your opponent it is awfully difficult to shake him off. He stays stuck to your tail. You try a steep turn. He's still behind you. Your own plane won't do any more, you've asked too much of it. Unable to turn more steeply it slips away and dives. Alas, the other is still there. A disappointing fight for me. For the two or three times I shot him down, he certainly got me a dozen.

This afternoon, for the first time in my life, I climbed to about 10,000 metres. It was bitterly cold up there and the higher I went the more numb my hands and feet became. The most curious thing was that I found it was enormously tiring to talk. Just giving my position and saying the usual short phrase exhausted me. I was not in the least upset by the oxygen, but after twenty minutes at that height I was glad to come down. As soon as I stretched on my bed in the evening I sank into a deep sleep. It is the mental crisis I am going through that causes it, but everything that concerns France affects me. The nights when I do not dream are rare; yesterday just seeing the coasts of France from that height plunged me into an abyss of bitter thoughts.

Two more killed in our training squadron this morning. They telescoped during a combat exercise. Poor lads, their courage has been in vain. To die in the face of the enemy, to go with the satisfaction of a task accomplished. ... But to die like that?

September 3rd

I think of nothing but my first combat. My little mother is in my heart. Remembering her will help me to win, for I am sure I shall win, just as I am sure of finding her in France again when we have chased the Fritzes out!

Grim record: six planes crashed on our aerodrome today. Two dead. I was the victor in a combat with one of my comrades. I am getting the hang of the Hurricane.

September 6th

My hours on Hurricanes are mounting up; I shall soon be one of those posted to a squadron. The great adventure is about to start. I practise combat whenever I have the opportunity. Simultaneously with the thought of the severe conflict I shall have to sustain, the memory of my mother and my family, the vision of my betrayed and violated country torment me.

September 7th

A liver attack is bending me double. I don't know why I mention it here, but I am as yellow as a lemon. ... Is it due to the bizarre food which is beginning to nauseate us, or has it some connexion with the bile I am accumulating on account of those I have left in France?

My mind is too busy. From time to time there comes into my heart a real terror of what has happened or could happen over there to those I love. *Then* I measure the immensity and above all the burden of my sacrifice.

September 8th

The systematic bombing of London has begun. Four hundred killed yesterday, 280 today. What will it be tomorrow? Is this the beginning of the great offensive Hitler promised? He announced the invasion of Britain for the end of August or the beginning of September. The English have been bombing Berlin since yesterday. That is routine. Our training seems to have been suddenly speeded up. There were several postings yesterday. Ours will not be until next week, unfortunately.

Chapter 5

In an RAF Squadron

September 9th, 1940

I did not think it would be so soon, as my training is not finished. When I got out of my plane just now, I was buttonholed and told that I was leaving the country in two hours' time. Where for? They must need pilots urgently.

I am being sent to Northern Ireland with only two comrades. The others are going near London, where they will certainly get interesting work almost at once. What am I going to do in Northern Ireland, where they never get a visit from the Boche? I am a little disappointed.

Bah! Let us follow our lucky star. In this business I have learned to be very fatalistic, even superstitious. I have my little mascots, my little fads, to which I attach an almost religious importance.

September 19th

I spent the night in London, in an hotel near the station. At about eleven o'clock the building was shaken so much that for a few seconds I thought it was going to collapse. Incessant bombing shook the city from nine o'clock on; the sky was reddened by the light of fires. The place being no longer tenable, we went out and visited the shelters to occupy ourselves. It really would have been too stupid to get oneself killed in that hotel on the eve of realizing what I have been waiting for for a year. The bombing stopped at about 5.30 a.m. We went back and were surprised to see that a house less than 100 metres from our hotel had been entirely destroyed by a bomb. Some people were still alive in the cellars, which the rescue party was making haste to uncover.

This morning we called at French Headquarters. This is in a very large building in the fashionable part of London. Received by Captain Chevrier, who was very friendly. We are to some extent his beginners. As the first French fighter pilots in England, from today we represent the nucleus of the French Air Forces. Up to us to be worthy of this unheard-of luck. The whole of France has put her last hope in us. Our example will perhaps make many a hesitant young Frenchman follow in our steps. What a fine task we have! He spoke to us in this strain at length and finished with tremolos in his voice. So, our little group is the reason for the existence of this sample of the Air Ministry! I am sure Headquarters is feverishly awaiting our first victories. They need a bit of publicity. …

Here I am in Northern Ireland. I am struck by the very crude colouring of the country. Everything is green. There is turf growing everywhere. Belfast, a very pleasant city, is just like the most modern English cities. Aldergrove Aerodrome is a good distance away: sixteen miles. We have only a restricted area to fly over, Eire occupying three-quarters of the island, and to fly over that country, it appears, might give rise to awkward diplomatic incidents.

Eire still proclaims absolute and stubborn neutrality. Thus, by night, the towns are illuminated as in peacetime. From day to day England expects a German landing, probably in Ireland; the sole fighter squadron is being reinforced by sending us there (Hum!). From all we have heard so far, the Boche is a rare visitor. In spite of the pleasant journey and the magnificent country, we would have preferred the London area.

We fly over the island, morning and evening, scanning the sky without seeing the least suspicious speck. We drive over the sea, fly above convoys. We soon get to know all the bays and lakes, which are so blue here.

Our English comrades are charming but they lament, as we do, our inaction. This morning a Boche came and bombed a ship out at sea north-east of the island. The pilots on duty, warned too late, arrived only in time to see the poor defenceless ship burning like a torch.

My comrade Guérin has just been posted to a squadron in the Shetlands. He could not have been sent further north. He who loves the heat! Even so, he has more chance than we of meeting a Boche.

This morning at six o'clock a German bomber laid an egg on Bathlin Island, north of Ireland. Bouquillard and I decided to go and patrol this area.

They sent us to England to shoot at a towed target. A sunny day which gave us a glorious little trip at high altitude. What wild country on both sides of the Channel, and how varied it is. My shooting was not too bad, but the joke is that they could not give me a mark: I cut the target in two with one burst.

We go on patrolling in a desperately empty sky. I am fretting to know why the Air Ministry has sent us here while at this very moment the Polish squadrons near London are covering themselves with glory.

45

I thought we should be staying permanently in this circle of good English friends but we are leaving for England. Will it be to a fighting squadron at last? I don't think so, for the aerodrome is near Glasgow, in Scotland, which the Germans hardly ever visit. They have given us one detail: the squadron to which we are posted is one of the most glorious in the R.A.F., with ninety-seven victories to its credit, decorated with the rarely awarded D.F.C. Unfortunately it seems that the unit has been decimated and has only three pilots left, resting at Prestwick.

I have just learned of my promotion to warrant officer. I can imagine the reaction of my comrades at Avord or Oran if they could see me with these splendid white badges of rank.

At Prestwick, our first question was whether there is anything doing, whether the Germans pay many visits to Glasgow. It seems even rarer than at Aldergrove. ... The food here beats all records. Breakfast, scratch lunch and tea, but no dinner. ... As for the quality, the less said the better.

We two French pilots are 'at readiness' and go up in turn, one day in two. Being at readiness means staying by your plane from dawn to sunset, ready to take off at the least alarm in a few minutes. Several times during the day we patrol, particularly in the area reputed to be dangerous, i.e., of interest to the enemy.

The aerodrome is on the coast south of Glasgow. Magnificent flights every day over splendid islands in the countless gulfs and bays which abound here. We discover something new each day, a castle hidden by a hill or a forest. A steep rock, about 300 metres in circumference, rises from the sea like a giant tower. It seems inaccessible; its sides are all vertical and look as if they were made of hundreds of thousands of organ pipes. ... Hosts of seagulls have made their nests on it and fly round it. The island really has a quality of mystery which a dark legend the local people tell has done something to develop.

The English pilots in the squadron are charming to us and we live on terms of close friendship with them, for I have only one French comrade with whom I can exchange melancholy memories. They do all they can to make us forget we are in a foreign land and we really are one family.

They are all officers, we are warrant officers, but it doesn't much matter. They are famous pilots with 8, 10 and 31 victories to their credit. We bring only our goodwill and precious little experience. They attach no importance to this and always try to create a strong bond of firm friendship between us. Combat will soon set the seal on our comradeship. ...

October 1st

Much excitement on waking up. Two of us are going to the outskirts of London. Alas! Ten times alas! I am staying. ... Another separation. Two Frenchmen here, in two different flights. The bitterness I feel is mixed with a trace of jealousy. Those who are leaving are going to the north-east of London, on the Thames estuary, over which all the German squadrons coming to England have to pass.

It is there that the Battle of London is being fought at this moment, upon which the fate of the world depends. Why have they been chosen rather than me? I make absurd suppositions which end in the conclusion that chance has decided it thus and that my turn will soon come. I am sorry to see the departure of two good friends with whom I had, in pure imagination, taken part in so many fierce battles. Must my dream of being the first Frenchman to shoot down a Boche be abandoned?

Two accidents in a few days, one fatal. The first was due to the pilot's inattention. He came down in the sea, near the shore, and was able to be picked up. The second is inexplicable. During a combat exercise, at 3,000 metres, the plane dived at full speed to the ground and crashed. ... The pilot had vertigo, probably, or a black-out. Combat at these speeds involves extremely steep turns and pretty fierce pulling out to shake off the enemy, which, on account of the centrifugal force, produces a rush of blood to the lower part of the body, causing blindness for a few seconds. With your eyes wide open, you see nothing but blackness. That is sometimes enough to make you lose control of the plane. They say a pilot cannot stand two minutes of black-out. During aerobatics and in combat in the Hurricane I am always having black-outs; it is rather unpleasant but I console myself by thinking that the man behind me, on my tail, certainly has a black-out too.

I have been here a fortnight, flying more than I ever did in France. I often go on missions, not very dangerous ones, for the Germans rarely show their noses here. Nearly all my French comrades are in the south and are certainly in combat every day. ...

October 8th

At last, we are leaving for London with the whole squadron. Perhaps in a few days I shall have my duel. At last, I shall be able to try and avenge my mother for all the misery she is suffering. Sometimes I have bloodthirsty impulses which astonish me, I should die content if I first slaked this thirst for revenge.

Each time my thoughts fly to France (God knows how many times a day) I am haunted by these memories; each time, I feel a weight on my heart, like a physical pain. Shall I have made all these sacrifices uselessly? I do not think so; I have faith in my star. I am sure I shall see France again; return to all I love. … But when? …

October 10th

We took off southward, sixteen planes. Shocking weather, very low cloud, thick mist in places. But it was absolutely necessary to go. We are replacing a squadron of tired Poles who are taking our place at Prestwick. No trouble on the trip; marvellously fast.

Chapter 6

At Northolt with the Churchill Squadron

October 10th, 1940

We have arrived at Northolt, a modern aerodrome with runways, at the gateway to London, since the Underground reaches it. It is much nearer the capital than Le Bourget is to Paris. We are at readiness from today. They do not lose time in England. For we are exclusively charged with the defence of the biggest city in the world. It was with some little pride that I learned I was to be one of the guardian angels of this very proud city.

'The job goes on all the time,' two Poles, who are leaving tomorrow for a rest, told me, 'you'll always be at readiness!' This Polish squadron has done a first-class job; in a month they have shot down 115 planes. This promises to be enormously interesting for us, but alas, what casualties! Nearly 50 per cent of their comrades have not returned from the battle and some are wounded. ... These last details left us thoughtful.

October 11th

My first fighting mission: an event. Greatly excited. We took off, twenty-four of us, in three minutes: a record. There is always a layer of mist over London which nowadays almost completely hides the city and its suburbs. We soon went through this ceiling and at once found ourselves beneath an immensely blue sky. The radio was guiding us, probably to meet a German squadron making for England. In places we saw the ground, very small, for we were already at 22,000 feet. I was thinking hard. Memories, ideas rushed into my mind, while my hands were busy.

I saw France. Far, far, very far off, the coast stood out clearly. Without wanting to be emotional, I abandoned myself to a feeling of great sadness and pity. ...

Instinctively I scanned the sky from which, fiercely and treacherously, might rush the danger we were fighting. Fighter work is like a dagger in the back. Each opponent dodges, escapes, returns, seeks the advantage of altitude, a spot in the sun, the better to achieve surprise, and at the moment when he is least expected he drops on the other like a stone and kills him from behind. That is the law. ...

The light patrol therefore has a plane to make S's behind it to protect it from surprise. A few metres to starboard I saw my squadron leader, his head continually turning to all the visible points of the sky. Behind us followed three groups of four, slightly below us, in perfect formation. From time to time came radio instructions, followed at once by the leader's answer, and the whole formation turned on a new course. What wonderful discipline and what a terrible engine of war we are handling! Still nothing in the sky. I was intensely awaiting the moment of meeting the Germans. ...

My heart beat faster, for far off, much higher than we were, I had just seen a cloud of furiously fast black specks. Would they be Messerschmitts? I pointed them out over the radio to my squadron leader, who signalled me the meteors' nationality: they were no other than Spitfires.

The time came to turn back; the order rang in my ears. I was not sorry; my hands were horribly cold. In the rush to get away I had forgotten my silk gloves. Also, I am not yet accustomed to breathing oxygen for so long.

October 12th

Our squadron has just had the honour of a visit, between two spells in the air, from Air Vice-Marshal Park. He shook hands with all the pilots. When he came to me, he asked me about my escape and, after wishing me luck, congratulated me on my English. He must be deaf. An hour later, Eve Curie came. What sweetness and simplicity!

After listening to us, she talked about her propaganda in America and her lectures on Free France. She told us of her faith in the future and in our early return to a liberated France. We French in Britain who go on fighting from here enable her to make her propaganda tours. She talked to us about her sister and brother-in-law, still in Paris. I am very proud; she has asked me to telephone her when next I go to London.

October 14th

Our flights over London go on almost without interruption. I am beginning to get used to high altitudes. This morning we put to flight a group of Messerschmitts much bigger than ours. They crossed the Channel again without our being able to get at them. I find the Hurricane is no longer fast enough for modern combat. The latest German bombers can almost keep up with it. In spite of these disadvantages in speed and manoeuvrability it has been noticed that the Germans generally refuse battle unless they have superiority in numbers and the advantage of altitude.

Every night, about seven o'clock, the sirens sound, and immediately afterwards the first bombs crash on London and the suburbs. We are not spared. All night, till dawn, the bombers keep coming over and dropping their load. Londoners have good nerves; during the day nothing of their nightly ordeal shows and work goes on everywhere.

October 17th

Yesterday I had my first engagement with Messerschmitts, for an instant. I confess I didn't see very much, the Germans being well above us. I saw a Spitfire dive earthwards at terrifying speed, trailing a cloud of black smoke after it. Poor lad! Another one. Up to us to carry on his work.

At this season of the year the sun is almost entirely lost in cloud, so that in the air the pilot is dazzled by the contrast between the white immensity stretching out beneath him and the limpidity of the sky. The Germans, who can go much higher than we can, therefore have the frightful advantage of seeing us coming far off and are consequently able to manoeuvre to approach unseen by us out of the sun; they have the advantage of height, speed, and often of numbers. Yesterday we flung our poor Hurricanes up desperately, throttles wide open. They wouldn't climb and we had the unpleasant impression of standing still. Appallingly unpleasant moments.

October 18th

The finest day I have had since coming to Great Britain. I long to shout my joy to the whole world. In London I met a woman who runs a club where Frenchmen often go. She herself is French, married to a Russian. She very kindly lent me her name to try and write to France. The letters apparently did not arrive so I sent a telegram to Cannes. My uncle has just replied, 'Family all well.' Now he will know I am here; I am happy.

October 19th

Two-hour patrol over London and Dover. Saw quite a few Germans. Always, alas, perched five or six thousand feet above our heads. We leap, but by the time we arrive they have long ago decamped. We landed almost without petrol. I was at the head of the squadron next to the squadron leader, when I noticed 50 feet from the ground that I only had one wheel down. I circled the aerodrome and tried the mechanism to lower the undercarriage several times. Nothing happened. I pressed the safety lever: no result. Looking at my fuel, I noticed that I had only four gallons in the reserve tank.

I climbed to 3,000 feet, and made a dive followed by an abrupt pull-out, hoping thus to dislodge my recalcitrant wheel. Nothing doing. …

I asked for instructions on the radio, not wanting to land without permission. I saw the whole squadron, which had landed an instant ago, with faces uplifted to watch me turning desperately, like a one-legged man. I tried all the mechanisms once more. No. My petrol exhausted, I should have to make a belly landing. A pretty prospect. Well, that was the order on the radio.

The ground came nearer and nearer. I had taken the precaution of retracting the other wheel. I was well strapped in. I made a very shallow glide. I kept the plane in the air as long as possible. Finally, the tail touched down first. The plane bumped savagely on the ground. I felt myself flung forward. But I was well wedged in and went about 60 metres with the nose ploughing up the earth. I stopped without hurting myself. But up came the ambulance and the fire-tender at full speed.

'Not worth the trouble, gentlemen!'

I had been expecting everything except the congratulations, and they came from every side.

October 21st

I have not yet succeeded in seeing any good reason for the necessity of balloons of the sausage variety, ranged in their thousands over towns and country. I remember having seen our balloons at an altitude of about 6,000 metres in Paris. They therefore put up effective opposition to the German raids. Here the sausages rarely go as high as 2,000 metres, giving the enemy no trouble; far from it, indeed, for comically enough, when a raid is announced, they are lowered lest the Germans should shoot them down. On the other hand, the barrage balloons are extremely harmful to pilots here who have to return to their base deep in very thick mist (nine days out of ten at this season). An Englishman touched a cable last week and was killed.

Five days ago, guided by radio, a patrol of three Poles crashed in the same way. Our landing-ground is literally ringed with balloons, and yesterday in particular I only just had time to yell over the radio to the leader of my patrol, 'Balloons! Balloons!' There was a monster less than 50 metres ahead of us. We made steep turns, each to his own side, and I immediately lost him. I must confess I felt far from pleased with myself, with visibility nil in that field of balloons. ...

In the end I managed, after much worry and perspiration, to find my way back to the landing-ground. They were waiting anxiously for me.

October 24th

I returned to London this morning and my first visit was to 'René Ignatieff', my letter-box. One never knew. ... In fact, my kind friend greeted me with a broad smile. 'Good news tonight, René; another telegram for you.' This one came from Dordogne. My uncle must have written to my sister and given her my address. So now I am in touch, but still without direct news of my mother.

Actually, a few days afterwards, a far from ordinary-looking letter came by airmail for me, covered with crossings-out, and censored. I opened it. Oh, surprise! It was my mother's writing! I did not believe my eyes. In a few words she contrived to tell me that she approves of my conduct and is proud of it. Poor mother, you are paying dearly for that pride; what fearful anxiety you must feel on my account!

Deep in action as I am, I have no more time for thought. I must not think. An excess of emotion can only spoil the top mental and physical form which is indispensable in the great fight we are carrying on. But you, over there, all on your own, are worn with anxiety. What sleepless nights you must pass! Leaning over the radio I imagine you feeling like the stab of a knife the lying news that a terrifying daily total of English fighters is shot down by the glorious Messerschmitts. ...

I wrote at once to thank the American lady who had agreed to forward this blessed letter to me.

October 25th

An engagement with three enemy planes this morning. This time again I did not see much. I could not take the initiative because I did not know where the danger was coming from; I followed the formation into a dive. I had a black-out. Then the shouting stopped, the squadron reformed and went up to the ceiling. Three Messerschmitts, apparently, attacked us.

They must have passed quite close to me for I was right in the rear of the formation, highest in the air. The cold is beginning to make itself seriously felt. At 9,000 metres thighs and hands feel the pin-pricking of the temperature. Tomorrow I shall wear more clothes.

October 25th, evening

I very nearly covered myself with glory; unfortunately, Providence wouldn't permit it today. Patrolling above the squadron, like a dog with sheep, I suddenly saw a big twin-engined plane 10,000 feet below us just above the cloud. I went into a dizzy dive, passing just in front of another Hurricane to draw it after me.

Unfortunately, the other saw us soon enough to have time to plunge into the thick cloud and disappear without trace. This is not a very interesting tale to tell, but it was such a disappointment to see the prey before me that I make a point of recording it. These pages are meant only to be read by me in a few years' time.

October 28th

Today is mother's birthday. I should love to shut my eyes and be transported to her. We would go out gaily, arm in arm, for a walk, talking about nothing and everything. One day, perhaps?

October 30th

Attacked by Messerschmitts, higher up than we were; we did not see them, the sun is so dazzling. They dropped out of the sky like three stones and climbed back without giving us time to say 'Ouf!' In the scrap that followed I saw two of ours shot down. One of them was my only French comrade in the squadron. Luckily, he was not hit and landed in a field. The enemy has a terrible advantage in superiority of altitude.

October 31st

It was our turn to attack this morning: an unhappy bomber, making off like the devil, turning starboard and port and diving desperately for France. Two comrades and I chased him three-quarters of the way across the Straits of Dover. He was hit and I think we damaged him; black smoke came out of his port engine for a moment.

I threw my hand in; I have no desire to be brought down and shot in France. That is what has just happened to three unhappy young men who bravely landed in Morocco with the intention of attracting other French pilots to England. Unfortunately, they were caught and executed at once. I knew one of them very well. Shame on the men who order such crimes! An obscure death, but glorious and beautiful. … Our task will not be done when we return.

November 2nd

615 has just had a visit from Mr Churchill. What a surprise! What an honour! We were all there, the twelve pilots at readiness, wearing our yellow

pneumatic life-jackets in case of coming down in the sea. He came in a car and shook hands with everyone, saying a few words to each. He speaks French very well. He is most informal and extremely likeable. To think that the future of the world depends on this man's will. ...

A square jaw; he certainly has the jaw of the English bulldog which grips but does not let go its prey. He talked to our squadron leader, smiling all the time and sucking the end of a match. He wanted to see our flying monsters. I learned that he is the godfather of 615. Churchill our godfather!

When he had gone, I was told that he has promised us, soon, a transcendent new plane with speed, altitude and armament superior to the Germans. Figures were mentioned to me; I dare not believe them; these machines are so prodigious.

I have just been a spectator rather than a participant in a terrific air battle involving at least 100 enemy fighters. They were everywhere. As fast as we saw them overhead (as usual) we saw more of them coming. It was like an hallucination to have them moving so fast and always above us.

We tried to get at them and were at our poor planes' ceiling when we were attacked by a squadron of Messerschmitts which calmly turned barely 100 metres above us and placed themselves in the sun to dazzle us the better. There was nothing we could do but clear out fast, which we did, I as fast as the rest, taking very little time to drop to 5,000 feet in zig-zags. At each turn I blacked out. We went at over 430 miles an hour. ...

November 3rd

This morning, patrolling towards Dover, we flew low over London, which for once was not hidden by mist. I could not help thinking of the hundreds, the thousands of wounds this valiant city receives every night. *Every night* bombs begin to rain down almost everywhere from seven o'clock onwards.

While I was flying over London I sought fallen landmarks, but I did not see any. I noticed Westminster intact. There was famous London Bridge, which I saw for the first time. Dense traffic on the Thames. But we were going fast. We shaved the balloons. Now we were over the estuary. The altitude and the cloud brought me back to other realities. ...

November 6th

We often take off in impossible weather. Rain or wind, we have to go up at the alert. The sun has just gone down; in a quarter of an hour visibility will be nil; even so, we shall have to go up. Yesterday afternoon the alarm bell made us all jump while we were reading or playing; some were conscientiously asleep. We ran to our planes. A low, threatening ceiling rolling with big black clouds. As usual we took off in close formation, soon losing sight of the ground. We went up into thick black cottony cloud for an interminable time.

At last, the blue sky appeared at 7,000 metres. The descent was difficult too, and the feeling of invisible balloons which we simply could not miss if we made the slightest error on our course did not make me in the least inclined to lose sight of my leader, whom I stuck to at about a metre's distance. On landing, one plane was missing. … A comrade gone, Heaven knows where, probably into the sea. …

This afternoon I was allowed to see the biggest concentration of enemy planes that has ever come my way. The radio put us on the track by announcing 120 'bandits', an imposing figure which made my heart beat faster. There were only twelve of us. …

We managed to see them, but always higher than we were. It made us despair. Throttle wide open, we tried in vain to cut across their course. They passed disdainfully before us and went on to carry out their operation. I think a fight with them would have gone hard with us.

November 9th

I am beginning to feel seriously fatigued. We go up on an average three and sometimes four times a day to eight or nine thousand metres. This has been going on for a month. Up twice this morning. … I have just finished lunch; it is 3.30. All morning there have been Boche from all directions. One of my comrades, in the position I was originally to have had, was shot down. He was fortunately able to land in flames in a field and I have just heard that he only has a leg broken. … The enormous amount of oxygen we breathe is killing us. One of my comrades in France told me that a dozen ascents a week to 8,000 metres requires some days' rest. For a month we have been doing twice that … without rest.

The Boche is waking up. We cannot climb without having an engagement, but the worst of it is that we always pay the piper. This morning again one of my comrades, a few metres from me, was shot down by a meteor dropping from the sun behind him. It climbed back without anyone seeing it but me, in the rear. The feeling of being an impotent victim is extremely unpleasant. I am always placed in the rear of the formation, a position which is always attacked. It doesn't strike me as sport; it is more like murder. Our planes lack wind and pace at these altitudes. Let them give us a more powerful machine or put us on different operations, not to act as targets for Germans on the spree.

AT NORTHOLT WITH THE CHURCHILL SQUADRON

There are beginning to be gaps in our flight; victories are rare. ... Did not France lose the war through lack of material? There are plenty of planes here but they are not modern enough. The papers are all full of the massive deliveries of American planes. But they are hardly ever seen in the air over London, where an aerial battle upon whose issue the fate of the world depends is being fought.

The Duke of Kent has been to pay a visit to our squadron. All the major English personalities seem to rendezvous here. Our Dispersal is very attractive. It is a big room with a hundred drawings and photographs of German planes on the walls. A few beds allow one to take a cat-nap before the ringing of the alarm bell.

Games and books prevent inactivity, which alone can sap morale. Some days I struggle wretchedly against a stupid depression which attacks me like a fever. Each comrade who falls brings back the mood, which I try hard to hide. It is no use reasoning. I cannot help realizing that on our daily operations, on which we only too often lose our feathers, there reigns a resignation to fate; each one senses beyond the duty imposed the impossibility of defensive action. The value of the individual and of initiative exist no more. We must go on and endure. ...

In spite of these ridiculous and inevitable moods of dejection, which make those who suffer from them to be pitied, the spirit of our squadron is very cordial and light-hearted. The most open friendship prevails and I have never heard one voice raised louder than the others. There is no distinction in rank here. Life goes on regularly. Every day we are brought the indispensable tea, reinforced by cakes, toast and jam. We form a most united family, whose principal purpose is to laugh. What curious and interesting studies there would be for a psychologist who analysed the characters of these fellows who are so young and calm!

At the door are the Hurricanes, waiting, like us, for the scramble. Whether it is a Boche signalled over Cherbourg or an enemy squadron in sight of Dover the bell rings immediately. Like one man, the whole flight leaps up, leaving games and books, each one rushing towards his kite.

In less than a minute the parachutes are adjusted, the engines started up, the pilots securely fastened in; rapid check-up of instruments, oxygen, radio, heating. A minute later the whole flight is off for some destination the radio will give it in a moment. According to the importance of the attack, two or three flights sometimes go up a once and this haste, with such apparent calm, has something both majestic and alarming about it. When I am not going up, I never fail to admire the get-away on the alert.

Twice, three times, the planes rise in perfect order and plunge into a gap in the clouds towards their fate. How many will return in an hour's time?

While the Messerschmitts circle over our heads, slowly, as if they were sure of seizing their prey, we do the same about 100 metres below, hoping, in gaining some altitude, to improve our poor position. In the rear of the formation, I give myself a crick in the neck by keeping my chin up in all directions. To lose sight of the enemy at this moment would be fatal. In the rear position, I could not help but be the first victim selected. By some irony of fate, the Radio Paris announcer is mixed up with our squadron's orders and replies: 'M. Molotov's journey to Berlin is regarded in official circles as a new stage in the expansion of the New Order in Europe.' ...

If my nerves were not so tensed by our situation, they would be put to a hard test. But we are suddenly got out of this sticky position by a squadron of Spitfires higher up.

November 14th

I have had the satisfaction of visiting the celebrated Operations Room, a kind of sanctuary buried 80 metres below the ground and as fiercely defended as a fortress. All the orders given to the fighter flights come from here. From this subterranean place those responsible take in at a glance positions, combats, altitudes, numbers, kinds, nationalities, speeds and directions of planes engaged all over the area. The heart of the R.A.F. is beating here; its mind is at work.

Round a huge table on which a map of England is spread are girls armed with rakes, like croupiers, to whom information comes by telephone. They give it form by moving the arrows and different multicoloured signs with their rakes. Other secretaries, grouped on the galleries along the walls with a view of the whole table, distil the information and pass it according to its significance to those in charge.

Dominating the whole, there are five or six men in a compartment reached by ladders which occupies a complete panel of the big room, situated at the height of the cornice. A mirror at forty-five degrees enables them to look anywhere in the room. From them come the orders to alert the flights. A vast luminous board on the opposite panel gives them the exact position of all the flights, even of all the sections of flights, of which they can dispose. From it, according to the situation, they order the planes into the air, giving direction and altitude. Like giant fowlers, by a single order, they can put hundreds of steel birds where they like.

Deep in these underground places, the conductors of the orchestra see more clearly than the fighter pilot in his sky. How often we hear some such sentence as this: 'Two enemy aircraft at 20,000 feet, six miles to port, such and such direction.' ... At these altitudes the purity of the atmosphere makes the sun so brilliant that it blinds one. ...

This visit to 'somewhere in England' left me thoughtful. What gigantic workings the hard laws of war make necessary! Each to his trade: this obscure one is just as glorious.

November 20th

The flight's black series continues: three missing last week, two in hospital, one lost in cloud, probably in the sea. I am now up to my third burial. This morning two comrades' deaths were confirmed. Linteck and Truaud. We sympathize like old friends. Poor lads! The war goes on, so do we.

December 5th

New faces arrive in the flight as fast as the gaps follow one another. The operations brook no delay. ... Two new comrades bring the number of French to four.

I am appointed leader of a section which is largely French. I hope that when the occasion presents itself, I shall be able to make us cover ourselves with glory. I never cease discussing with those who fly with me the best dispositions for attack, so that when the time comes, we shall act together with rapidity, safety and the maximum cunning. To know each other well is to understand each other well, which is what we want. I dare to believe that they have faith in me.

December 8th

As the days pass, enemy activity is less and less apparent. The bad weather does not trouble us but it stops the Boche. The cold is becoming intense. At 15,000 feet I can no longer feel my fingers; at 20,000, pain; at 25,000, intolerable; at 30,000, I would rather not think what it must be like.

We have been photographed by a man from the *Daily Sketch*. A double page is devoted to us: 'With the pilots of the Churchill Squadron.'

December 10th

I am in a terrible state of over-excitement. Tomorrow morning two of us, both section leaders, are leaving early to fly over France and try, by hedge-hopping, to machine-gun some aerodromes. I volunteered at once; they told me tomorrow will only be a try-out but that as I had asked for it, I could go on the second attempt.

Obviously, I am not hiding the risks of the adventure from myself. If one is hit while hedge-hopping there is no chance of coming through alive. If fate intends me to be captured, my death sentence and execution as a Frenchman who is a 'rebel' and 'traitor' to his country are likely.

I admit I no longer recognize myself. What is it in me that drives me on and stifles all apprehension? I had always promised myself that I would wear an English uniform when I flew over France, have Canadian papers and take the maximum precautions in case I was forced to land. Today, on the eve of a volunteer mission, inertia prevents me, so sure am I of success. I have no illusions about what might happen to me, but I am fascinated by my certainty that all will go well. I have become (or so I think) appallingly positive, making an abstraction of anything that might lead my mind astray among the byways of emotionalism. The only reflections I allow myself I confide to this notebook. My life here has become shamefully material. I eat, I sleep and I fly. My other occupations are few. I should be a little ashamed if all the others were not like me.

I had leave to go to London, and having nothing to do I set myself to go and find Duvelleroy's[1]. I thought the sight of the shop and its fans would give me the feeling of recalling a family memory, something a little less foreign in the very cold England where, despite the magnificent welcome I am given everywhere, I sense the distance which separates me from people and things.

I could only see one fan, on its own in the depths of the shop in a showcase; feminine underwear was displayed in other and larger ones. A showcard indicated that customers were welcomed on the first floor, where tea and even lunch were served. ...

On account of the bad weather, they have just offered me six days' leave. I have had none since January. What should I do with six days? I refused. If only I could have flown to Paris. It would not have taken me long.

The Boche are making themselves scarce. They only come at night now, when the bombing goes on with more or less intensity, according to whether the sky is clear or overcast. The cold and fog increase from week to week. When, after a mission at 25 or even 30,000 feet, at an outside temperature of 50 or 60° below zero, you come down in a matter of minutes to the

---

1. A shop famous in the annals of French fashion since the end of the nineteenth century. It specialized in the making of stylish fans and was founded by René Mouchotte's great-grandparents.

ground, not only are you usually blinded by thick fog but it is rare for the plane, especially the hood perspex, not to be covered with half a centimetre of ice.

To open the whole thing is the only solution. Then the nose freezes. Half blinded, straining your eyes to pick out anywhere at all to land, in case the radio won't work, each instant dreading the embrace of a balloon, you watch the petrol supply running out in terror. That adventure happens nearly every day. Yesterday morning, after chasing two Messerschmitts in vain for too long, and circling round a comrade who had baled out, we wandered about looking for our aerodrome in the mist and found a minute emergency landing-ground. Alas, I had mechanical trouble. No more air pressure, no brakes. I collided, not very violently, with an asphalt lorry. Result: forced to go back via London and by train, my parachute on my back, in boots and flying suit; people looked at me as if I were a Boche prisoner.

December 13th

Friday the 13th: I shall certainly not fly today. First because I have no plane, also because all over the country there is one of those wet white fogs that cut visibility down to five or six metres. Friday the 13th, too.

Suddenly there arrives a posting order as unexpected as it is secret. Tomorrow morning, we leave for another aerodrome, south of London and nearer to it. It is Kenley, next door to Croydon. We shall know the delights of being bombed even better there.

Chapter 7

Kenley Aerodrome

December 17th, 1940

We arrived at Kenley only today. The aerodrome is quite small. Beware of misjudged landings! A big Norman castle, formerly a private home, is completely reserved for the pilots. I had told such a pitiful tale to get my old wartime pal Charles Guérin, lost in Northern Scotland, posted to the squadron that my squadron leader was moved and has succeeded in getting him and another comrade for 615.

That makes six Frenchmen in the house; we have been cleaning and decorating it all day. If the room temperature were not freezing it would be a positive palace. The aerodrome is pleasant; women soldiers swarm. The French uniform has a good deal of success. They serve at table in our Mess. Everything goes on very much as it should.

December 19th

We have no luck. A thick fog has extended over the whole area for several days. Impossible to fly. The Boche is not much talked about, except in the evenings, on the radio.... Charles Guérin has arrived among us. When he was in Scotland he danced with impatience and envy whenever he had a letter from me. Knowing I was in London, fighting without him, while he, for whom the verb 'to fight' conjures up thousands of images, each more wonderful than the other, remained up there straining at the leash!

December 21st

Our first sortie at Kenley nearly turned out badly for me. I had returned to the aerodrome with so little petrol that it ran out just as I was turning to land. Thirty or even fifteen seconds later and I should have had a silly accident which, in these fast machines and in the region south of London, might have had troublesome consequences for this character. Lord, how cold it is up there! Even on the ground it is freezing hard. ...

December 23rd

A day off. I had promised myself a trip to Brighton. Today I borrowed a plane and landed at Shoreham. But before I took off, I had the surprise and happiness of a second letter from my dear little mother.

The affection, the certainty, the calm in those few lines. I am proud of her. I was so afraid of panic and despair. Instead of them I find complete confidence in Heaven and in my fate, and great patience. Let me return soon, and all her hopes with me. She does not doubt that I shall: 'Suzanne will stay with me until you come back.' Neither do I. I have never doubted for an instant.

December 24th

Christmas Eve. How many homes will be lighted up in France tonight! Unaware, the children will utter their cries of joy at the sight of their shoes filled with toys. Some, perhaps, will wonder why their playthings are not so fine this year as last. ...

Here, as always in England, there is an avalanche of Christmas cards. Are the English trying to drown their anxiety in sending these care-killing cards or rather expressing their hope for the future? As for me, from eight to nine o'clock every evening I hang over the radio, concentrating hard. I listen to Radio London: *'Les Français parlent aux Français'*. I know now that my little mother listens religiously every evening and I feel a little as though I were in the room with her. ... My dream is to be able to speak to her through these broadcasts, and when I have shot down my first Boche I shall ask to do so.

An English officer of my squadron, a great Francophile, has forwarded my application to volunteer for operations over France. We are very good friends and I felt sure that through him I should get a favourable reply. They needed a lot of coaxing, it seems, such flights not being meant for the likes of us. Moreover, an application for a false identity card, which is regarded as indispensable, is a matter of almost insuperable difficulty at the administrative level. They also have to take into account the possibility of our escaping in France, with all kinds of material and information.

Whereupon conversations took place and it emerged from them that though we have been trained to escape with stolen material, this is no longer to be feared. 'Bah! We can take the risk. There may be good stuff in these Frenchmen.' ... We'll show them what we can do. So, there we are. I have permission, and so has my inseparable companion Guérin. It would have pained me to do on the venture, without the man who has flown at my side for the past fifteen months. Some last-minute news has come, as absurd as it is incomprehensible. We are to go on these operations over France wearing plain pullovers ... thus, if we are forced to land, we can be under no illusions. We shall be shot at once. *Alea jacta est*. The English are doing the same: so will we. Preparations begin tomorrow and we must observe absolute secrecy. ... Is the Churchill Squadron going to be in on a good thing at last?

Snow on the ground, frost in the air. Without radio we could never get back to the aerodrome. The dirty sky makes take-off very difficult, so all flying is suspended.

The English attach a religious importance to their Christmas. Everything is closed in London. Nothing open but the restaurants. The streets are deserted. At midday a letter came from France for me, this time from Cannes. There I was, wandering about empty streets darkened by thick, yellowish fog. Never have I spent a day in such deep dejection. Even our little club, where I could have got warm, was shut. I should have done better to stay in my room. Even so, Christmas Day! I never cease turning over in my mind the problem that was presented to me before I escaped.

If I had gone back, what should I have been but a source of constant anxiety to my mother? Sent into a factory or a camp, I could not have submitted to German discipline or to working against English interests. Despite myself, I should have done everything I could either to sabotage or to get to England. Would not that cause my mother even more worry? If General de Gaulle's movement did not exist, what state of prostration and shame would the French be in? Life sometimes is far from bright, but it does seem that the future is lighted up by the accomplishing of an ideal: *the liberation of France*.

My uncle seems to be reproaching me with having acted inconsiderately in taking a decision fraught with such serious consequences. Have they seen in my desire to do what is right an irresponsible jump into a new life of adventure of perhaps a wish to escape from an existence that in France is inevitably hard on young people? God! What am I to think? Yet this letter gives me a very clear impression that they are holding something against me over there, at home. ...

What a sad Christmas I have had. My little mother is alone, too.

January 1st, 1941

A new year, full of troubled hopes. Shall I be back in France this time next year? Bitterly cold. It is snowing.

January 2nd

Devastating news has just burst among us like a bomb. No foreigner, French, Polish or Czech, is to take part in the hedge-hopping raids planned for the near future over France. ... So, we have come to London to serve the propaganda of the gentry at French Headquarters! Our pictures appear in the papers, the whole world knows there is a handful of French pilots fighting in the Battle of London. But what they don't know is that we are forbidden dangerous operations. What would become of the noble structure of publicity if the effective strength of us twelve pilots were halved in a month. ...

Yet they never miss a chance in London, with their innuendoes, to say with a paternal little smile, 'Well, no Boche shot down yet this week?' So, we shall be seeing our English comrades take off without us on the flights we have been dreaming about for weeks. Why don't they want us? There's a war on and we are as much combatants as the English. They tell us, almost with tears in their eyes, that the game isn't worth the candle for us, the risks are too great.

I retort that they are less for us than for an Englishman; in case of a forced landing, we French would be able to manage better. As prisoners, we should be shot. But I think the English are very naive to imagine that they could land without trouble during hedge-hopping or that if they were captured the Germans would sleep them on beds of roses. 'Three Poles have just been tortured for three days and then shot.' I certainly should not think my position a very cushy one if they broke my toes one by one to drag some information out of me. But ever since the Poles fought in France, before the Armistice, have they refused to send them over Germany? Did they make use of these ridiculous sentimental formulae with the trembling in the voice to them?

I am disgusted that I have sacrificed so much and that I feel so useless now I have made the effort. I am going to apply for a posting to Canada as an instructor.

January 4th

It wrung my heart to see the first Mosquitos leave. After emptying their pockets and loading the clips of their Colts, they took off eastward. We followed them by radio; their objective was Dunkerque. They attacked south-east of the town. Altitude zero. I imagined them flying along the roads, shooting up all suspicious uniforms, convoys and lorries with their eight machine guns.

Spitting flame right and left, shaving the tree-tops at 300 m.p.h … They came back smiling all over their faces; the report has been drawn up. … Till next time. And as for us, we stay here.

January 5th

We consider we are being bullied by the measures they have taken against us. I dared to hope that as an old member of 615 Squadron I should take part in all interesting operations. There are six Frenchmen in the unit now, six I have got here after much insistence to my squadron leader.

From the six I eliminate two who lack aggressive spirit and are never happy except when they are on the ground. Out of the other four I shall not mention Guérin, whom I have not seen in combat, but whose ardour and will to attack I know only too well. I should be very surprised if he did not come up to my expectations. Bouquillard, whom I got here from North Weald, is not only a delightful comrade but also an astonishing fighter pilot. He is never nervy for an instant; he is only happy when he is in the air. When he scents the Boche he cannot hold himself back. He is the most reliable of the lot. Lafont, who has always been with me in 615, has stood out from the beginning on account of his extreme youth. He is rather a wild youngster but there is no badness in him.

As far as the job is concerned, he is an excellent pilot and has surprises in store for us, I am sure. Lastly, myself. We are so disappointed at being put aside thus that we have held a meeting. The theatre of operations now is the Mediterranean. Here the English are taking the offensive. We are excluded from it. Why not make an application to the Air Ministry for postings to Greece or Egypt? The Germans have just landed in Sicily. There is a job to do there.

January 6th

In hospital with flu.

January 8th

I was surprised to receive a visit from the squadron leader. It was kind of him to put himself to the trouble of coming so far to see me. I am very flattered, for I know others he would not have done as much for. I took advantage of it to raise the famous business of the Mosquitos again. He, too, raised no end of objections against sending us to France. I was able, from my long consideration of the question, to rebut them all heatedly. At last, I saw he was hesitating a little. Was he going to tell me the real truth? He spoke.

'If you were taken prisoner, it would be too easy for the Germans to identify you and make you give information; to confront you with your father or mother. Who would remain silent while his mother was being martyred?'

I admitted the force of the argument. What horror that it should even be conceivable! Shall I one day have my opportunity to sate my loathing of that race?

Our squadron leader is young and a good sport. He is Australian and his accent makes it difficult for me to understand him. He is full of fighting enthusiasm but his is an intelligent ardour which will not make him throw himself and his men heedlessly into the struggle, without getting all the strategical advantages on his side: sun, altitude, dispersion, etc. But he detests the lukewarm, those who follow the squadron like sheep in a flock. He regards them as assassins, for they can cause the deaths of those behind them.

January 11th

I read in the papers that another Goéland has flown from Oran to Gibraltar with two Frenchmen on board. They have just arrived in London. I immediately rushed off to try and see one of them, whose name I shall not mention. It is difficult to describe his face when he saw me. He admitted he thought we were dead.

Our flight made a terrific sensation in Oran, he said. The day before, there had been two or three armed vehicles on the aerodrome; the day after, the landing-ground was surrounded with automatic guns and there were troops everywhere. It appears that the colonel had given his word of honour that no one else should take off, and that same morning two planes escaped – one of them his own Goéland! We had stolen the colonel's plane! He was informed at once, in spite of the earliness of the hour, and gave orders for three fighters to pursue us, which they could very easily have done, for everyone knew our catastrophic cruising speed. It was regarded as a miracle that we had been able to take off, especially with six on board (but they did not know we had such a load).

The act committed by that colonel was thus an absolutely criminal one. Instead of preventing escapes by taking the magnetos out of the engines, dismantling the propellers or other parts to make take-off impossible, he preferred to leave the planes apparently serviceable so that victims in love with liberty should kill themselves after leaving the ground.

67

'Besides, some of those who saw your flight thought it was an acrobatic one: they distinctly saw the plane brush the little direction-finder at the end of the airfield and go dragging heavily along the ground. They would have sworn there had been a crash if they hadn't heard you coming back on your tracks five minutes later.'

In short, the colonel had perhaps decided it would be unwise to let three other pilots take off in pursuit; it might mean three more escapes. It was left at that.

'But next day there was a rumour that the colonel had received a telegram from Gibraltar to the effect that you had been fired on by Spanish troops and that the plane had crashed in the harbour, killing you all.'

That was obviously the plane that had arrived in the afternoon from Morocco, the four occupants of which had been killed. I asked him if our identity was known in Oran after our departure. He could not be sure but does not think so. There was so much coming and going at that time that my flight commander, who was fond of me, would easily have been able to show me present. But in any case, I would rather be officially dead, so that my family run no risk of being bothered.

The measures taken after our escape were incredible it seems, troops, automatic guns, each pilot, having to give his word of honour not to escape, planes partly dismantled and many comrades posted to 'youth camps' in the south. We know what that means. The man who told me this story took advantage of the Italian Commission's visit to fly off at full noon in their plane, which apparently contained important papers into the bargain. Well done! Now he was in London, rather surprised to find a whole people with all classes united by a common purpose, fighting with smiling faith and keeping its good humour despite hard knocks.

January 18th

One sometimes wonders whether England – or rather, the people – fully realize that they are now in a besieged citadel and that victory is a matter of life or death. What administrative slowness there is! Selection, then manufacture, testing and distribution involve a waste of precious time.

We were promised new planes by November 20th. Churchill himself assured us of it. Spring is near. The Germans are about to mount a most shattering and deadly offensive. They are going to throw the whole of their air force into the assault, twenty to one. Against their new types of aircraft, we shall still have only our old Hurricanes, which used to get out of breath last September chasing German bombers.

Here is an amusing instance of the English state of mind.

The district in which one of my comrades lives was plastered with delayed-action bombs. Not knowing this, he went back to his hotel in the evening and was astonished to hear no sounds next morning. At eight o'clock, not having had his breakfast, despite repeated ringing of the bell, he got up and was surprised not to find a living soul, even at the reception desk. He went out and came across a policeman, who told him that the whole area had been evacuated on account of the bombs and that he should have gone to spend the night in a shelter.

They would have forbidden him to enter the hotel if they had noticed him. He then asked if the specialist squads would remove the bombs before night and if he could return to his quarters in the evening. 'You are forgetting, sir,' said the man, 'it is Sunday today; the squads will not start work until tomorrow.'

January 22nd

My squadron leader has just recommended Bouquillard and me for commissions. We thought at once of the troublesome effect this might have on the rest of our comrades. I foresee stupid arguments. It would have been a hundred times more sensible to have commissioned the lot of us rather than give the appearance of some being singled out, and perhaps spoil our good relations.

January 24th

The Germans announce a shattering attack on Great Britain before next April. 'A fatal and decisive blow!' An important American commentator estimates the number of planes they can put in the air over London at 35,000.

I have rarely been more indignant than I was the other evening when a comrade told me of the conversation between two French Headquarters bureaucrats; they remarked that we have no Boche to our credit and spoke of us as 'debunked'. Now that my anger has passed, I can regard them with the contempt they deserve. Is it jealousy because they are not in our shoes, rancour and bitterness resulting from a stupid life of pleasure and inaction in London? Or is it more simply popular opinion, which expects a fighter pilot's courage to be measured by the number of enemy planes shot down.

'How many Jerries have you got?' That is the eternal question one is asked in London and elsewhere. Success in fighters is undoubtedly a question of courage, but no one will deny that luck has an equal share in it. How often, last October, did we patrol without seeing an aircraft, while the flight that went up after us landed an hour later with two or three victories? It will not be so next month. But I must not disclose what our job is to be. I only desire one thing: to be able to give the lie once and for all to these scatterbrains who talk without the slightest knowledge of a game that is often pretty tough.

February 7th

Our flight went over France today, driving in as far as Arras. It was a black day for the squadron: three out of twelve planes did not return. It is supposed that one of them has landed safely in France, shot down by an Me. 109. Let us hope he got away. He knew a little French and may get by. The second crashed in the sea; the third came down in England and, thank God, there isn't much wrong with him.

What humiliation it is to look on as we did today when our comrades returned. They knew perfectly well that we would have volunteered, that the only barrier was an order which goes against our wishes. But when we put ourselves in their places it is easy to imagine what those who are lukewarm in combat and who are left cold by these Mosquito operations must inevitably feel. Moreover, we are French! That is the heart of the matter. The least mistake through inattention, in handling the plane, will never be forgiven us, while it would pass unnoticed in an Englishman. It is brought to light and remarked upon. 'He's still a Frenchman!'

Of course, the English admit our qualities, but they must be often displayed. A plane saved under difficult conditions, an engagement with the enemy, any lucky initiative on our part, will never produce any sign of satisfaction. We are French. Two friends, Perrin and Bouquillard, were shot down by the enemy. The former baled out; the latter, with many bullet wounds, landed in a field. In France they would have been mentioned in despatches; here they only just escaped being regarded as imbeciles. A delicate situation; sometimes it needs a lot of patience and courage not to let our morale go.

February 8th

Charles and I have been to Air Headquarters. Colonel Pigeaud has been in charge for three days. He almost embraced us. He told us he would never forget the morning of our arrival in Gibraltar. He gave us some good news: he has just lifted the ban which his predecessors inexplicably imposed on our flying over France.

70

At last! Knowing we had volunteered for operations of this kind, it would delight him, he said, if some of our exploits made the skeleton group of French pilots' shine. It seems he has great plans for us.

So, we left his office, our hearts uplifted by huge hopes. At last, we feel a commander behind us.

February 16th

A gale is blowing over the squadron. Nothing is going well. From orders badly given to planes deplorably maintained. We miss the little French mechanic who loved his 'kite' and formed one team, one conscience, one will with his pilot! No one would think this is a squadron on active service. The English mechanic repairs the part whose maintenance has been entrusted to him. *If he notices a defective part, he has no orders to deal with, he will not touch it.*

Apart from the periodical inspections, it is the pilot and the pilot alone who examines his plane each morning. If he finds anything wrong, however slight, a verbal order to the mechanic is not enough. He has to enter it in a book for the purpose. What a waste of time! How many human lives risked by negligence!

Since I have been with 615 Squadron, I have four times seen forced landings in the country for lack of oil! I have not once heard the least protest or the least murmur on the part of our C.O. or our chief mechanic. Once it was sure that the pilot was safe, the affair was hushed up and not mentioned again. People have always boasted to me of English coolness and phlegm, but pushed to this extreme they are disquieting. ...

This morning at nine o'clock three planes left on a special operation over Northern Belgium and Holland. One had to land shortly after taking off, before reaching the sea, over which he had 140 kilometres to fly. Reason: shortage of oil, shortage of glycol, the engine-cooling fluid. The other two, Stewart and Foe, reached Ostend but they have not returned. Is that due to combat or rather to ....? All these matters are ill-calculated to keep up a squadron's morale. We are not far from confusing negligence with ill-will. Stewart was a good pal and a 615 veteran. The squadron keeps getting replacements. There are only four 'originals' left.

February 17th

I have this moment heard that the German radio has announced that two Hurricanes have crashed in Holland. One is reported to have had engine-trouble. ... One of the two pilots is safe.

The recommendations have gone in to the Air Ministry. According to the custom, Bouquillard and I are going to be given the King's Commission. Our position is a curious one. Shall we have the rank of sous-lieutenant or that of pilot officer? I should love to see the face of a certain officer in Oran with whom I was not particularly friendly. He gave me eight days' C.B. for flying too close to the ground the second time I flew an M.S. 406! Not knowing I had been an instructor he could never stomach such a performance on the part of a trainee, while he himself always kept to a cautious horizontal flight. 'Don't bank your turns too steeply, it's very dangerous.' He was one of those most active in putting obstacles in the way of pilots escaping to England after the Armistice.

February 18th

At last, we have our new planes. A new Hurricane, faster than the one we have, whose climbing power is apparently prodigious. According to its 'theoretical' performance it will go up to 13,300 metres. It gets from the ground to 10,000 metres in eight minutes.

February 19th

The snow has begun to fall again. But it has not stopped me getting astride the new war-horse which has just been allocated to me. What an engine! As soon as the wheels have left the ground, the plane itself takes a terrifying climbing angle and, even more incredible, it keeps its climbing speed without seeming to flag. To spare the engine, I gave it no more boost than plus two. I found myself going at a speed of 250 m.p.h. As for its diving speed, I reached, without forcing, in a medium dive, 640 km. an hour.

The meteor! It must do more than 850 in a rapid one. I am thinking delightedly of the little Messerschmitt which, if I am lucky, I shall have in my sights. I blacked out several times in my turns, giving the machine a good shaking to get to know it. Spins and pull-outs were sweet. There are upper and lower rudder-bars. In turns or high-speed movements one can put the feet on the upper bar so that the feet and knees are level with the chin. This lying-down position apparently counteracts the effects of black-out. Now for the Boche!

February 22nd

An artist from the Air Ministry has been to sketch me. Posed for nearly two hours to get my sorry mug (to which the artist wanted to give the look of an aviator) down on paper. For its specimen of a French pilot, the Air Ministry is going to be done!

February 23rd

I have just beaten my altitude record. This morning I reached 24,000 feet and the plane wanted nothing better than to go higher. Our interception task, however, was limited to that height. Forty Messerschmitts on one side and eighteen on the other made a half turn. We were flanked by Spitfires and I was pleased to see the ones we used to be unable to support were having trouble keeping up with us this morning.

Ten more Frenchmen sentenced to five years' hard labour for trying to join General de Gaulle's army. Shameful.

February 25th

My first raid over France. Escorting bombers over Calais. They dropped their bombs on the harbour. Impossible to see the explosions but impossible not to see the hundreds of shell-bursts from the Boche ack-ack round our Blenheims. All went well.

February 26th

A sad reckoning today. One plane on its nose in a field. Pilot safe. Another, Foxley-Norris, shot down. He baled out and woke up in hospital. Our squadron leader, Holmwood, was hit and baled out. All would have been well if his parachute, for some inexplicable reason, had not blazed up at 4,000 metres. Another, Hone, is also in hospital. Score: one dead and two wounded.

On the other side, I am delighted to know that little Lafont, youngest of the French, has just shot down his first Messerschmitt.

I have this moment learned that Holmwood baled out from his burning plane; his parachute caught fire and he hit the ground from 7,000 metres. Hone got a burst and his plane turned over. He landed upside down! To have come through that with a few bruises is a miracle. I did not take part in the operation, having run short of petrol in the morning and had engine trouble for half the day on an emergency aerodrome.

So young Lafont has his Boche, the first shot down by one of the French. Unhappily our delight is much diminished by the squadron's mourning. We loved our C.O. He was a great Francophile and often took our part. It is to some extent due to him that Bouquillard and I are getting commissions. His frightful death, not in combat, is upsetting everyone. Three planes lost without anyone seeing a thing.

February 27th

A letter from France has reached me, from my uncle. After the state of confusion into which the last blow threw the squadron, I have now reached one almost of despair, for I cannot see how I can possibly get out of it.

My mother's health has taken a serious turn and he twice asks me to go back to France, *as only my return can help her to bear the great mental and physical suffering she is going through.* I have re-read his letter fifty times and each time I find a more alarming meaning in the words of his appeal. A tragic problem! Even to think of deserting England? The shame for me! Yet why, if it would save my mother?

My comrades tell me that my return to France would mean my being sentenced to death or imprisonment. The horrible impotence! And feeling so alone, so alone. If I could sob and shed tears, I think it would relieve me. The bombing is raging tonight. My uncle asks me in his letter if the bombing is not upsetting my nerves too much. If only he knew! The war, the country occupied, the only son on the other side of the barricade, the impossibility of his return, the worry, the physical privations, frail health – what an agony I am making my poor mother suffer! If only I could clasp her to my heart, if only for a minute! I am like a madman dashing himself against the four walls of his cell until he injures himself.

February 28th

I re-read my uncle's letter; he complains of no longer having a car! … I do not know what will come of the mental depression I am passing through. I act like a body without a soul, driven on by I know not what; I have neither pride nor bitterness. I am a destiny. I move at the will of events. Only today I am afraid of being afraid, for I am anguishedly measuring the change that may take place in me if fear should take the place of the indifference that dictates my actions up there in the sky. I am not thinking. I am afraid of thinking too much.

March 3rd

Holmwood's burial.

March 4th

Until Foxley-Norris recovers from his parachute jump, I am appointed leader of B Flight. In the air I am therefore responsible for six planes. An honour rather than a reward.

We went up to 35,000 feet today. At this altitude I have frightful trouble with my stomach. I suffered so much I thought I should faint, but I would not have left the formation for anything in the world. Violent hiccups tore my chest. In spite of the oxygen, I had great difficulty in breathing. I vomited in my mask. ... When I have to go up three or four times a day shall I be able to resist the exhaustion?

French Headquarters are taking good care of our publicity ... and their own. They must have found the document relating to our escape at the bottom of a drawer only today. They hastened to send it to *The Times*. ... We were far from foreseeing that on June 29th, 1940.

March 6th

When Hone crashed on February 26th the shock so unbalanced him that he was insane for hours. As he got out of what remained of his Hurricane, he suddenly drew his revolver and fired in all directions. Soldiers had to overpower him and take him away. He was lucky they did not take him for a German and shoot him down.

March 8th

Engine trouble again forced me to break formation. Cockpit full of smoke, engine stopped. Above an ocean of cloud, very near the ground, position not known and in a modern fighter aircraft, there was nothing very funny about the experience. However, my engine started again, with dubious goodwill, and I was lucky enough to get to Shoreham aerodrome.

March 10th, evening

I have just had my worst nervous shock since I began to fight: as an impotent onlooker I have just seen the terrible end of one of my best friends, little Bouquillard. We went up on an alarm this evening at 6.30, dirty mist clinging to the clouds. In a few minutes we climbed to 30,000 feet. We were warned of 'bandits' everywhere.

My own plane being out of commission, I had been given one which had a defective supercharger. I did not succeed in staying with the squadron and found myself in the critical position of being a solitary aircraft. At each turn I managed to manoeuvre nearer to them but I soon lost the distance gained. I therefore saw distinctly what happened; I was the only one to do so.

Two planes, visible by the white smoke from their exhausts, appeared 1,000 feet above us. They had already been in sight for five minutes. At once I knew that not a single pilot except Bouquillard and myself had noticed them. Poor Bouquillard, whose job was to fly S's above the squadron, went for them immediately, climbing. I saw them turn and then, at once, I saw a plane dive earthwards like a stone. With my powerless plane I could do nothing whatever. I cannot understand why they did not also try and fall upon the isolated and easy prey I offered.

The death of our poor 'Grand-Père', as we affectionately nick-named him, has left us all in a horrible state of depression. Henry shared my room; the empty bed and the sudden silence give me an overpowering sense of isolation. Without family and without friends, too, in this land of exile, we drew close enough together to think of each other as brothers. In whom should we confide, to whom should we confess our troubles and talk of our hopes, if not these same brothers who share the same dangers and obey the same law each day?

I had made a real friend of Bouquillard and the day never passed on which I failed to admire his qualities of uprightness and courage. Savagely determined, he gave himself body and soul to his purpose; he took hard knocks without ill humour. Now there are three of us, a little more united, perhaps, and ever more determined to go on and avenge our poor little Bouqui. May God grant it.

March 15th

Our poor 'Grand-Père's' funeral was this morning. My room is appallingly sad now. We bore him to the cemetery, broken-hearted. ... Goodbye, Bouqui.

On March 10th, Bouquillard and I were commissioned as sous-lieutenants by General de Gaulle. We knew nothing about it; I have only heard about it today.

Today, March 15th, the day of our comrade's burial, young Lafont shot down his second Boche. I had been patrolling over a convoy for an hour and a half without seeing anything. Lafont relieved me and had the luck to chase six Messerschmitts which were attacking the ships. He thinks he got one of them; he saw it making for France, losing altitude, with a cloud of glycol escaping.

It is magnificent that he should have been successful on a day like today, but you are not sufficiently avenged yet, Bouqui.

March 18th

This afternoon there is something amusing to record. The whole squadron was flying at 35,000 feet. I was at the head, to port of the leader. After an hour and a quarter's flying, I realized that in a few minutes I should have no oxygen left. There was only one thing to do: signal the fact and break formation to get down fast into a more hospitable atmosphere.

The Boche was patrolling in our neighbourhood so I must waste no time going down on my own. Alas, they were too busy keeping a look-out for bandits and no one heard my message. I turned over, without further delay, and went into a vertical dive. Just as I was landing, I was surprised to see the whole squadron behind me.

They had all thought I was attacking some imaginary plane and had raced into a vertical dive on my tail. Some even thought I was the bandit! That is how, unconsciously, I brought the pack back to kennels.

Three hours later, at the same altitude, we were attacked by a squadron of Spitfires coming out of the sun; we took them for Messerschmitts. We received orders to beat a retreat, all the advantages being with the other side. There was a disorderly flight into the sun, some upside down, some spiralling, some in S's. I went down 10,000 metres in a few seconds on my back. The plane vibrated terribly. My air-speed indicator showed 430 m.p.h. The stick was as hard as iron when I hauled on it to pull out. These two dives have exhausted me, and I have to fly again tonight.

March 20th

I can't do any more. And the great German attack has not come yet. We are on our feet from 5.30 in the morning until 10.30 at night, at readiness most of the time, ready to leap into the saddle. This has been going on since September. I am going to ask for a few days' rest. It would be too stupid to be immobilized for more.

March 22nd

I have been to French Headquarters; they told me there is a Rest Home near Oxford. I have a week. I am royally installed. A huge park. I laze, with a regiment of English nurses and adorable French nurses, too, at my orders. Some French naval men and flyers keep me company. This is rest on the grand scale and it is doing me good.

But I am tired, dreadfully tired, as much mentally as physically. I can say without hesitation that Bouqui's death gave me a terrible nervous shock. Our incessant overwork and the exhaustion have got me down. I needed a month's rest.

March 26th

I have been for several walks in the park and surrounding country. I am friends with everyone. What a joy it would be to be awakened every morning at Kenley by such pretty nurses, all kind and of excellent family. Their beauty is remarkable. I have observed that in England the women are either frankly unattractive or else have such pure and regular faces that one seeks in vain for some small defect which would tire the eyes. And here I have fallen into the midst of this gathering of Madonnas, rendered even more angelic by the head-dress which gives them heavenly profiles.

One of them, like a tiny doll, always smiling, took me to Oxford yesterday by car. Alas, it rained and I saw nothing but grey walls. We only stayed half an hour. She is the daughter of the principal directress of the British Red Cross. She insists that I must go and stay for a day or two at their country home near here. Another, whom I call Joan of Arc because she is so beautiful, is the close friend of Churchill's daughter. Another, who has just honoured me by taking a walk in the park, is merely a Princess of the Royal Family. They are all unspoilt; they coo and splutter in French, which causes a great deal of laughter, of which there is abundance in this place.

As for the French girls, physically pretty as they are, they are far from approaching their rivals' beauty. I say rivals, for there is open war. I think jealousy is chiefly responsible. I need diplomacy all the time.

March 28th

I must leave this earthly paradise. Three of them came to wake me up. I am not too dissatisfied at going because I am re-joining my squadron, which is beginning to miss me, and I have promised everyone here to come back by plane.

At Beaconsfield I met Sergeant-Pilot Dubourgel, who has an arm broken in an accident due to the instructor's fault at the training unit. His case really is worthy of the greatest admiration. Before escaping from France last June, he telephoned his mother to let her know and learned from her that his two sisters, nurses at the front, and his three brothers had been killed; his father was a prisoner in Germany. His brave mother, quite alone now, had the sublime strength to say, 'Go and try to avenge them.' And here was my poor friend, dragging about like a soul in torment, going from bad luck to worse. They refused to post him straight to a fighter squadron. He was forced to begin his training as a pilot all over again, though he had been flying a Bloch 151 in France. Time passed. Then his accident. I found the poor fellow in a most frightful mental state. I have promised to move heaven and earth to get him into my squadron as I did Charles and the others.

During my absence Admiral Muselier has been a guest of honour in the officers' mess at Kenley. The wing commander spoke in our praise.

He even went so far as to say that if he had to start again, *he would wish to be commanded in the air only by Frenchmen.* Such a compliment is flattering indeed.

April 4th

Disappointment, disappointment. This morning at ten o'clock they asked for volunteers for the Mosquito raids: hedge-hopping and machine-gunning over France and Belgium. I was given a section to lead and had the luck to have Guérin with me. The weather was good: low, continuous cloud.

I studied the route I meant to take in great detail; I planned Le Touquet, where there are, I know, one or two Boche squadrons. But when all our dispositions were made and we had innumerable wild ideas in our heads, we were told the banquet is postponed. This did not prevent our C.O. saying to another officer, 'Out of eight volunteers, the three Frenchmen stepped forward as one man, the Czechs and the Poles as one man, and I am surprised to see that out of ten Englishmen only two came forward.'

April 15th

There are only three of us French round the big mess table tonight. Young Blaize, who joined 615 after our poor Bouqui's death, has just met a horrible death, too. Our squadron was over the Channel, patrolling at 30,000 feet. Blaize imprudently let himself fall behind and was attacked by two Me. 109s. He baled out and, followed by a Hurricane, came down in the sea 15 kilometres from the coast.

Unhappily, shortage of petrol forced the pilot back to his base, and when the patrols of ships and coastal aircraft arrived, they found only the parachute. He had drifted away, supported by his safety-belt. The icy water condemned him to a shocking end. The search was abandoned this evening. Guérin and Lafont are now my only brothers-in-arms.

The horror of such an end only confirms the more profoundly the lust for vengeance which makes us instinctively grit our teeth when the enemy comes in sight. The job is hard physically but all the more so mentally. We never have the solace of confiding in a beloved being, a mother, and hearing from her the sweet words of affection and consolation that would make us think we were going down a few steps towards childhood, when the mother so often healed a grief-stricken little heart with a smile.

Our position as exiles, rejected by our own people, is becoming appallingly hard. The balance of our morale is maintained only by a constant effort of the will; when a wind a little more violent than usual blows, we are the first to fall victims to it and it takes us days to build up again. The English, less emotional, were so surprised at our depression after Grand-Père's death that they could not help notifying the Air Ministry of it in one of their reports on us.

April 17th

A grim order to the effect that the squadron is leaving the defence of London to devote itself to that of the Welsh coast, protecting convoys in particular. We shall fly at lower altitudes, which does not displease me. Unfortunately, when we change over, we shall have to surrender our beautiful Hurricane IIs to the pilots who take our place and ride once more upon the ancient war horses that pant after the bombers. ... We shall also be flying a lot at night. Those with cat's eyes are lucky!

Last night London suffered the worst bombing of the war. From 8.30 p.m. the enemy air force came not in ones but in full squadrons to pour its loads on the city and the surrounding country. We were not spared at Kenley. Habit, fortunately, saved me from insomnia, in spite of the bombs and the guns on the aerodrome. This morning a dense mass of smoke over London was reflecting a sinister red light which extended for several miles. London burning. ...

What a contrast with the blue sky to the south! Tens of thousands of people will be homeless; hundreds have certainly met their deaths. Whole districts will be nothing but smoking ruins. And yet, when I return to that very brave city, I am sure I shall find it as animated as before, the people as carefree, their spirit as determined and as *sure of victory*.

April 18th

I have considerable cause for pride. It so happens that our squadron leader and the two flight leaders are on night-flying and it was necessary to appoint someone to be responsible for the whole squadron, as a squadron leader is. I have been chosen. I thus have proof that they esteem me as a pilot as well as a man. With twenty pilots to choose from they select a Frenchman. I do not want to be taken for a fool or a braggart but I am happy in the faith the English have in me.

Chapter 8

Valley, in Wales

April 21st

We took off at nine o'clock. The whole squadron. After circling widely, we passed in majestic order over our base, taking a friendly farewell. A last glance at the scene of so much adventure and so much mourning. The memories we leave behind us! To starboard, London was still smoking from that night's bombing. It is a scratch squadron, four-fifths replacements, young and unassimilated elements, flying from the battlefield to dress its wounds and forge new arms.

We were making for Wales. At the end of our journey, we found mountains still showing traces of snow. It took us forty-five minutes to do 200 miles. We landed on our island. A desert place! Not a village less than twelve miles away. Not a tree. Sand – sand! It is windy and the wind penetrates everywhere. Very cold and comfortless. We shall have to fight against depression here. The planes they have given us in exchange for our own are in a deplorable condition. The propellers are peeling, there is play on the controls, the sand covers everything, dries up the oil, gets into the engine. Despite all this the machines must fly, which is something of a miracle.

April 26th

The days pass slowly. Every second day we rise at 4 a.m., before sunrise. Bed at 10. Patrol over convoys all day. Whatever the weather, we go far out to sea to find them. This morning a young comrade and I went out more than 80 kilometres to protect a single ship for an hour and a half. Often there are fifteen of them, sailing in line astern like soldiers marching, while one or two little destroyers play at being hounds from a hunting pack, ahead or astern. They sometimes have balloons which they drag like children's toys, to prevent dive-bombing.

I often amuse myself by flying at sea level between the ships. I see them wave a kind of salute. A senior officer who lectured us once on convoys made no secret of the impression the arrival of British planes makes on a convoy. The tension relaxes; everyone feels such confidence in the speed and armament of these winged brothers that the whole convoy seems to come to life again. The captain's nerves relax, all the men on deck watch the great birds as they ceaselessly turn and dive and sweep the air above and below the clouds. Reassured, they smile at such friends.

April 29th

Eyre, our squadron leader, is leaving us. It appears he has too much operational experience. It is the most exasperating thing that could happen to us. Thanks to him there still prevails in 615 some of the magnificent spirit of the period when I joined at Prestwick. Bit by bit the squadron has been decimated. We have seen the best fall.

Others have come; then the great hecatomb of March decided the squadron's fate. Eyre thought a lot of me, and as old men of the squadron Hugo and I both had his confidence. Another squadron leader is coming and some new pilots. Goodbye, dear old 615, you are definitely dead now.

April 30th

Here I am, stuck in this hole, probably for several months, long enough to form a unified squadron. The monotonous job will be devoid of all interest, the Boche being totally absent. I did not come to England to be the patrol leader of young men in training and I have decided to send in my resignation tomorrow to the new squadron leader and apply to be posted back to what I call a *fighting* unit. They tell me that an experienced pilot only has to ask and he will be welcomed. I am going to have a third shot at getting to Egypt. There must be some warm work out there.

We do nothing but protect convoys. We fly in pairs; I have got Charles in my flight, so we always fly together. I prefer having him beside me; he knows me well, better than anyone else.

This morning visibility was nil, or very nearly. We literally shaved the waves, flying right out to sea without being able to see 200 metres ahead. It was a miracle that after a quarter of an hour's flying straight through a grey cotton mist we suddenly saw the outlines of ships rising before us.

I have sent a long letter to Headquarters, explaining the reasons for my resignation. I do not think they will refuse it, for on the whole my motives are quite praiseworthy, but I should be very surprised if they authorized me to leave them. What would become of them if one of their few pilots for the defence of London left for the Middle East?

The Mouchotte Memorial at the Louis Bleriot Aerogare, Dunkerque.

The Memorial to The Few, on the cliffs at Capel-le-Ferne, overlooking Folkestone and the English Channel, where Jan Leeming's deeply personal journey and search for René Mouchotte began.

Left: Jan Leeming at the
Sir Christopher Foxley-Norris
Memorial Wall, at The National
Memorial to The Few site, on which
René Mouchotte is commemorated.

Below: Hubert de Lisle, husband
of René Mouchotte's niece, with
Jan Leeming at the Sir Christopher
Foxley-Norris Memorial Wall.

The Mouchotte family tomb at Père Lachaise Cemetery, Paris.

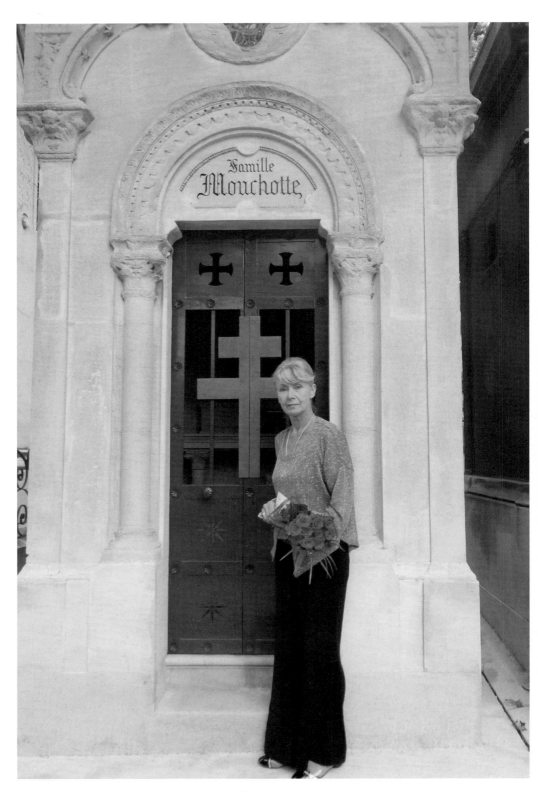

Jan Leeming at the Mouchotte family tomb.

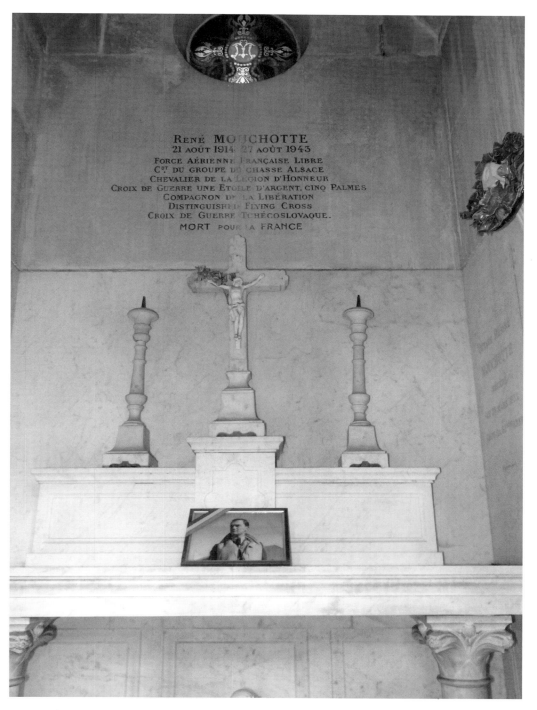

RENÉ MOUCHOTTE
21 AOÛT 1914 - 27 AOÛT 1943
FORCE AÉRIENNE FRANÇAISE LIBRE
C^{DT} DU GROUPE DE CHASSE ALSACE
CHEVALIER DE LA LÉGION D'HONNEUR
CROIX DE GUERRE UNE ÉTOILE D'ARGENT, CINQ PALMES
COMPAGNON DE LA LIBÉRATION
DISTINGUISHED FLYING CROSS
CROIX DE GUERRE TCHÉCOSLOVAQUE.
MORT POUR LA FRANCE

The plaque commemorating René Mouchotte within the family tomb.

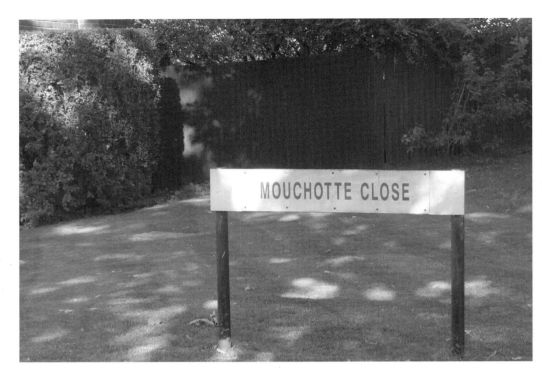

Appropriately, Mouchotte Close, at Biggin Hill in Kent, also commemorates this gallant French airman.

René Mouchotte and Charles Guerin at controls of the Caudron Goéland in which they escaped to Gibraltar – a photograph taken by Henry Lafont.

René Mouchotte aboard the *President Houdouce* – an armed merchant ship, Liverpool bound.

Commandant René Mouchotte and Squadron Leader Jack Charles, who jointly shared RAF Biggin Hill's 1,000th aerial victory.

Commandant René Mouchotte and Squadron Leader Jack Charles. Henry Lafont is behind the former.

René Mouchotte in flying kit. (Courtesy of the Mouchotte Family)

A favourite photograph of
René Mouchotte. (Courtesy of
the Mouchotte Family)

An exhausted René Mouchotte, resting between sorties. (Courtesy of the Mouchotte
Family)

The Commonwealth War Graves Commission section of Middelkerke Cemetery, Belgium, where Commandant Mouchotte's body was first interred.

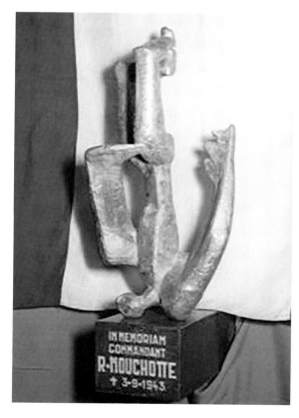

The Mouchotte Memorial in Middelkerke Town Hall.

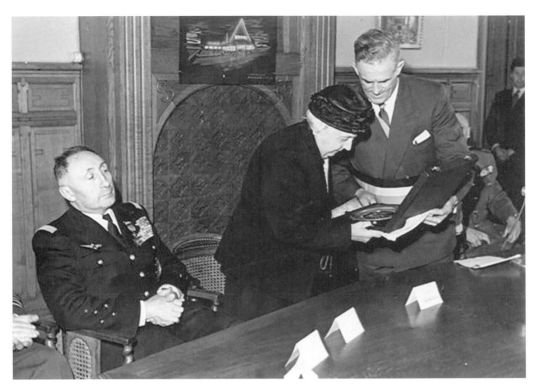

The presentation of a commemorative plaque to Madame Mouchotte, René's mother. At left is Colonel Valin.

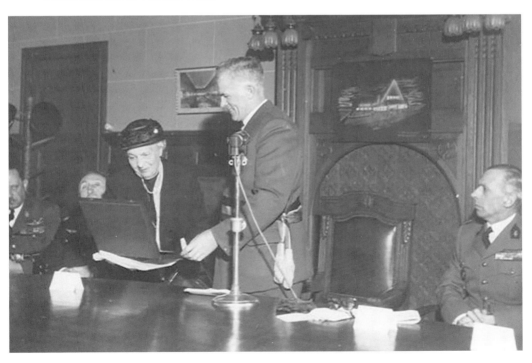

Plaque presentation in Middelkerke Town Hall.

The Middlekerke Plaque. (Courtesy of the Mouchotte Family)

Saluting the flag.

M. Mouchotte cutting the ribbon at the naming ceremony of René Mouchottestraat.

ICI EST NE
LE 21 AOUT 1914
LE COMMANDANT RENE MOUCHOTTE
HEROS DES FORCES FRANCAISES LIBRES
COMMANDANT LE GROUPE ALSACE
CHEVALIER DE LA LEGION D'HONNEUR
COMPAGNON DE LA LIBERATION
MORT EN COMBAT AERIEN
LE 27 AOUT 1943

Mouchotte Plaque outside the family home.

The Mouchotte family home, where René grew up – now apartments.

One of many streets dedicated to René Mouchotte, this one adjacent to Gare Montparnasse, Paris.

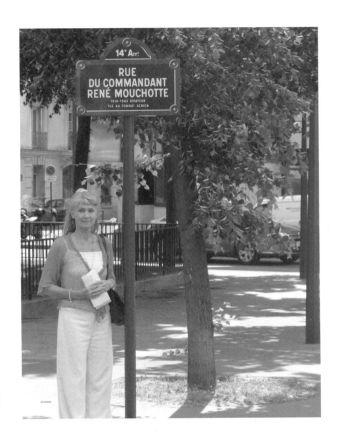

Jan Leeming with Art Nouveau street sign adjacent to Gare Montparnasse.

The Mouchotte sign at Luxeuil air base, France.

Left: Jacqueline Quentin Mouchotte, René's sister, with her daughters and sons in law.

Below: René and Jacqueline Mouchotte as children. (Courtesy of the Mouchotte Family)

Chapter 9

Charles Guérin's Death

May 10th, 1941

It happened on Saturday at 3.45 p.m. and now that several days have passed, I can write about the frightful catastrophe which cost my best friend, Charles Guérin, his life.

On patrol over a convoy some fifty miles out to sea, we had been flying for over an hour when I suddenly saw the fatal white cloud which indicates escaping glycol stream from his machine. There is nothing to be done about it: it is complete engine-failure. I immediately got in touch with him. He asked me for a course back to the aerodrome. As we made for the coast, I advised him to bale out; we were at 4,000 feet.

At last, I heard his voice; he told me he could not get back. He was going to try and ditch near the convoy. My poor old Charles, if only you had listened to me! I kept as close to him as I could. He had opened the cockpit hood. His propeller was barely turning. In spite of that, a great cloud of white smoke completely enveloped the plane and must have blinded him. I talked to him to the very end, encouraging and advising him.

Alas, when we were at 50 feet, the most unforeseeable thing happened. I can only explain it by the density of the glycol which must have completely blinded Charles. He straightened his plane out, thinking he was at sea level, then with a savagely swift movement the plane lurched to starboard, skimmed the sea, turned over and vanished in less than a second. With my eyes fixed on the spot I could not realize the horrible truth, so rapidly had it all happened.

Against all common sense, I dived desperately at the little yellow lifebuoy flung overboard in passing by the ship near which Charles had gone down. The destroyer came up at high speed. I circled and circled at sea level. I skirted the destroyer. I saw the seamen making gestures of despair to me. I stayed there for a quarter of an hour, seeing nothing but the flat sea closed above my poor old Charles, swallowed up, imprisoned in his plane.

I had to leave the spot; my petrol was running out. The cruel reality was borne in upon me. I went back alone.

My companion throughout the war, who left France with me, who escaped from Algeria with me, my brother-in-arms with his great hope for the future, has left me for ever. We were inseparable, and it was to be my fate to hold him by the hand until death. I could not repress the sobs that were choking me. Flying Control called poor Charles for the second time. I answered brokenly. Then at a third call, unable to stand it, I cut off. The way back was one long torment and it was a miracle I did not kill myself in landing.[2]

I sent a desperate letter to Headquarters immediately after this. My nerves are at breaking point. I cannot remain with this squadron, pursuing us with its horrible ill luck. I want to go to London, to fight somewhere else, to fly no more of the tin-pan planes we have here. Three engine failures this week! For the third time I have to pack a poor comrade's effects. The horror of this war. I swear, I swear to avenge them all, especially you, young Toto, who so longed for a sight of the Boche. I have taken his private papers and will give them to his father myself. Now I am alone with Lafont and Brière.

I have been to London by plane to break the news to Charles' fiancée. A painful duty. Also called at Headquarters. They have been favourably impressed by my two letters and I shall soon be back in the south. Colonel Valin asked me to lunch.

Have just come back from London. I feel appallingly lonely. I have sad news from France. My mother, through some Fifth Column machination, heard I was dead. She had a cruel time for three days or more until my telegram arrived. My uncle writes that her health is poor. The horror of being exiled like this.

May 11th

I am getting letters of sympathy from all over. Among them one from Lady Sinclair, who was very fond of poor Toto. Another, from a comrade, tells me they are asking for volunteers for a very special kind of mission – accompanying convoys from America as pilot on board a ship. It often happens that one of the famous German long-range Condor aircraft surprises a convoy in mid-Atlantic and bombs it.

---

2. Charles Guérin received a posthumous mention in despatches. It ended with this astonishing note: 'This citation does not carry the award of the Croix de Guerre.'

The pilot's duty is then to go up, catapulted, shoot down the big four-engine plane, then bale out from his Hurricane and be picked up by one of the ships of the convoy. I would take any job to get away from this squadron. In any case the Boche is rare in England now and the Battle of the Atlantic is vital to Germany. I am therefore putting in for it, provided I can definitely come back to England when the first French squadron is formed. I sent my application in this afternoon.

May 13th

Brière, in his turn, has been lost in mid-ocean and was drowned in his plane in the same circumstances as Charles. There were seven Frenchmen in the one squadron at Kenley. I am now alone with Lafont. Whose turn next? I prefer not to think about it, thinking hurts so much. I want to live like an animal from now on. What is the use of going in circles like a lunatic round this idea of the ill luck which curses us. I avoid pitying myself for my fate; there is nothing like it to lessen courage. I have done my job until now and I can go on doing it.

May 13th, night

I am at readiness for night-flying again. I confess I would not mind being replaced tonight. Our poor old Brière's accident haunts me. I tested my plane at ten, not long ago. A black night, my God. Impossible to distinguish the sea from the land. I tried to plunge through the clouds. ...

For 2,000 feet I lived in unreality. Only my panel lights gave me any sense of life. Then the stars. Coming down was agony. Trusting nothing but my instruments, I dived back into the bath of blackness. I found it hard to know when I was out of it or what my altitude was, so dense was the darkness. And it was only by the course I had been given for my return that I found I was over the sea.

I was sweating when I landed. Ten minutes after my return the chief mechanic came to tell me I had a glycol leak and that my plane is definitely unserviceable. Another ten minutes in the air and it would have been my turn.

May 16th

Despite myself I am pursued by the memory of the two comrades who fell at such a short interval. I have had a telegram from Colonel Valin, trying to restore my courage. If he thinks I have lost it, he is deceiving himself; never more than now have I gritted my teeth in despair at not being able to avenge my poor lost ones. I should be so ashamed to go back empty-handed to France. ... How can I justify myself? I have a sacred duty to perform in avenging my brothers-in-arms who did not have the chance to fulfil their ambition to serve before they died.

I have not yet had an answer to my application to ship as pilot on board a convoy. I am flying like a madman while I wait. Patrols from dawn to dusk. I am even running the training of an acrobatic patrol it has amused our flight commander to form. We do rolls and loops in close formation. I confess the results aren't too bad.

May 20th

I am going to London, to Headquarters. They must get me out of here. I cannot remain any longer protecting convoys in a theatre where I have so little chance of seeing anything. Colonel Valin's promise is slow in being fulfilled. I hear they are asking for pilots specializing in night-fighting. I am going to talk to him about it.

May 25th

I have been to see Lady Sinclair. She seemed very moved by my two friends' deaths, especially Charles'. I did not talk to her of my wish to leave the squadron; she might have thought I was afraid of flying these bad machines.

At Headquarters they made no secret of the fact that this posting involves great difficulties with the Air Ministry. I am sinking into despair of ever being able to do anything useful. On the other hand, I learn that they have been officially informed by the Air Ministry that I have been appointed leader of a flight. A lot of good that will do me. I was better off as a sergeant at Northolt than as a pilot officer at Valley.

June 5th

Poor visibility this morning. I plunged into cloud as soon as I had taken off. Climbed to 10,000 feet without seeing the sky. I decided to come down. The altitude decreased slowly. One thousand feet now; I should soon see the ground. Suddenly the dense mist split and instead of the horizon an enormous cliff rose in front of me. I owe my life to the speed of my reflexes, for I was facing the side of a mountain.

Then I found myself involved with a valley, then an amphitheatre, all the ways out being blocked by cloud. I did the only thing possible; I plunged back into the dirt. Navigated by the compass for fifteen minutes. I came down, slightly faster heartbeat. This time I was over the open sea. Ten minutes later I was back on the aerodrome. They had sent me up to see what the weather was like!

June 6th

My squadron leader broke the news to me. He did not look in the least pleased about it. 'Mouchotte, you're leaving us.' He told me they all like me and that he is short of experienced pilots. I am posted to 601 Squadron, the City of London Squadron. It is a day and night squadron. I could not tell him the truth about this posting, which has sent me wild with delight.

At last, I am going to feel my heart jump again at the sight of Messerschmitts. If I run into a Fritz, I swear he shall repay me for the loss of all my poor comrades. My squadron leader does not understand why I am going. He seems really worried. 'But do you really want to leave us?' What could I say? I told him of my desire to fight and how useless to me it was to rest or to carry on here. Then he told me that 601 Squadron has been in the south for eight months and will be rested shortly while we, on the other hand, will soon be getting the new Spitfires, in order to get used to the highest speeds because we shall be getting Typhoons, new ultra-fast planes, and we shall not be staying here long, etc. Before I could reply he stood up and said he was going to write to Group to tell them he wants to keep me.

Strickland, Haywood and Timewell have just heard of my posting. They are sincerely sorry. My only regret in leaving the squadron will be in leaving these three friends; they have been real brothers to me. Haywood is furious and threatens the C.O. that he will go too, after me; the others say the same. The C.O. is scratching his head. He keeps saying he is short of experienced pilots and that he will go up to Group himself and make a fuss in order to keep me. … I am all at sea.

June 10th

It is full moon. I have been up the last two nights but the Boche is scarce. Last night was so light we could see almost as well as by daylight. The mountains forty miles off were outlined against the sky and the moon's reflections were shining on the sea. If I could, I would have spent my whole night in that star-studded sky.

June 11th

At last, I have had two long letters from mother. There are plenty of details. She seems quite reassured about me. I have told her, of course, in all my letters, that *I am an instructor*. Poor mother! It would kill her if she knew.

French and English troops have gone into Syria. I ask myself bitterly what I am doing here in the heart of England while other comrades are fighting without respite and getting themselves killed.

June 16th

I nearly killed myself this morning. Engine-trouble caused splashes of oil on my windshield. I was blinded, and while flying low along a valley another plane passed so close that despite the deafening roar of my engine, I heard the sudden scream of his. We passed in opposite directions; by miraculous luck he was a few metres above me.

June 17th

One of my comrades has just brought down a Junkers 88 but his companion, who was also in pursuit of it, was hit and had to make a forced landing in Eire. They are keeping him there as a prisoner. The irony of fate, to be made prisoner by the Irish!

June 23rd

Fate still has it in for our poor squadron. Two youngsters have just been killed in a light aircraft. Another has crashed and it is a miracle he escaped without breaking a limb. I hear from Malta of the death of a brave young English comrade who was with us for three months. Our first squadron leader has been shot down in operations over France, where more and more sweeps are being flown.

A day never passes without two or three of these vast sorties which prove, alas, appallingly costly. At least we are succeeding in keeping the Boche from our coast and in a constant state of alarm. The roles are reversed but it costs us dear, especially when our planes are inferior in speed to the enemy's.

We shall soon be going south. I hope I shall open my prize-list there. Let me get at least one Boche, for Heaven's sake.

July 2nd

Yesterday I celebrated the gloomy anniversary of my escape. Today I scarcely dare believe my eyes and I can't help turning the envelope over to convince myself the letter is really addressed to me:

> Sous-lieutenant Mouchotte, mentioned in divisional orders. Excellent fighter pilot. Volunteer for all operations. Has, in

past months, taken part in more than seventy engagements or convoy-escorts.

His moral qualities and professional worth have led to his being appointed leader of patrol. Recognized by his senior officers and his comrades as one of the best pilots of his squadron.

My first mention. Here I am, decorated with the Croix de Guerre, with Star. How happy and proud my poor mother would be if she could share my joy.

July 6th

We are still marking time here. Each week I hear of the exploits of the few Frenchmen who fly daily over France, and the daily reading of the R.A.F. communiqué gets me into an indescribable state of exasperation. I missed the great air battle of September; am I going to be kept out of this no less important phase of the air war? We regard ourselves as being 'rested' – I fly night and day without the Boche ever showing up. I shall join the A.R.P. Did they think they could keep me quiet by sending me the Croix de Guerre?

July 11th

Another name on 615's roll of tragedies. A young Canadian pilot whom I counted among my friends. Engine-trouble over the sea. I flew about for an hour above the waves, hoping to find him swimming somewhere near the point given. What could be more tragic than this despairing search? I searched over fifty miles out to sea. The radio at last specified that he had tried to land on a beach. I found him then, the plane smashed and overturned. Two hours later we learned he was dead.

July 12th

I have just learned that poor Stéphane was only superficially injured on the cheek; he was drowned, a prisoner in his plane, in less than 50 centimetres of water.

July 14th

Symbolic date. Day of liberty in the France of yesterday, day of mourning in the France of today. Day of hope in the hearts of all the French who have not sold themselves to Germany. The V Campaign has begun.

I listen to and read about the developments of this game with the keenest interest. In France, unless I had already been thrown into prison or put up against a wall for some attempt against our generous Nazi masters, I should be an ardent and enthusiastic distributor of V's.

July 18th

While patrolling above a convoy I suddenly took it into my head to dive over the escort and, as I was skimming the waves, I was most surprised to see a destroyer flying the French flag. Nothing more symbolical of this strange war than to see an English convoy escorted by a French ship, while a few hundred kilometres to the south the entire French nation is imprisoned and paralysed.

July 27th

An inquiry has been opened only now into all the accidents (glycol leaks) of which we have been victims. Two more this week: a comrade who made a forced landing and myself, who succeeded in getting my plane back to the aerodrome, dragging it along like a wounded ant trailing its leg.

The inquiry finally revealed that there has been *sabotage*. The glycol the squadron is using contains, no one knows how, a little acid which slowly eats into the metal and causes these terrible leaks. I do not yet know what measures are going to be taken, but I cannot help thinking that if they had been taken sooner my poor old Charles and so many others would still be in this world.

July 28th

Our flight commander is leaving. We are losing a very pleasant chief and an excellent pilot. He has just been posted to a squadron in Scotland. We always flew together and were forming a team which meant to give a good account of itself in the south. We know who we are losing but not who his successor will be or whether he will be posted to us from another squadron. This departure has quite upset the squadron.

90

Chapter 10

Flight Commander

July 29th, 1941

An incredible thing, which I certainly did not expect, has happened to me. Our squadron leader has just called me into his office to inform me that, having referred it to Group and got their approval, he has decided that I shall succeed Haywood as commander of the flight.

I was so surprised that he burst out laughing. Then I mentioned Claude Strickland, who has been with the squadron as long as I have, Timewell and others, but each time he refuted me by saying he had weighed it all up and thought of everything. He added, very courteously, that his choice could not be bettered. I did not conceal from him that I am bound to have certain small difficulties, being French, but as I am one of the oldest members of the squadron it may turn out all right, with a bit of tact.

August 5th

I have been to London for three days. I went to French Headquarters. Everyone congratulated me on my appointment as flight commander. Captain Bouderie said it was a great feather in my cap as there was no other instance in England of a foreigner being called upon to lead an English flight. He knew about it before me, the Air Ministry having asked their permission to promote me to lieutenant, to which they agreed at once, though I have only been a sous-lieutenant for four months. Such is war! They had also sent a cable to General de Gaulle, signed by the Admiral, but in the meantime, I received a telegram from Valley, announcing that my promotion is official. So, I am a lieutenant.

At Headquarters they spoke in laudatory terms of the future French Squadron which is in process of being formed. The few French pilots, alas, who remain, and who have been in English squadrons since last year will obviously form the backbone of this squadron. The other pilots will be drawn from the best officers in the training units – I might say from those with most influence at Headquarters.

91

There will be a terrific struggle to get into the first French squadron. It would even appear that the list is already closed. I confess the whole business leaves me cold, for in spite of all the trouble 615 has had I shall miss the good old squadron in which I made a start as a combatant and which has so often seen me in a cold sweat. Moreover, English camaraderie is so pleasant and sincere that I am afraid I may not find its like where they send me.

I am required to command one of the two flights of this squadron. They have not concealed from me that I shall perhaps have captains under me. I am vaguely worried about all the publicity there will be about the whole affair.

August 6th

Yet another catastrophe. I got back to Valley today only to learn of the death of my poor old Timewell, nicknamed 'Time-bomb'. The news upset me awfully. Engine-trouble, the plane caught fire, he baled out too late and went screaming to the ground. What upsets me most is that if I had not taken three days to go to London it would have been I and no other who would have gone on that mission and in that plane. His poor young wife came today. They had only been married for thirteen months. I have just heard of the death of one of the Frenchmen in the squadron, Garnier, shot down by a Messerschmitt 110. How many of us are there now, and who will come out alive from this lottery?

On account of this, all training flights are cancelled. We only go up from readiness. All my young pilots therefore are inactive. We are awaiting orders to start again, or else (I suspect) new planes.

August 7th

Patrol over convoy 50 miles out at sea. Very bad weather. I thought I should perhaps have had some mental reservations, a reflex of fear, some sort of apprehension. I was never touched by any such feeling for an instant during the flight. Am I hardened to danger or is it a feeling of fatalism or of resignation which makes me take and seek out all kinds of missions? I do not know myself whether I think that whatever happens I shall survive or whether that as a fatal outcome is inevitable, I cannot avoid it and should therefore do my duty without analysing anything.

A psychologist would love to study this kind of mental state at close quarters; I must confess it is the first time I have faced up to it. On the other hand, I often recoil instinctively from certain flights, as if something were warning me of danger or an inevitable accident. Then I have to fight the animal in me. In the air I do not feel comfortable, but I inspect my plane scrupulously. The least defect brings me out in a cold sweat. I am appallingly careful. But if nothing unusual happens, I am myself again, the bad moment is over. I often tell myself, 'You must go, nothing must stop you getting the better of this weakness.'

Often, when the night has been very dark, thick cloud obscuring all light, I have been ordered to go up into the inky ceiling. When it would have been easy for me to stay below it, I have been ashamed to find it took some seconds of inner struggle with the animal. But in spite of night, the sea, the cloud, I went in with teeth gritted. Was I afraid? I was so glad at having overcome that cowardly dread. By this means I have certainly acquired more assurance and self-confidence. Each time a touch-and-go mission is proposed, I think I am always first to take it because I am hastening towards the inner joy I get from a victory over myself.

August 8th

I took my flight up today for the first time. It will be a great day when I lead it into combat.

August 10th

I thought my turn had come this evening. Night was falling over the convoy. I was attacking a grey shadow, full throttle. Suddenly I had the fatal leak of glycol which has caused so many deaths. My immediate reaction was to bale out. I tested the engine. It seemed sound enough, but each instant I dreaded to see the flames leap out. The sea did not look very hospitable. I decided to leave the convoy and turned for the coast. The glycol leak stopped all at once. By gradually losing altitude, I managed to land on an emergency aerodrome. Just an excitement.

August 16th

This morning I sent the young Canadian Albert Boulanger up on patrol. A few minutes before landing, while he was circling the aerodrome, one of his petrol tanks caught fire. He crashed at full speed, a few miles from here. Poor dear old Boulanger! A young pilot, but so ardent and full of enthusiasm. He had extraordinary qualities as a fighter pilot and dreamed of nothing but 'shooting one down'. I have just read a splendid letter from his sister, a nun in Canada. She calls him 'my beloved young hero'.

I opened his diary, which he began the day he left Quebec. In it he tells of his hopes, his adventures, his posting to 615. I stopped at this sentence: '9 July. The English have appointed my French comrade Mouchotte as Flight-Commander. It is odd they should accept a foreigner to command them. It is true he is a jolly good sort, all round.'

August 23rd
Tony Eyre, our former squadron leader, has just flown in to visit us. I was glad to see him again. Alas, like us, he is sick of not being in the south, fighting. He told me he is soon going to be sent to command a new Spitfire squadron to make sweeps over France. I was overjoyed when he said he had decided to give me one of his flights to lead.

Chapter 11

The First German Plane

August 26th, 1941

A bit of excitement yesterday. I was 'scrambled' and went up. A bandit was signalled over the sea, somewhere between Ireland and us, at 10,000 feet. I went up to 13,000.

After half an hour's search I suddenly saw a bomber clearly outlined against a cloud. I went to meet him, manoeuvring all the time to keep the sun behind me. He certainly did not see me, for he did not change course. Terribly excited, I recognized an unmistakable Junkers 88. The monster was black all over. I saw its round nose and thin tail. Its shape was as clear as if I had a model in front of me. I was surprised that I was so calm and at the preciseness with which I prepared to attack.

The moment of action came. He was to port of me. A rapid turn in that direction, followed by a steep diving turn to starboard and I found myself in a dead straight vertical dive upon the Boche. The speed became incredible. The swastikas grew bigger and bigger in my sights. I opened fire. I just had time to avoid a collision. I was concentrating so hard on aiming that I forgot to pull out; I cannot have missed the Boche by much. I realized my companion had followed me into the attack when I made a steep turn as I climbed and noticed him behind me.

The speed was still so high that as I turned, I blacked out. I was blind for seconds, with my eyes wide open, desperately striving to see. At last daylight came back and I just had time to see my Junkers disappearing into the cloud. I shot after him at full speed. Unfortunately, it was a thick black rain cloud. Stay up or go down? I decided to go down. Three thousand feet. It seemed a long time. At last, there was the sea below me. I turned then and looked everywhere, without success. I saw my companion. I called him and we returned to the aerodrome, rage in my heart at having missed such a lovely opportunity. The Intelligence Officer is counting it to us, nevertheless, as 'damaged'.

Two hours later

Hurrah! I cannot believe the news. Operations have just phoned me that a Junkers 88 has just crashed in Eire. An endless procession of cars is now arriving at my flight. The wing commander, the C.O., the Adjutant, Ops., etc. I have had to tell the tale twenty times. They are so little used to seeing a Boche here, and besides, it is the station's great official report today. The C.O. is delighted that it should be B Flight.

Then it is the wing commander's turn to be congratulated. The news is spreading. I am happy about this victory but it was so easy and so swift that I inwardly find myself a little ridiculous in accepting so many compliments with such beautiful false modesty. I made no second attack, did not have the merit of a fight, not even the satisfaction of an enemy bullet leaving a nice little hole in my fuselage or wings. But the job was done and that is what matters.

The C.O. admitted to me that he is delighted, for he thinks a lot of me. He says it is very rare for a pilot to shoot down the first Boche he attacks and that in his career I am the first example. I am particularly fond of attacking in a vertical dive. One is less vulnerable. The target cannot escape and one strikes more easily at the most sensitive parts of the enemy. During exercises I have amused myself several times by attacking the C.O. thus. An excellent pilot, with eighteen victories to his credit, he was virtually knocked out each time despite cunning attempts to escape.

When I told him of my identical attack on the Junkers he jumped enthusiastically. He put my modesty to the test for a quarter of an hour, especially in front of all those surrounding me. I did not know where to hide my head but I found a way out by suggesting that we should celebrate in the mess. My young companion was in on the party. All the officers succeeded in clearing the bar of great stocks of whisky, gin and beer by 11 p.m. We beat a retreat; I cannot say in good order. For once I had to stand cheerfully up to the double whiskies everyone insisted on buying me; it would have been ungracious to refuse.

August 27th

Got up at midday. Not very good on my feet, head heavy. I shall not be cutting capers in a Hurricane today. Received a telegram of congratulation from Group, another from French Headquarters.

I have made my combat report. My first report! Shall I make any more after this one? The agonizing and mysterious question of my future is before me once again. Why think of it?

Tomorrow evening, a grand gala in the mess. I shall put on my French uniform as lieutenant for the first time. I have just received confirmation of my promotion in a telegram saying that General de Gaulle has approved it.

I am not flying today but I vow never again to make yesterday's experiment with the whisky.

Two letters from my sister Jacqueline. They know about my Croix de Guerre. Good news for my little mother.

August 29th

Yesterday's ball brought us all the elegant ladies of Anglesey and even of Bangor. A vast buffet, in spite of the rationing, succeeded in appeasing all appetites. But the bar attracted most customers. As usual, my uniform aroused a fair amount of curiosity. I am beginning to get used to it. My comrades, who find it very smart, think it puts them at a disadvantage with the girls.

At about one o'clock in the morning, when the party was at its height, a dreadful thing happened. The orchestra stopped playing, the doors were closed, everyone was quiet and the wing commander spoke. A few brief words on the success of this pleasant evening, then these alarming remarks: 'I should not like to finish without mentioning to you the names of Flight Commander Mouchotte and Sergeant-Pilot Hamilton, who distinguished themselves brilliantly yesterday by shooting down an enemy bomber.'

Then, after the usual applause, and some details of the 'exploit' and my 'dive to the attack', he turned and drank to me, my future victories and France. I was most upset, for I did not expect such applause for one poor victim lost in our sky. But my torture was not yet over. Another officer, speaking in his turn, also congratulated me and then announced that he had brought some champagne especially for me which I must drink with them. He ended by asking me to say a few words. I had to perform. I passed lightly over 'the accident' and congratulated the operators who had guided me so well to the objective by radio. I drank the health of the squadron and the station. Ouf! It was over. The orchestra struck up again.

August 30th

A horrible accident took place yesterday 500 metres from the aerodrome. A Beaufort bomber came down in the sea, near the shore. All the population of Rhosneigr hurried there but were powerless to help the unhappy men striking out desperately for the shore barely 100 metres away; in vain, for the sea was too rough.

I took off immediately in spite of a wind that threatened to turn into a gale, taking a small rubber boat which I meant to throw to them. The sight was pitiful. Some good swimmers dived in and were themselves caught by the huge waves and swept away in the storm. A boat with six rescuers in it capsized and there were six more victims. I flew a few metres over their heads and it was a desperate, tragic sight, these poor creatures so near at hand, struggling in vain with the elements. One of them raised his arm towards me but I passed too quickly. I made several attempts; each time the wind exerted such pressure that it was impossible to throw the whole thing out of the cockpit.

I succeeded at last but the dinghy hit my tail unit violently and, flying very low, I thought for a moment I was going into the sea. My aim could not have been very true: the boat fell too far from the unhappy men. All afternoon I flew over the sea, hoping to find some debris or other with a man on it; alas, although there were three of us our search was fruitless. The reckoning this morning is fifteen drowned, and there will be other names to lengthen the list. Two men from my flight are missing, which brings the number of dead to seventeen.

September 1st
An air vice-marshal at the aerodrome. After lunch he came to B Flight, congratulated Sergeant Hamilton and me and told us that a radio message from the Boche to its German base had been intercepted: 'Have been attacked by two Spitfires. One engine stopped, the other damaged. Intend to land in Ireland. Destroying papers on board. We shall soon return, after victory. Don't be long. Heil Hitler!'

September 2nd
We are all terribly depressed; we have heard it is possible we shall spend the winter here. We refuse to believe it and will volunteer for anything, even to go and fight in Russia this winter, rather than stay in Valley doing nothing. We have also written a letter to Churchill, our Honorary Air Commodore.

September 3rd
My squadron leader has just heard, how I do not know, that a French squadron is in process of formation and that perhaps I shall be posted to it. He does not want to lose me and has sent for me to his office to tell me so.

He says he is very proud to have me in his squadron because he expects I shall have a great career, not only because I have shot down a Boche with so few bullets but also because I am an example (hum!) to everyone, both in the air and on the ground. He added he will approve all I decide on for my flight. He ended by saying he will not release me for this French squadron unless our Headquarters decide to put me in charge of it.

September 6th

Great commotion in the squadron this morning. The C.O. has just announced the news. The squadron is at last being sent into battle.

Chapter 12

Manston Aerodrome: Attacking German Shipping

September 10th, 1941

Once more I have crossed England with my squadron. No trouble. Clear weather, a little cloudy, some storms. Then, north of the Thames, the legendary fog which, whatever the weather, envelops the British capital for nine-tenths of the year. Landed at Manston. A big turf landing-ground, very bumpy, on account of the many traces of bombs and the work on the mines which, if necessary, would enable the whole aerodrome to be blown up by electrical means.

The squadron we are replacing and which tomorrow will have the ... pleasure ... of flying to Valley have told us about 'the job'. They are delighted to be going, they don't much like the job and they imagine, poor mutts, that they will only be at Valley for a month. I met Captains de Scitivaux, Dupérier and old Labouchère, who have been fighting like me in England since the beginning. All three are changing squadrons and coming to us so that there will be four French officers together.

Our machines are still Hurricanes, but are armed either with twelve machine guns or four cannons. The damage they must do on the target!

Main duties: attacking convoys, with or without bombers, whole squadron, single flight, section or even single planes. The cargo boats are armed to the teeth and spit flame from all their weapons. They are usually escorted by flak ships, motor boats and light vessels armed like fortresses which surround the units of the convoy in great numbers. There will be venomous insects for us to distract, too, while the bombers are dropping their perilous load of bombs on the precious cargoes.

To avoid being picked up by radio, we fly at a constant altitude of zero. Except for the attack, when we have to go up to 3,000 feet to make a better dive, our flights will always be made at sea level. The work is terribly depressing because there is no satisfaction from it and it is appallingly costly. Much loss and little profit. No possibility of getting a Messerschmitt, for they dive to attack from above and the engine power of the Hurricane precludes equal combat. Flight is the only answer. A wild flight, zigzagging as much as possible, while the Boche dives and dives and you get soaked with sweat. Our manoeuvrability protects us against their higher speed.

September 18th

We have made several patrols near the coast of France, over Belgium and even Holland. When I came back this morning from two days' leave in London, I learned of the death of young Hamilton, who seconded me so ably in shooting down my Junkers 88.

On their way to attack a convoy, with three Blenheim bombers, only one of which has returned, and that holed like a colander, they were attacked by at least fifty Me. 109s. De Labouchère got one. Another comrade baled out in mid-Channel but was picked up. The target, a big cargo boat, was abandoned while huge flames were rapidly consuming it.

Much excitement this afternoon and a handsome success for the squadron. To my great disappointment, I did not take part. Four comrades made repeated attacks on four German minesweepers. *The latter were all annihilated.* Two blew up and vanished like smoke from the surface of the water, the third was left with flames more than 100 feet high and the fourth also caught fire and turned keel-upwards in ten seconds. The C.O. had half his tail shot off by a shell but managed to get back to the aerodrome by holding the stick in both hands.

I am very excited, like everyone else, and at the same time in despair at having so stupidly remained on the ground.

September 19th

A big attack is in preparation. I forbid myself to talk about it. One never knows; some accident may befall me and this notebook would be read by someone else, which might lead to a great catastrophe. Anyway, I hope before two months are past to record the success of a bold scheme which De Scitivaux, Dupérier, De Labouchère and I are going to attempt on a certain date. Our chief at Headquarters, General Valin, approves and is very keen.

The Air Ministry have been informed and are going to put up our plan at a forthcoming meeting of the Air Council. If we four really determined Frenchmen succeed, it may have incalculable consequences. I am trembling with impatience. By going to work on it in advance we are preparing our blow and cutting down the risks, which are considerable.

I have just received my second citation, this time in the orders of the *Armée de l'Air*. *My* Junkers 88 has got me my first Palm. Will it be followed by others? I must write to mother about it, she will try and read between the lines.

Received two photos of my little nephews. I am as wild with delight as if they were mine. Lord, the size of them! Will they recognize their uncle? Especially if the life I am leading, with its excitement and exhaustion, makes me look older. They are so young, happily, that they do not yet understand the horrors of a war and the tough school I am attending. But though society transforms assassins like us into heroes, the daily experience, the sad and routine sight of such young men struck down in the great lottery, will have made me a little better than I was. It is as though by accepting such a lot, the kind of fatalism which enables me to tackle anything has filled me with a great compassion and a need to be always doing more for others, without religion necessarily entering into it at all.

September 20th

I was over Ostend this morning. Nothing special, no ship sighted. On my way back, perhaps 35 or 40 miles from the English coast, despite the mist which was cutting down visibility, I noticed a tiny rowing boat. I turned, leading my three comrades. I was surprised to see men on board it. There were five of them, all on their feet, at the risk of upsetting the frail skiff, waving everything they had, handkerchieves, coats, etc. One whom I saw distinctly was wearing a mackintosh and waving a soft hat as high as he could.

There was no doubt whatever that they had escaped a few days earlier from the Belgian or Dutch coast. After making a few turns, while the other three planes continued to circle widely, I went up to get better radio contact. When I had given the information and the position I went down and we left our new friends. Not far from the coast we met two fast motor launches. Our wild gestures persuaded them to follow us. An hour later our fugitives and the launches were safe. ...

Telephoned Dover. We are going to have tea with them this evening.

September 23rd

I have been for a ride in a tank, which took me at high speed over rough ground. A speed test, with a swift turn round on the spot, which sent up clouds of dust. I certainly prefer the Hurricane.

September 25th

We are still attacking shipping. Yesterday, flying through fog, always just above the waves and sometimes only missing them by a miracle, we only spotted the French coast when we were on top of it. After landing, Scitivaux, who was my number two, told me he had never been so near death. He lost sight of me, then suddenly saw me flash in front of him in a turn. He says he passed only a few centimetres away, after a savage wrench to avoid me.

This evening, in slightly less dense fog, we flew to Ostend – twenty minutes at 200 m.p.h. – at sea level. A fierce turn to miss the coast rising at us. Then after a few minutes' flying parallel with the shore, while the coastal batteries opened up at us as we passed, we attacked a 2,000-ton ship 100 metres from Dunkerque, which was making ready to enter the harbour. My number two tells me he later saw me surrounded with ack-ack fire, bursting a few metres from my plane. He counted five bursts, apart from tracer bullets. My plane was not even touched.

September 26th

This morning I took my flight over France. We were surprised by thick mist at sea level in mid-Channel. I went through it without gaining altitude, rightly, for it thinned a little when we suddenly saw the beaches of the French coast 200 metres away. A fierce turn, but all the planes followed me. We scraped over a lot of fishing boats, on which many arms were waved to us in happy greeting.

Nothing particular between Calais and Dunkerque, but after the latter port I suddenly saw the silhouettes of six big ships before me. Too late to manoeuvre and attack them. The water was already splashing all round me and I saw tracer bullets coming straight at me. I turned to port and had time to see my comrades vanishing at full speed into the mist. My number two followed me. No damage done; we could attempt an attack.

While endeavouring to circle widely in the mist, I came across another ship. No hesitation this time. I went in, ordering the attack over the radio. I set my machine guns spitting and saw the havoc the bullets caused on the deck. Twelve machine guns at once do a lovely job. But I had attacked on my own. My young number two had vanished in the mist.

September 28th

A great party this afternoon. Visibility 50 miles. I saw the French coast as soon as we took off. De Scitivaux and I were alone and made for Gris-Nez,

Boulogne, Le Tréport, Dieppe and Fécamp. A devil of a long way. Not the smallest ship to shoot up. Not a single Messerschmitt after us.

At Fécamp I noticed a minelayer or, rather, a flak ship, preparing to make port 100 metres away. It was really too good to miss, and although we should have to fly over the port itself, we climbed to attack. They opened up everywhere, from the port, from the coast, all the guns on the ship in action. I dived more or less vertically, aiming at the red flashes coming up at me. I avoided the masts and pulled out as I fired. Why not another attack? De Scitivaux, with his four cannons, was surrounded like me by black flak and tracer. The excitement was at its height and we attacked again. The ship's fire was less intense, proof that we had done some damage. I disengaged rapidly after my second dive. The water was splashing all round my plane. I zig-zagged like a madman. Ouf! It was warm. I had just come out of hell. No trouble in the heavens! Our return was like a pleasure flight.

Young Robert has just been killed, shot down by a ship, too low to bale out. Another jumped from his burning plane so low that he hit the water immediately after his parachute opened. He was fished out 35 miles from the English coast half an hour later.

October 3rd

Unsuccessful attack over Fécamp. We were on our way back to the English coast. The time was passing slowly. Following like a sheep, I was day-dreaming and letting my reflexes fly for me, while my thoughts, lulled by the monotony of the sea passing at 350 kilometres an hour a metre or two below, strayed to distant lands.

At last, we saw England. As usual, we went up to 300 or 400 metres for the batteries to recognize us and then crossed the coast in impeccable formation. We had gone three or four miles and were turning port and starboard. I must admit I absolutely did not recognize where I was. I saw sand dunes, then firs. Odd. Then, as if seized by a sudden madness, all the planes went into a frenzied dance.

A second later we were surrounded by shell bursts and tracer. All the ack-ack batteries opened up at us and at 300 metres we were an easy target. In my aerobatics round their deadly black circles, I had time to recognize – Le Touquet! I went back over the coast at full throttle, accompanied by hundreds of those nasty little arrows of flame that go past you and make the water splash round your plane. I flew a few metres to port over a little fishing boat. The two fishermen waved wildly at me. Landed with a bullet in my wing. The funniest part of it is that our C.O., *like everyone else*, thought he was over England.

October 4th
Four of us attacked a ship over Holland, south of Walcheren. I had time to see two traditional windmills. Two attacks set it on fire. Nothing to report.

October 7th
Perhaps it is time to talk about the famous French squadron on which so much ink has already been expended, the formation of which has been the subject of such numerous orders, discussions, counter-orders, hopes, disappointments and lists of all kinds on the part of those 'in charge' at Headquarters. They certainly must press on with it.

The great difficulty lies in the fact that our former chief, Admiral Muselier, naturally wants to sponsor it. Our new chief, who has taken the air forces under his control, General Valin, also wants to sponsor it. The admiral needs the Army Air Force pilots, the general needs the Naval Air Force mechanics. The admiral cannot form a squadron essentially 'Navy' because he lacks a sufficient number of naval pilots. The general cannot accept the naval pilots in a squadron essentially 'Army' without being obliged, to avoid injustice, to pay the others at the naval rate, which is nearly twice as much. Each has his own programme, his own nominal rolls and his own squadron leader to wish on the other, and each thinks himself the more competent. ...

This has been going on since last March. The formation is thus put off from month to month. We remain with the English squadron, and things might be worse.

The projected French squadron seems to be enjoying great success. We hear it discussed everywhere. At the Ministry, in the French bars in London, in the Press; only our little group is uninterested, being too worried about the possibility of a fiasco. Slippery and well-connected persons are manoeuvring at Headquarters. They are busy inserting one name instead of another in the list of a thousand erasions.

According to the latest reports, the admiral-general quarrel has been made up; the squadron will be formed on November 1st and we are to have the most modern aircraft. I say 'we' because all our little group will be in it. The C.O. would be Captain de Scitivaux. The choice could not be improved on: an excellent pilot, alive with grand aggressive spirit, supported by long experience. With him to lead us, we could not fail to do really useful work, especially with good planes, but ... I doubt whether the famous list will have been settled by November 1st.

October 8th

My C.O. wants to promote me to captain. He says my present position is abnormal, because I have three captains under my orders. He told me he has already sent in the recommendation; it had been approved by the Air Ministry but French Headquarters have rejected it, being unable to conceive that I should rise from sergeant in October 1940 to captain in October 1941.

In England only the worth of the officer is considered, setting aside the question of age. Thus, one often meets wing commanders of twenty-three in the R.A.F. who, having shown their value and acquired real experience of aerial warfare, have been judged fitter to command a wing of three fighter squadrons than an officer with greying hair whose physical powers would no longer be compatible with those required by modern aircraft and modern war. But such violence to routine procedure makes our gentry raise their eyebrows, and although Captain de Scitivaux has interceded in my favour they seem to be resisting energetically.

October 10th

One of my comrades has shown me a letter he has just received from France. It contains truths far from flattering to the Vichy Government. The writer calls its representatives Hitler's lackeys and makes no bones about foretelling the day when they will be put up against a wall and shot. He concludes by hoping that 'the swine of a censor' will not open his letter.

It had, however, been opened in France, and in red ink, in one corner, was written: 'The swine of a censor has opened your letter and has read it, but he has let it pass just the same.'

Churchill came to see us today. He took tea with us very democratically, while the cameramen and press photographers dutifully shot us. Still accompanied by his wife, smoking his traditional cigar, our 'godfather' left us on the best of terms.

October 11th

Now I can speak of the famous special mission we four Frenchmen wanted to attempt. After several discussions, the Air Ministry refuses its approval, the experiment being too dangerous. The idea was to take off on November 11th in ultra-fast planes, specially adapted for us. We should have made for Paris, arrived over the capital at about eleven o'clock and made a fantastic dive over the Champs-Elysées, passing as low as possible in perfect formation. Three containers of smoke-producer would have poured one big trail of blue, one of white and one of red smoke, while the fourth plane would drop in its wake millions of tiny French flags. The avenue would be black with silent crowds, contemptuous of the Boche troops marching past for their famous changing of the guard.

Nothing need have prevented us firing a short burst at their greenish uniforms, for the avenue is wide. What a sight for the French, to see their persecutors killed before their very eyes! The joy for them to see them running from French machine-gun fire! The propaganda for De Gaulle and Free France! The encouragement for those who are suffering and hoping there!

Messerschmitts, ack-ack, balloons? We should have got through somehow. The return would have been difficult, the small amount of fuel in a fighter aircraft not permitting long flights; it would have obliged us to come back the shortest way, which would have meant encountering the strongest opposition from the Boche squadrons.

We had weighed everything, anticipated everything, envisaged everything. We accepted the risks, so long as the thing came off. One of us went to the Air Ministry and saw some high-ranking people who not only approved keenly but put the idea to the technical arms. Spitfire Vs of the latest make were going to be specially modified: bigger petrol tanks, smaller armament, smoke-producers, etc. They were nearly ready and were going to be tested, then we learned, to our great consternation, that Air Marshal Sholto Douglas would not let us go.

October 15th

Each day that passes brings us a stage nearer the end of the task entrusted to 615 Squadron alone. We can truthfully say that no enemy ship can leave a port between the mouth of the Scheldt and Fécamp without being machine-gunned by our planes. The daily contact with danger has hardened us to the extent of making us too daring. I say 'too' because the luck we are having cannot last long; it encourages us to venture more each day. At first, we only attacked targets two or three miles from the coast. Now, this evening for instance, we go seeking ships in harbour. They dare not come out.

At Zeebrugge this evening we made a concentric attack on three flak ships in the harbour. I have never seen such fireworks round my plane. It bordered on the fantastic. My fire seemed to do a good deal of damage on one ship; it caught fire before I pulled out. I climbed vertically, made a few zig-zags; shells were bursting all round. A second attack. I escaped in haste, banking port and starboard like a crazy man.

Yesterday morning there was not a single ship between Dunkerque and Holland. We went over Ostend, not without being greeted on the way by the ack-ack batteries. Despairing of a target, we made for the coast and penetrated into Holland north of the Scheldt. The fields, the cows and the windmills did not induce the desired peace of mind. Invisible machine guns pursued us and I saw nothing to shoot up. All the good peasant-folk were on the doorsteps of their farms. They seemed quite calm.

I passed a few metres over the head of one old man driving his horse and cart, and despite the thunder of my engine he did not even deign to lift his head, very vexing. Chimneys on the horizon; suddenly we flew into a terrifying barrage. We had to go through it. I kept as straight as I could because of the danger of collision with the others. Tracer bullets poured after us like jets of water. I dipped suddenly, though I was flying at tree-top height, to dodge a barrier of fire. It followed me and I was in the middle of it. In spite of myself, I put my head down. I do not know how I avoided a screen of trees.

My speed was frightening. I plunged to starboard; another Hurricane was coming at me without having seen me. Then I saw light machine guns letting fly at me. A turn and I fired back. My four cannons planted some hits at short intervals. The whole thing blew up. I went on firing rapidly. There was nothing left of the machine-gun post. I was skimming the ground. It was a miracle. I went over the coastline, followed by my number two. All the batteries opened up at once. I had lost nearly all the others. I was safely over the open sea. I saw some of them attacking a ship. I turned back to use up my ammunition. We met once more over the sea. We counted up. There was one missing. Poor Aldous! Dead? Prisoner?

October 17th

This morning for the first time we were attacked by four Messerschmitt 109s which fell on us like birds of prey. Alarm. Each one escaped as best he could. Nothing but damage to the planes, luckily, except one Boche which someone managed to shoot down. A young Norwegian pilot, in his excitement, made a little error in navigation.

With his plane rather badly damaged –a blade of his propeller broken, a wingtip shot off by a shell, part of his tail unit smashed, his instrument panel in bits, oil leaking – he found himself over Calais, believing himself in England. He thought the ack-ack barrage which greeted him was a mistake on the part of our anti-aircraft. Seeing the aerodrome, he went down, slowed his shaky engine, put down his landing gear and was getting ready to land when he suddenly saw three Messerschmitts quietly lined up beside a hangar. It did not take him long to reverse his operations and make for the English coast, fast.

October 18th

Our squadron leader has just been awarded a bar to his D.F.C. for the magnificent work he has done with us since the beginning. It is a great honour, for the D.F.C. itself is a very difficult decoration to get and the bar means it has been earned twice. The whole squadron is greatly honoured by it.

October 19th

I have been to the cinema in London to see 'my' film. The C.O. had told me it was being shown in this week's news films. I have the luck to have a camera on my plane which takes pictures whenever I fire my guns at a target. We sometimes get very good ones and it is fascinating for us, a few days after an attack on a convoy, to re-live the breathless seconds during which we see our own bullets hitting the target and the enemy's surrounding the plane.

I noticed that on a cinema-theatre screen the details stand out better because they are brighter. They showed fifteen attacks by the C.O., Hugo and me; I realized more than ever before what terrifying damage we must inflict on all these enemy ships. Though they do not all sink, most of them catch fire. The morale of the crews cannot be very wonderful, even if one judges only by the ever-decreasing number of those who risk leaving port.

We have just had a visit from the Air Minister, Sir Archibald Sinclair. It is eight months since he saw me but he remembered my name and told me his wife has often spoken of me to him and would like me to repeat the visit I paid her five months ago. He honoured us with a speech, congratulating us on the 'formidable' work we are doing and assuring us that we have done a lot to help Russia by forcing the Boche to withdraw several squadrons from the Eastern Front to protect his western coast.

October 21st

We take some elementary precautions before flying over enemy-occupied country. Above all, I never fly without my English uniform, which will give me a few hours' respite if I am taken prisoner before being recognized as French, in which event. . .

Handicapped as I am with an unshakeable French accent, I doubt whether I shall be taken for an Oxonian. I have anticipated this difficulty by wearing the word 'Canada' on my shoulders. So now I am a citizen of Toronto, as long as I roll my 'r' as they do in Périgord. Without any papers whatever, my pockets absolutely empty, I go off with a light heart, in the conviction that my lucky star and my guardian angel will turn aside the bullets meant for me.

These precautions are unnecessary, really: we fly like swallows scenting the storm and there is no likelihood whatever of our being taken prisoner and every likelihood that we shall test the temperature of the Channel deeps or the resistance of the English plane when it crashes at 400 kilometres an hour in some kitchen garden in one of the New Order countries! But regardless of these lofty considerations, the English amuse themselves by encumbering us with a quantity of small objects of undeniable usefulness 'if' fate should make us the quarry in some absorbing manhunt.

More than once, I admit, I have thought about this kind of sport. It must be extraordinarily exciting, and once the first agonizing minutes were over being French would make my task easier. We go with our pockets stuffed with odd paraphernalia: compasses hidden almost everywhere in the form of trouser buttons, propelling pencils and collar studs; miniature hack-saw sewn into the belt; maps, on silk, of Holland, Belgium and France hidden in shoulder pads. We carry nutritive chocolate, pills to stop us going to sleep, an ampoule of morphine with a needle to inject it, tablets to purify water and a great deal of French and Belgian money. With all that, we are ready to face the terrors of a grand pursuit.

October 29th

Operations go on. In a week, however, I have only flown on four. Attack on a seaplane base this morning, in a basin behind Ostend harbour. The alarm was hotter than ever. We were surrounded by a curtain of flame. In spite of the terrific scuffle we succeeded, miraculously, in avoiding collision. Three seaplanes at anchor were set on fire. Scitivaux set fire to a gasometer.

Eight of us went, six came back, one with a frightful glycol leak. We flew close to him. He climbed and got ready to bale out. The sea was rough below. It was terribly cold. Poor devil! We were over the open sea and minutes were precious. The smoke grew denser. I saw great holes in his wings. He was suffocating; he opened the cockpit hood and sat higher. His head emerged, enveloped in smoke. A quarter of an hour later he succeeded in making a crash landing on the aerodrome, without injury.

But young Sergeant-Pilot Potts is missing and my best English friend, Claude Strickland, has not come back. I have lost a grand companion. We have been together constantly for thirteen months. Some say there is still hope, that perhaps he succeeded in landing. I think not. What I admired in him was his courage. He was cruelly nervous before each operation. He thought too much of the danger itself instead of thinking of the end to be attained. His faith in his own powers as a pilot was not sufficient to balance his chances of coming through. That was the root of the obsession that rode him, as it does certain young pilots, of the nervousness which shook him long before we took off.

I admired Claude because in spite of this terrible handicap (which he had succeeded in concealing from everyone) he was always among the volunteers for special operations. Painfully sensitive, he had to struggle with himself to take on such duties, perhaps in the hope of curing himself by the evil itself. Did he seek to deceive himself that, like us, he found 'excitement' and happiness in fighting? Was it his self-respect that was at stake, making him vie with us, quarrel like us, for who should go and who remain? Claude carried out some lovely jobs with great courage and inconceivable merit. I emphasise that.

October 30th

I am leaving 615 Squadron suddenly for Hornchurch. How many memories I leave behind me! Before my departure, General de Gaulle came to lunch with us. A great reception: the English incurred expenses they would not have incurred for Churchill or the Air Minister. Other comrades from different squadrons joined us and, after reviewing us and saying a few words in English, General de Gaulle came and chatted with us for a long time while the photographers shot us.

For the first time I have been near our Chief, *the great leader of Free France, to whom go out the hopes of all the true French in the whole world*. At Headquarters, where inevitably there are endless intrigues in the darkness of the lobby and where more or less malevolent tales are always circulating, as in any self-respecting French ministry, I have always been glad to find that the General enjoys the unanimous respect and admiration of his colleagues. He rises above all the mischievous rumours. He is above all that. He loves his country and thinks of the end to be attained.

We are leaving Mansion. This evening I learned that in the afternoon four of 615 went to Belgium. Only one has come back. Must we believe in Providence?

November 1st
Here in London, having a short rest. We are in waiting at Hornchurch, posted to Turnhouse, near Edinburgh, to form the French Squadron.

November 5th
Met two severe policewomen in London, marching in full awareness of their importance; long, slow strides, hands behind their backs. I passed them.

'Hello, Ronny!' cried one of them. I recognized an old friend from the Chez Yvonne Club. Who could have suspected that the tall blonde girl was entrusted with the task of preserving law and order?

Chapter 13

'Ile-de-France'

Turnhouse, Scotland.

November 10th, 1941

Goodbye, London! I am on my way to 340 Squadron, the first *Free French Squadron!* Sleeping-car. I woke up 10 miles from Edinburgh. The green countryside of Scotland was passing beneath a greyish sky. The cold was not too bitter. I had trouble collecting my four suitcases and two fat kitbags.

I travel with all my lares and penates, including an electric fire. Why be uncomfortable? Turnhouse, where I have arrived, is a big station. Nearly all the French pilots have been here for some days. We are up to our necks in papers. The business of the mechanics is a hard nut to crack, the sailors not wanting to be under the 'erks' and vice versa.

November 15th

We have just received two planes. And what planes! So old that the exhaust pipes are dropping off, the undercarriages won't retract and, more serious, won't let down. In the air they are in the tin can or flat-iron category. Add to this that fog and cold are giving us a lot of trouble.

Fortunately, a dear old lady in the knitting department of a charitable organization called France-Argentine has sent me a thick, hand-knitted, blue sweater. A pity I do not know the lady's name to thank her. Anyway, why shouldn't she be young and pretty?

November 17th

Captain de Scitivaux is commanding A Flight; I am his second-in-command. Captain Dupérier is commanding B Flight; Fayolle is his second-in-command. An English squadron leader, Loft, will be commanding us for several months. He is a great Francophile and also an excellent fighter pilot.

How long shall we stay here? I haven't had much luck. I vegetated nearly five months at Valley and was unfortunate enough to have only two months on operations at Manston. Once more I am far from the theatre of war. My family in France must have a poor opinion of my stomach for fighting.

I have just heard of the accidental death of Captain Laurent who fought with us at Manston. He crashed into a hill, blinded by one of those mists that cling to the ground almost daily near London at this time of year. Another comrade fallen. …

I have had a third citation, which gives me my second Palm. It refers to the many ships damaged and the work at Manston.

November 25th
Edinburgh can be regarded as the handsomest city in Britain. Great squares, wide avenues, fine monuments – but what gloom! How chilly it is! The character of the people is apparent merely from their way of walking in the streets. One might fancy it is against the law to laugh. In public places people stand motionless, talking in low voices. The shops close at four o'clock. The 'black-out' and the winter make the place even more dismal. I understand it is the same in peace-time.

A French voice hailed us in the street while I was walking with Claude, a naval lieutenant who has been three months in England. It belonged to a dark young woman, slightly moustached, who announced herself as General de Gaulle's representative here. All in a flutter at having the first French squadron on her doorstep, she promised to get us books, gramophone records, radio sets, furniture, magazines, parties, etc. This called for a cup of tea in a select establishment.

Our entrance caused a sensation, to the great delight of our little moustached lady, who quivered as if it were a prize-giving. To show off her rare birds, she made us walk the length of the room by going round as many tables as possible. … Two hours later we were still listening to the interminable tale of her life of suffering and of the various plans and projects she would discuss with 'the ladies of the committee, for our valorous pilots' happiness and comfort', etc.

December 1st
We are on the move already. One flight at least, mine. We are going further east, to Drem, on operations. Why? High military commands have reasons that reason does not understand. First impression of the mess at Drem: a huge room, comfortably furnished, is the anteroom. In the middle is a deep

fireplace, very wide, above which stands an enormous copper goblet, taller than a bucket but a little narrower. The name of some generous donor is inscribed on the base.

Once or twice a week some volunteer comes forward, fills the cup to the brim, which represents more than twenty full pints and makes a point of drinking the lot before going to bed. I have never been able to see the humour of this joke. To judge by the pallor of his complexion, I suspect the hero does not either. I shall not be a candidate for it.

December 7th

Japan has attacked America. Now the whole world is disrupted by the most monstrous war that humankind has ever suffered. The centre shifts like the heart of a whirlwind. Poland, France, England, Russia, Libya.

Now the Pacific has caught fire while the German armies, beaten by the Russians and the cold, are retreating on all fronts. Negotiations: Goering rushes to see Pétain, Ciano sends for Darlan; the French Fleet is at stake. The question is being decided without consulting French opinion, as if it concerned no more than a few wagon-loads of corn; acts which may compromise the future of the whole world are being decided by unscrupulous men and traitors to their country. What an observatory England is; here, more than in France herself, I have learned to think French, to watch, judge and criticize the blows being exchanged, the vilenesses and intrigues being plotted! The war with Japan has begun with a great naval defeat. So much the worse! So much the better! It will be a lash of the whip for the United States.

December 10th

I have just had a letter from the manager of one of the biggest London restaurants. He has decided to give three free meals to each French pilot who shoots down a Boche. He therefore sends me this invitation, plus a box of preserves and a book. His wishes are much appreciated.

I have recently made the acquaintance of a French-Canadian pilot. After he had talked to me of his *demoiselle* in Quebec, we naturally came to a subject close to both our hearts: France. He confided to me that he had sworn never to return home without seeing France and the inevitable parallel was drawn between 'our' countries and England.

The Canadians say openly that they went on fighting after France's collapse with the sole object of liberating her. The state of mind of these French Canadians was such that after June 17th, 1940, they were all confined to barracks for a month. They wanted to desert and go home. For them the war was over, France having signed an armistice. It took endless trouble to convince them that, on the contrary, they must redouble their ardour now. And it is with that idea that they are fighting bravely today. 'Montreal', said my companion, 'is the biggest city in France, *after* Paris. Quebec comes second, Marseille third.'

December 25th
Christmas this year was spent quietly in the mess; a dance had been organized.

January 7th, 1942
The Boche is retreating on the Russian front; he is retreating in Libya. German invincibility is a myth. The mechanism is out of gear. The hour of collapse is at hand.

Chapter 14

The Cross of Lorraine in the Air

Ayr.

January 8th, 1942

We have moved again. West coast of Scotland. Training is going on slowly while in London the drums of propaganda are beginning to beat. There was a great to-do yesterday when we were told, 'The Air Ministry is publicizing the French Squadron on a scale allowed to no other squadron, Polish or otherwise, not even the famous American Eagle Squadron.'

About thirty journalists arrived on the aerodrome this morning, accompanied by radio and newsreel vans. The whole British Press was represented. The most extravagant questions from this avalanche of civilians about our memories, our impressions, our adventures, our combats, our escapes, our victories, our hopes, etc. ...

Pencil and notebook in hand they sprang from victim to victim, torturing the discreet, exhausting the garrulous. What will they make of this mixture of adventures scribbled down in shorthand? The photographers had no luck.

No one volunteered. The measure of caution which restrains us was very well understood; they will soon come into their own when we fly twelve Spitfires over in close formation. The French radio in London and the B.B.C. were also represented. They recorded some voices. I refused, as I have always done since I have been fighting, to speak on the radio. My mother does not and must not know what I am doing. All the publicity is annoying. Our squadron has not yet given the slightest proof of its worth. Only six of the pilots have been in action.

January 14th

Bad weather is proverbial in this region. Despite frost and fog our squadron, and particularly our flight, perform wonders of ingenuity to accumulate a few flying hours. The planes shoot into the mist and the pilots, goodness knows how, come back an hour later only too glad to log up another hour.

Our mechanics, too, are French. We have had a lot of trouble in matters of discipline and organization, etc. Certain malcontents claimed they had come to the squadron with other intentions than to do this work. But everything is gradually settling down and even the latter, on occasion, boast about and defend the qualities of their respective pilots, when foreigners are present.

My two mechanics are naturally interested only in their plane, which they maintain very conscientiously. I am already forming a team with them as I did for fifteen months in 615 with two excellent Englishmen who – I do not think I am deceiving myself – liked and esteemed me.

Apart from this vital interest in having a responsible team, the pilot must wholeheartedly recognize the devotion of these good lads. In all kinds of weather, rain, frost, at night, they carry on an ungrateful task with no glory attached to it, which every mechanic worthy of the name knows to be necessary and of high value. He, on his side, as a rule appreciates his pilot's merits; he will admire him before all others and his team-spirit will function. I have always regarded these principles as essential during my life as a pilot. I think I now have two excellent lads: Gruget is very skilful and hard-working, always beside the plane, his hands in the oil and his head in the cockpit. He has an affection for his kite and will never be satisfied until he has repaired whatever little imperfection I have pointed out to him. Moureau is very young and of a very placid type; he is less eager for work but he will still carry out his pal's instructions faithfully. He has a perfect contempt for all that does not concern his machine.

I augment their miserable pay each month with a present. They too are anxious to be off to the south. We have a number of Tahitians, not specialists, who are useful in several ways. They and their mandolin are inseparable and often play it for us so that we can hear nostalgic songs about their country. Their singing is very rhythmical and arouses keen interest. They sing with a sad smile, as if their memories were painful. What do they understand of all the chaos that has exiled them from their native land? Their happy songs are rapid, some of them mingled with bad French. Despite the guttural accent, the tone is sweet and compelling.

Poor devils, they suffer terribly from the climate, especially that of Scotland. One of them owns a two-masted yacht. Here he cleans the planes.

January 17th

I have just seen the news film which was made on the aerodrome about ten days ago. First our flag, floating from the top of a mast as tall as a telegraph pole. Very successful. Then we saw a scramble, a handful – what am I saying! – a glorious phalanx of pilots who fear nothing, rushing bravely towards their planes to give chase to a redoubtable horde of the foe. To get there quicker, we even saw one jump through a window.

If one listened carefully, it seemed that there was a murmur of admiration in the cinema. The last man went past the camera's eye like a thunderbolt, racing gallantly to the battle, perhaps to death. Bad luck, the effect was a little less successful. He ran on his heels, knees outspread, his rear remarkably far behind him, giving the camera a wonderfully vacuous smile … which the English censorship has allowed to go down to posterity.

Then came the impressive fly-past of our planes in perfect alignment. They taxi'd past one by one to take off. The formation was filmed at an altitude of 200 metres in two parts, one first, three second and two following. The bad weather prevented us practising and forming the flying Cross of Lorraine, which is particularly difficult to execute.

February 1st

Loft, our English squadron leader, is leaving us, leaving our squadron to its fate, letting it go without even having flown with it on its first adventures, as he had expected. As a result, Captain de Scitivaux, promoted commandant, takes command of the squadron.

February 6th

No official handing-over; just a simple speech. All the French personnel, men and officers, gathered round the flag, about 250 of them. Scitivaux came forward and simply announced that he has taken over. At the same time, he appointed his successor to command A Flight – your humble servant.

Once back in my own lines, I thought it useful to call the men together and say a few words to them. I did not forget who I had to deal with. Plenty of tough characters, some of them discontented with being here with their hands in the oil instead of fighting, which was their reason for risking everything and escaping to England.

A great many of them were naval men, leading seamen and quartermasters; the others came from the Army Air Force. I addressed myself to the former, knowing the importance to them of the difference between military and naval air forces. I emphasised the unity of the squadron. These men's desire to see us fighting is as great as ours. The training of pilots, the condition of our going south, depends on them, on the sound maintenance of the planes.

Finally, a few words of comfort about the forthcoming revision of their pay. I hope I did not sound too much like a visiting fireman when I wound up by exalting the value of the French mechanics and appealing to their sense of duty, England and France having their eyes on the beginnings of the first Free French Squadron, etc.

February 7th
First accident. A young pilot arriving here from his training unit turned over as he landed. A miracle he was not killed. Last week another made a belly-landing, smashing the plane at the edge of a wood. Two days later a sergeant forgot to put down his undercarriage and came down proudly in a belly-landing in the middle of the aerodrome. The bills the Air Ministry will be presenting at the end of the month to General de Gaulle will be steep.

February 8th
I have been promoted flight lieutenant by the Air Ministry, the R.A.F. rank corresponding to that of captain. A curious position, mine: I am a captain when I take it into my head to wear my English uniform; dressed as a Frenchman I come down to lieutenant.

February 9th
General de Gaulle is coming to visit the squadron (recently christened the 'Paris' Squadron) next Thursday. I am beginning to get the flight ready for this visit, which is apparently to be a particularly splendid one. I am having all the planes painted and a handsome small Cross of Lorraine put on each one. A brand-new flag is flying near my flight. Artists (whom I acknowledge in the person of Lieutenant de Tedesco above all) are boldly attacking the grim business of decorating the pilots' room. Others are knowingly fixing maps to the wall. Lieutenant Mouchotte does not know which way to turn; he is absorbed in his many tasks, harassed by one after another, feet on the ground but eyes watching the sky where his planes are.

Not a minute to breathe. Tore strips off a few people, which was some relief. A Heinkel III is hanging perilously on two slender threads. It weighs five or six kilos at least. I hope it stays up when de Gaulle passes under it. We speak in whispers, for fear of its moorings snapping. ...

THE CROSS OF LORRAINE IN THE AIR

February 10th

We have just practised the Cross of Lorraine formation for the second time. Not too much wobbling. I have the impression it will be all right. It looks fine from the ground. If only the weather is decent!

February 12th

Catastrophic! It has rained all night. This morning the wind is blowing a gale and there is a very low ceiling rolling with horrible black clouds. It will be impossible to present the Cross of Lorraine to our chief. Everyone looks disappointed.

I went to the flight. My sailors had assembled, their collars dazzlingly white. The Army Air Force looked like poor relations beside them. I felt I ought to take my shoes off before going into the pilots' room; this is the result of long days of work. For two hours the phone kept ringing; even Monsieur X, General de Gaulle's civil representative in Glasgow, was put through to my office, goodness knows why, to ask me if I thought the General would receive him and his staff if they came. Then came the news which demolished the organizers' noble edifice: the General's train is hours late. ... It is still raining.

Six o'clock

The day has gone very well. The General seemed in better form than at Manston, if I may venture to say so. ... But he is still as great. Cocktails in the mess.

'I have seen you before somewhere.'

'Manston, General.'

General Valin in his blue shirt, Commandants de Rancourt, Delahaye and fat Pompéi accompanied him good-humouredly. Two other officers and I managed to corner General de Gaulle and questions came thick and fast, which he answered with very good grace. He seems very pleased to have played a trick on the Americans over Saint-Pierre and Miquelon. He foresees some small landings in France this year. *Perhaps* we shall keep a small foothold somewhere. He is not too confident of a favourable development in Russia this year. He told us there will very soon be an all-French division and a Polish division fighting in Libya, both under the command of General Catroux.

And the squadron will soon be on operations, which overjoys us. A succulent luncheon. How did they manage it? De Scitivaux talked to the General about me. Hum! I assumed a detached air. After the meal, Captain

Dupérier, in great good humour, told me he had talked in a similar vein to General Valin. What have I done to deserve it? I must confess that the flight would carry on just as well without my being given a third ring, and that when I make a mess of my landings, they would be less noticeable as a lieutenant's than as a captain's. And try and make them understand that I earn more as a flight lieutenant than I should as a captain: difficult to believe, but true.

The sky cleared: the C.O. took the heroic decision. We went out to the landing-ground, where the planes were drawn up in perfect alignment. General de Gaulle inspected us, then we took off. Agonizing moment for everyone, especially for me, when my engine wouldn't start. At last, it behaved itself and I soon took charge of the three who were to fly on me. All went well.

We ended the display, hearts racing, with the famous Cross.

'Steady, lads! Hold on, we're nearly over!' cried de Scitivaux's voice. The formation was horribly blown about but we all set our teeth and did our best. …

It was perfect. The Air Marshal was enthusiastic, there were endless congratulations, films were made and everyone was pleased. It would not surprise me if this success hastens our departure south. They talked of the Cross of Lorraine tonight in the streets of Ayr.

February 14th
I gave chase to a Boche this evening but did not even see him.

February 15th
Filthy weather. I have been tackling some English history with my grammar. They have certainly shown us something since we made them a present of William the Conqueror. But we are quits. And friends, too, for the good and bad days ahead.

How many great statesmen, down their centuries, hard, keen men, have thought incessantly of the nation's greatness. But I do not think they have ever had a greater one than Churchill – who already belongs to the history of the civilized world, like Roosevelt and, I should like to hope for France's sake, like de Gaulle. …

February 21st
Dubious weather this morning. I hesitated over letting my pilots go up; very low white cloud. I decided to see what it was like for myself. Once in the

air, I thought it was very bad. A ridiculous curiosity made me want to go through the cloud. The climb through the dense mass seemed interminable. I went up to 9,000 feet, eventually coming out under a magnificent blue sky overlooking a sea of spotless white cloud. How I should love to stay here in the infinite immensity!

I flew in wide circles so as not to lose my position, knowing there were mountains all round whose peaks were enveloped in thick cloud. Ten minutes later I was back in the cloud, but cloud denser than when I came up: 6,000 feet, 5,000, 4,000, 3,000, 2,000, 1,000. ...

Now I was in the midst of a snowstorm. I began to feel rather uncomfortable and throttled back. It was dark, my windshield was blocked with snow and the speed was making the plane vibrate strangely. Provided there were no mountains. ...

Provided the frost or snow did not interfere with my instruments, especially my artificial horizon, and I did not fly on my back near the ground ... 500 feet, nothing yet. The cloud broke at last at 200 feet above a landscape buried in a whirlwind of snow. Visibility barely 500 metres. ...

Now I knew why Flying Control had been calling me for the last half hour. At last, I found the aerodrome and landed safely. This flight will have been a lesson to me. Luckily, I took no one with me.

March 10th
Anthony Eyre, old Tony of 615, who was in turn my flight commander, my squadron leader, and latterly our wing commander, has just been shot down over France. Fortunately, he has only been taken prisoner. He was married about a month ago.

March 15th
A surprise this morning: I have got my promotion to captain.

March 20th
Commandant de Scitivaux has just told me – at last! – the news: we are going south. We leave on 1st April for ... Manston. In spite of the disappointment of going back on the terrible operations against enemy shipping, I am glad to be leaving this country.

What will the reaction of our pilots, especially the young ones, be when in a few days' time we announce their new destination? I am sure they will do the job well, but being transplanted without an intermediate stage into the front line to do a job as thankless as it is murderous will be tough at first. God protect our 340.

March 23rd

It is not Manston, but Merston, near the Isle of Wight, to which we are moving. We shall not be doing Jim Crows over Holland. Cherbourg and Brest will be our new theatres of operations. Goodbye, old Scotland, with your icy gloom; we shall leave you without regret because we are going nearer France. We shall soon be flying over St. Michael's Mount and Saint-Malo. Our wings will shine over Normandy. The first French squadron will try its guns in a real French sky, encouraged by the idea that French people are watching it and praying for its victory without suspecting that they are praying for their own countrymen.

We have just got brand new Spitfire Vs. I take morbid care over running-in the engine of my plane, chosen from a score of others. It is the handsomest, the newest, the most complete and the most perfect! No other flies as fast or is easier to handle. No one but me will fly her. I am more jealous than a tigress of her young. I hesitate to turn too steeply for fear of spoiling her, and my mechanics, who have adopted the newcomer with affectionate respect, look after her as zealously as nurses. The least scratch is promptly dealt with by a tiny stroke of the brush. I trim my ailerons with such solicitude that flying this beloved newcomer is a perfect joy.

I shall anticipate her slightest reactions in the air. The least tremor will go right through me. I want to make her a living thing, all of whose instincts of sensitivity and obedience will meet in me. Man's pride in the machine! I live with my plane; I have a physical sense of her efforts in tail-spins at speed. I suffer with her when she gets a violent buffet, that gives her too severe a shock. I worry about her when I feel one of her organs vibrating or failing. I inspect her every morning, almost stroking her with my hand as if she were a proud charger about to bear me into battle. ...

Colonel Pigeaud has died a hero's death. He will be among my memories as long as I live, receiving us at Gibraltar, telling us who was waiting for us in England and who our chief would be. I shall remember him in his office in London, too, greeting me so kindly each time I called there. Another pioneer gone.

April 2nd

We had a magnificent trip, covering the whole length of England. At the last moment, on March 31st, we learned we were going to Redhill, south of

London. Landed without trouble on this very open aerodrome. Gargantuan food and, what is more, it is absolutely first class. It is the first time I have eaten thus in an English mess.

It is true that the cook is a Czech and was a chef at the Crillon in Paris before the war. He is very proud of the Frenchmen's very acceptable praise. My mechanics came in a heavy troop-transporting plane. They were frightfully sick, which, I fancy, has finally cured them of any desire to be pilots.

Chapter 15

Sweeps over France

April 7th, 1942

This time we left for Tangmere. Near the Isle of Wight and its formidable defences, right at the gates of Portsmouth, this aerodrome and its satellites, Merston, Ford and Westhampnett (our destination), are in the vanguard of No. 2 Group's Fighter Command. While at Manston, where we were attacking shipping, we had to fly between zero and 100 metres, this part of Great Britain is the most advanced bastion for sweeps in the direction of Cherbourg, Fécamp, Boulogne, Calais, Lille, etc.

The fighters go over in waves to win mastery of the French sky. The Germans must attach some importance to this station because they bomb it regularly. Our quarters being on the aerodrome, we shall have to take sleeping tablets.

April 8th

Choron has just got himself posted to our squadron. He, Fayolle, de Labouchère and I are the four oldest Free French fighter pilots. The memories we love to recall! I hope we shall do a good job together. General Valin is forming a second French squadron, which he intends to send to Russia. He will give the command of it either to Choron or to me.

April 10th, five o'clock

The squadron took off for its first sweep. The majority of the pilots taking part must have had a far from ordinary baptism of fire. Wing Commander Robinson, one of the best wing commanders in Fighter Command, himself took over our squadron for its first contact with the enemy. I would not have missed this first flight of the squadron for all the money in the world. De Scitivaux, Dupérier, Choron, de Labouchère felt the same. I had chosen my most resourceful pilots to go with us, all enthusiasts, determined to put into practice the many exercises and lessons we had taught them in

126

the past six months. We thus had all the trumps in our hand to make a brilliant start.

Alas, this air-battle, whatever the rest of my adventures may be, will remain engraved on my mind in its minutest details as long as I live. Twelve of us took off, three abreast in fours; we gained altitude slowly, here and there picking up other squadrons, punctual at the meeting points, progressively coming in to join us, taking up position on either side, above and below, so that we formed the point of an enormous arrow of about 250 fighters. All 2 Group had sent their squadrons – Northolt, Hornchurch, Kenley, Hawkinge, the Poles, the Czechs, the famous American Eagle Squadron, etc.

We left England by Beachy Head, climbing to 20,000 feet beneath a dazzling sky. I could already see Le Touquet in front, with its blue swimming-pool. Why did that detail strike me? I scanned the sky, pretty sure that no Boche would ever dare to attack such an enormous force as this. A violent wind at our altitude soon brought us to the spot. The total lack of opposition from the coastal batteries at once put me on my guard and immediately I heard a concert of shouts: 'Look out! A 109 behind you! Ten 109s in front. We're attacking.'

Then the voice of Wing Commander Robinson, magnificently calm, speaking to us: 'Buck up, chaps, we're going to have some fun!' Then we went into hell, attacked from below, while four Focke-Wulfs fell on us from behind, out of the sun. Our squadron was the centre of the whirlwind. There were shouts on all sides. De Scitivaux dived suddenly, turning to port; followed by my number two, I kept close to him. Looking over my shoulder, I saw four 109s diving; we were in the best possible position to be shot down.

Our speed was terrific. I used both hands to pull the stick back and fly straight up to deal with them, which gave me the worst black-out I have ever had. I hoped to make the Huns turn tail or at least change their plan, thus allowing de Scitivaux to continue the attack on his Boche – which I hadn't spotted. As soon as I could see again, I was flying almost vertically and just had time to glimpse a 109's tracer coming from above. Our two planes had just missed each other, but his bullets and shells both missed their mark. I never saw de Scitivaux again.

I regained both consciousness and my balance. A swarm of planes was whirling all round. It was hard to distinguish Huns from friendly aircraft. Twice I saw a plane spinning down in flames. A solitary Spitfire seemed very pleased to join forces with me. We gained altitude, zig-zagging wildly; I have never watched what was going on behind me with such attention.

A score of Focke-Wulfs passed very close, apparently without seeing us. They were painted a fine dark green.

Not being a lunatic, I was not going to stop them. In the scuffle that followed, eight Spitfires appeared from goodness knows where, spinning madly. I joined them. It was frightful, for we were hopelessly entangled, shaving past each other by miracles. I saw swastikas, then Spits, dived after one of them, it vanished, I pulled out. Nothing! I was all alone with my inseparable number two, alone in the huge sky, almost over Saint-Omer. Still cries of 'Look out to port! Attack to starboard!'

Then the most pitiful thing of all, a very calm voice: 'Maurice here, I'm baling out, see you soon!' Maurice Choron, one of the four veterans, with Fayolle, Labouchère and me. ... That was agonizing. The wind was strong. I seemed to live through an eternity before I was over the sea again. Then, following the coast, I climbed towards Calais, in the hope of finding the others. I arranged it so that I stayed in the sun, ready to fall on the first Boche I saw. To the north I saw hundreds of planes flying back to England. Gradually the radio quietened down. The most terrifying air battle I had ever seen was over, after fifteen long, sweating minutes. I returned to the aerodrome, ashamed of not having fired a shot. When I landed all the officers who had not been up were in the Operations Room in a terrible state. They greeted us, dreadfully anxious to hear the news. The planes came back, one by one: except three. Robinson, de Scitivaux and Choron are missing, three of the best fighter pilots there are. ...

April 14th, twelve o'clock
We took off this morning to accompany twelve heavy bombers, surrounding them in close-formation escort. They were going to bomb a power station near Caen. The weather was lovely. Crossed in 35 minutes at a mere 8,000 feet. We throttled back our engines to fly at their speed. I noticed Le Cotentin to starboard.

We crossed the coast without the Germans reacting either on the ground or in the air. Flew over Carpiquet, the aerodrome where I spent a week a few days after war was declared. Then Caen. The bombers were in perfect order. They flew over their target. 'Let them go!' And the heavy bombs dropped from their bellies and vanished towards the ground. I was expecting an enemy attack. ...

Nothing happened. Huge curls of dust rose right in the middle of the vast works below. The blighters were right on target.

We made for the coast again. A hundred planes, perhaps, were visible above us; from time to time some of them shone in the sun. What an impression of power it must have given to the French watching us. Twenty miles beyond the coast we were at last tackled by the Focke-Wulfs. I suddenly noticed five planes where I should only have been able to see four. A shout over the radio, the four made a steep turn – luckily, for the fifth was a Boche who opened fire too late, narrowly missing his target, Coignard escaped with a big hole in his port wing and a slight wound. Later I learned that as the diversionary sweep was late, the Boche thought we were feinting when he saw us making for Caen.

Thinking it was a trick and expecting the diversionary sweep over Le Havre and Fécamp, they threw all their fighter strength over Le Havre. Then, realizing their mistake, some of the enemy contrived to meet us over the sea. One funny thing was the story of Béchoff, who was swearing, blinding and making our dispersal echo with his bad temper after our return.

'A fine thing to be doing! What a bloody awful war! I'm going to resign. I've had all I want. I'm packing up!'

'What's the matter, Bechoff? Did you take the seagulls for Messerschmitts? How many did you shoot down?'

'Oh, go to hell! I think it's pushing patriotic zeal a bit too far to go and protect the bombers of a nation that goes over our country to bomb a power station I'm a shareholder in.'

April 15th

General Valin has been to Tangmere. Lunched with him, also Dupérier, de Labouchère and the air vice-marshal commanding the station. After lunch he called everyone together and said a few words, of which I remember only these: 'You have had the appalling bad luck to lose Commandant de Scitivaux and Captain Mouchotte. We will pray that one day they will come back to us. May their example ...'

Full of compassion, three or four comrades came up to me with tears in their eyes to shake hands: 'Poor old chap! How quick you've been getting back!'

I heard from the General's own lips that he means to send a French squadron to Russia in the very near future. The slight drawback is that it has been decided in high places that either Labouchère or I will be chosen to go and form it. Before Choron's disappearance it was he or I.

April 20th

During an exercise over Dunkerque, I took advantage of favourable circumstances to hand over as leader to a comrade. The weather was splendid, especially over there above France. I could not resist the temptation to fly round a bit.

Once over Calais, Cap Gris-Nez, I noticed that two Spits had followed me. So much the better. If we were attacked, we should be better able to defend ourselves. What a joy it was to be free from the rigidity of flying in huge formations! I could turn when I liked and look around me so comfortably.

Were we really at war? No opposition, no flak from the ground. I reached Le Touquet. Visibility marvellous; I saw Le Havre. I returned towards Boulogne. No black speck in the sky. I was at home. A few more turns and I went regretfully back. Operations called me and I heard Flying Control laughing like a hyena at the other end of the line. I had apparently caused thirty Boche to take off and they had gone into the sun to intercept us. Bad luck.

It was at the moment when I made a 180-degree turn. There would have been some sport. They told me cheerfully that though the Boche hadn't been seen for a week, since they dared not attack forces equal to their own, they had not hesitated to send up thirty planes to intercept three Spitfires. They added that though I had good fighting spirit I had been extremely rash. …

Letters from patronesses are flooding the squadron office. Numbers of English ladies are asking for French pilots to adopt. One even offers her car. The Canadians' generosity is touching. The City of Ottawa has adopted us. The first fruit of their kindness, London tells us, is the arrival of 25,000 cigarettes and a great quantity of tobacco.

Visits shower on us. More or less official personages come to see such rare birds at close quarters. The last was Jean Oberle, the writer-artist, who did a flowery eulogy the next day on the B.B.C.

May 1st

I have already made eleven sweeps over France. Three yesterday during the day. No success whatever. Losses: young Hauchemaille and Waillier. Yesterday I led the squadron and was attacked by two pairs of Focke-Wulfs. As one was attacking from behind, I yelled into the radio for the squadron to tackle it immediately.

The Boche broke off the attack. Then the other two attacked on the other side. I had to wait until they were close, then, turning steeply, I made for them. The turn lasted an eternity. Impossible to keep them in the sights; they disengaged out of range, refusing battle all the time. I succeeded at last in getting after one of them but he turned over and dived for the ground. This fantasia took place over Abbeville.

Despite all my efforts, Blitz got two cannon shells in his engine. He managed to get down but crashed his plane 200 metres from the aerodrome. Leg broken. We thought of Hauchemaille, a heart of gold, whom everyone loved.

This morning I had the most memorable combat of my life. Ten minutes' dog-fight with a Boche who, unlike his fellows, would not let go. And no one to help me! The bandit attacked from above and I could do no more than turn at the opportune moment, trying to give him a few bursts in passing. He must have been a tough one, one of those veterans who hang on to their prey.

Each time he made for me. I clenched my teeth and everything else, wondering if this was it. I was alone over the Channel with this bellicose brother, showing me his white belly, his fine black crosses and the dangerous red lines of tracer. He let me go in the end, in disgust, but I admit that more than once I should have liked to say, as in my childhood days, when I realized I was losing a game, 'Pax! Pax! The game's over. I won't fire at you anymore but do let me go!'

I thank Heaven for having given me such good sight and such a long neck. Unfortunately, I have a very sensitive stomach which makes its presence strangely felt before each sweep, but once I have my backside on the pilot's seat and my 1,200 horses are crackling, I couldn't feel better! The mind works fast in the air but if I meet the enemy, I know perfectly well that I do not *think* what I am doing. My nerves respond like clockwork. I no longer have time to think, to feel, to consider. There is no trace of fear but an enormous excitement, an intense mental effort. The proof that one does not think during these moments of combat is that on landing it is very hard to remember all that has happened.

A few images or impressions are photographed, but the more one ponders them the more they change. A striking incident may remain before the eyes, but the most difficult thing is to remember what one has done in a particular situation. After a good night's sleep, it is rare for any details of a combat on the day before to be remembered. ... So many things happen in so short a time that I can compare this phenomenon to a kind of mental indigestion. The thing that is by no means an illusion or distortion of ideas is the state of my shirt, wet through with sweat when I come back from a sweep. But what a great life I am leading!

May 3rd

As there was an unusually leisurely programme for the sweep, this morning I decided to let Lieutenant Gibert, whom I have been gradually training for the job, lead the flight. I have rued it and I shall have a grudge against myself for a long time, for the squadron won its first victories during that hour. I let the flight go with a heavy heart, too, watching the take-off with some apprehension.

Captain Dupérier shot down a Focke-Wulf which he followed down and saw crash. Fayolle and Lieutenant Chauvin got another and saw the pilot bale out. Lastly, Lieutenant de Tedesco shot his down over the Channel. A brilliant success for the squadron. Our joy exceeded all expectations; the English who were present caught it from us and even they became exuberant.

We shall celebrate this tonight. And I shall never miss another sweep.

May 4th

Once more escorted six bombers over Le Havre. We were attacked from above, out of the sun, by four Me. 109s. They passed like meteors to port of me and disappeared behind me –not without one of them leaving his mark on me. I turned my Spit to port and went after them. A single pilot from my flight followed me.

The movement was barely executed when I found myself on the last one's tail, to which I could only give a short burst from my cannons and machine guns. With black smoke from his engine following him, I saw him suddenly make a timid turn to port, going into a vertical dive. My job was to protect the bombers, not to follow the Boche. I climbed back as fast as possible without seeing the issue of the fight, which took place 10 miles from Deauville.

When I landed, I realized that one of the pests had put a bullet through my port wing and made a great hole in the tailplane. A wing will have to be changed and I shall therefore have to fly a plane which is not my own, which I dislike.

The moral of this story: I cannot claim the Boche as destroyed, probable or damaged. No one has reported a parachute. Only my number two and I saw the black smoke, which, it seems, proves nothing. We took off very quickly and, in my haste, I forgot to switch on my camera, which robs me of further proof. But in my heart of hearts, I am almost certain, that the Me. 109 has been struck off the effective strength of the Luftwaffe. Only very bad luck prevents me having it confirmed.

May 10th

The sweeps continue on the same scale. We invade the sky of France from early in the morning until very late in the evening. The bombers we escort are pounding the minefields and ports in the north, from Ostend to Cherbourg. Yesterday evening, it was Dieppe; today, Hazebrouck and Dixmude. And it is just beginning, the rhythm is stepping up. The American factories are turning out 5,000 planes a month. Not counting English and Russian aircraft. The Boche is certainly going to get it in the neck.

I have been told today that they are testing a new fighter aircraft, the Spitfire VIII, fitted with a more powerful engine and capable of going up to 60,000 feet.

May 11th

The weather has suddenly taken a turn for the worse. We can review our successes and have a breather after the cracking pace they have made us keep up for the past month. On the 8th, Sergeant Debec shot down a Messerschmitt which turned up as an easy prey at sea level near the English coast. He had just taken off from the aerodrome with another sergeant and quite by chance they suddenly found themselves with a dozen Boche below them. They dived and set one on fire, which sufficed to put the rest of the gang to flight.

Yesterday I was on duty from morning until five o'clock. B Flight takes over from us then. Alarm at 7. Fayolle took off with Béchoff. Half-way between here and Cherbourg they met a Junkers 88 which Fayolle shot down. It caught fire as it hit the water and the petrol burned for over an hour; thick black smoke could be seen from the coast.

The luck they have in coming across such easy victims! I remember, with a retrospective shudder, my ten minutes' dog-fight with the Focke-Wulf the other day, to whom I could not give my visiting card. When will it be my turn? We have just got some young pilots, among them André Moynet.

May 20th

I have been in command of the squadron for a week, Dupérier being on leave. Unfortunately, the weather has continued bad so I could hardly exercise my talents at the head of the squadron. One small advantage is being able to use the car when I like, especially considering the interminable bother caused by papers from Air Headquarters and the Air Ministry accumulating. Letters to answer, reports to make, claims to put in! ... Debec, de Tedesco, Boudier, Coignard and Fayolle have just received their citation and Croix de Guerre. We are celebrating tonight.

On the 17th a visit from Air Vice-Marshal Leigh Mallory; on the 18th, from the Air Minister, Sir Archibald Sinclair; today from the great chief of Fighter Command, Sholto Douglas. Sinclair remembered my name well. He made a very cordial speech to us. Then he took me aside and asked me the most indiscreet questions, but with such good humour and kindliness that I did not hesitate to open my heart to him.

I took advantage of this to express the great desire we all have to get the new Spitfires quickly. Leigh Mallory cross-examined me too, in front of the whole squadron, but he had the delicacy to ask none but official questions. I know nothing more reassuring and informal than these visits of senior men to our dispersals; I imagine what they would be like in France with French officers. They would immediately be invested with the atmosphere of the Fourteenth of July, with flags, march-past, pompous speeches. ...

May 22nd

Yesterday, at a cocktail party given by a famous woman painter at the Air Ministry, who lives in a delightful studio in a vast park, I met the wing commander from Ford aerodrome. He asked me to lunch today to introduce me to his mess and also so that I could try a new American fighter aircraft, the Mustang. My Spitfire deposited me at Ford at midday.

After a wonderful meal, we went and admired the rare bird. Unfortunately, I could not try it as it was not ready to fly. Postponed. It tempted me terribly. Its wings are clipped square, like those of the Me. 109, and its broadly balanced fuselage gives it a solid, thick-set look. I made a date with one of the pilots to compare its performance in the air with the Spitfire's.

May 24th

Great news for the squadron. A card has just been received in London from de Scitivaux. Wounded in both legs and both arms, he came down in France and is a prisoner. What a joy for his fiancée; she took eighteen months to reach England via Algeria, Portugal, South America, the Bermudas and finally reached Great Britain two days, alas, after Philippe was missing.

June 9th

Less frequent sweeps than in the last fortnight. Dubious weather, apparently. Or would it perhaps be a pause, in preparation for some tough work? Lots of things make me hope that something is being plotted secretly, in which we shall not be the last to take part. Thousands of invasion barges are being towed behind the Isle of Wight each day. Whenever I have a chance to go over there, I always take it and each time there is a surprise.

London is full of Americans, Canadians and soldiers of all nationalities. The Russian successes give every reason for hope and the terrific English bombing of Cologne allows one to expect anything. The day before yesterday we covered the withdrawal of a Commando raid on Boulogne and Le Touquet. They tell us the manufacture of the new Spitfire is being speeded up. The Americans announce that they have abandoned their 1942 building programme to give the maximum concentration to that of 1943. Shall we be in France this year?

June 11th

A bit of excitement this afternoon. Took off with my number two, young Sergeant Bouguen, to patrol to St. Catherine's Point, southern bastion of the Isle of Wight. 'Get up as fast as you can, bandits at 16,000 feet.' I put the nose of my Spitfire at the clouds and climbed like hell to 20,000 feet. There I saw two suspicious black specks, which I chased. They disappeared but not without taking me up to 24,000 feet.

Barely back in my patrol area, the radio sent me due south. My heart leapt. I cocked my guns, lighted up my sights again, cut in my camera (I never forget to do that now). A few minutes later I heard, 'Steer 170', then shortly afterwards, '190', then '200' and finally '240'. I scanned the sky. ...

Four planes appeared a few miles away, coming from the south-west. How had I missed seeing them earlier? I was already above them. They were in pairs.

Attacked one of the rear pair immediately, manoeuvring to put my number two in a good position to open up at his. My adversary saw me just before I could fire and turned steeply to port. I pressed the button, without hope, for my speed took me past behind him. To catch him again I gave myself one of the finest black-outs of my career. Blind, I went on making the turn. When my sight came back, I saw one of the Focke-Wulfs going up vertically in front of me. Was it the first one? I do not know.

My high speed enabled me to follow him in a vertical climb and to see him with his big black crosses quite close. Fixed well in my red circle, I let

135

him have it with my four machine guns and two cannons. Tiny luminous points lighted up in his wings, followed by little plumes of smoke. He tilted over to starboard and seemed to stop, immobile in space. A horrible feeling attacked me: I could feel the Boche, visibly out of control, falling back on me from above. My obviously undesirable position was that of a Spitfire fastened by the hub of the propeller to a thread at breaking point. I remember the rest very vaguely. After a sideslip, I recall a whirlwind of planes, lots of black crosses. I attacked again but did well not to fire: it was young Bouguen. Then a shout hit me: 'Look out behind'.

I disengaged without seeing my adversary. Then I found myself in a vertical death-dive behind an apparently disabled F.W. 190. At full speed I had trouble keeping the nose of my plane strictly vertical. The noise becoming intense, the vibration alarming, while I thrust with both hands on the stick. My ears hurt horribly. A shot in the cockpit; the Perspex at my side was torn away. The altimeter needle whizzed round the dial. Three thousand feet. ... I had to pull out, get the stick back gently or it would be all up and the old man with it. ... I climbed again, going like a bullet.

Once my controls had lost some of their stiffness, I tried to turn to port to find my Boche again. I turned and looked everywhere without success. I thought it unlikely that he would have come out of it when I had had difficulty in doing so with a more manoeuvrable plane. I think I got up a nice little speed in that dive. I wonder if that Fritz was the one I opened fire on from above? I can only claim one F.W. 190 damaged. One for Bouguen, too.

June 12th

Posed from 9.30 a.m. until 6 p.m. for an English artist who had come to the squadron to make a pastel drawing of Commandant Dupérier, Fayolle and me. My back hurts more than after two hours in a Spitfire. Clot! I have just heard it was the famous Kennington, the painter and sculptor, who priced his work in peace-time at the modest sum of £500.

Apparently, I have come out well. I think I must have been thinking about yesterday's combat, for he has given me the very wild and wicked look of Donald Duck in a rage. The drawing is very beautiful, the colours exact and fine. It seems it is to be exhibited in a month's time at the National Gallery. Kennington was a great friend of Colonel Lawrence.[3]

---

3. In 1947, by a graceful and much appreciated gesture, the Air Ministry handed these portraits by the lamented Sir Eric Kennington over to the French as a gift to the pilots or their families.

June 15th

While on leave yesterday I went to Reading, where I made a magnificent find: discovered a statue erected to a man called Palmer. Crowned with a majestic top hat, he carries a mighty gamp in his hand. What a ninny the good man must look, carrying his rolled umbrella, when it pours with rain.

June 20th

We went with twelve Boston bombers in close escort over Le Havre. My position was protecting the rear. I was thus a few dozen metres behind and slightly above them. Other squadrons were on either side and more in echelon overhead.

Once over the target area, the fire from the ground came up at us and surrounded us. My plane was shaken each time I crossed through one of the balls of black smoke that burst ahead of us, and almost everywhere, with reddish light. We had to follow close. Anyway, shows of this kind, excellent for a novice, now leave me quite cold. What is this, after all, compared with the receptions the gunners of Zeebrugge, Ostend, etc., gave us when we were attacking shipping in the Manston days?

But what makes me *furious* today is to see how clumsily the bombers have missed their target. Until now I have always been a witness of their great accuracy. Obviously, beginners, completely bewildered by ack-ack. Coming in over Deauville, they swung to port too soon to attack Le Havre from west to east and arrived over the target at the end of their turn, still diving. Deplorable positioning, when no enemy fighters were bothering them and the ack-ack was not too fierce.

The results wrung a cry of indignation from me. A great part of the bombs fell like a string of beads right along the principal artery of the city. Heavy plumes of smoke came up; I thought with horror of the wretches buried beneath the debris of their houses, smashed by their friends of yesterday. Did they know that the monsters who were ravaging their homes were protected by Frenchmen?

When we returned, I insisted on making a detailed report, and with the aid of a map of Le Havre I was able to fix the bombed street. The terrible apprehension each time I am sent on this kind of operation.

June 24th

Apart from the bombing of Le Havre on June 20th, total inactivity for a fortnight. The calm before the storm, people say everywhere. The weather is radiant. The time drags. The Boche has just retaken Tobruk. Rommel is advancing rapidly towards the Egyptian frontier. Eden has signed a pact of friendship with Molotov for twenty years and an engagement to open a second front in Europe before 1943.

Every day we smell gunpowder more strongly here at Tangmere. The wing has just been expanded by four squadrons 'on exercises' for a week only. It remains to be seen whether the 'exercises' succeed. Among them is the Belgian Duvivier's squadron, specially trained for attacks on the ground. Talked to him after dinner. He seems scarcely enthusiastic.

Every day the question is the same: 'Will it be tomorrow?' We watch the sky anxiously. Rumours, all amounting to the same thing, make us stamp our feet with impatience. I haven't taken a minute's leave for the past fortnight, and don't want to, for fear of missing the big show. I have waited two years for that date!

An English pilot has just flown over the Champs-Elysées, doing in less spectacular fashion what we wanted to do on November 11th last. While admiring his boldness and applauding his success, it is hard for us not to feel some bitterness; the idea was ours and the mission should, by its very nature, have been entrusted to the French. The execution of it was denied us without reason, though it was of a patriotic nature and would have done magnificent service to our cause and our propaganda. General de Gaulle has made no secret of his dissatisfaction to Fighter Command, adding to his other reasons that he should have been informed of it in advance. Apparently, he did not mince his words; the official excuses do not alter the facts. ...

So, we are busy with Dupérier, working out a lovely idea. We shall have the sense this time not to mention it to anybody before we carry it out. We will ask for authority after the dice have been thrown.

June 30th

Anniversary of my escape to Gibraltar. Two years. This morning, at last, the great news. We shall attempt the invasion tomorrow. Tomorrow, at several points on the French coast, a combination of air, sea and land attacks will be let loose on a probably enormous scale.

Whatever it is, my pilots and I are good and ready. I spent this morning inspecting all the aircraft of the flight. The maintenance is excellent from every point of view. I even have the satisfaction of knowing it is better than the other flights. I must admit that in anticipation of this inspection the mechanics had been working on the kites all yesterday. As for the pilots, they have had time for a week's rest while we were just training. I have cancelled all leave, not without exciting some comment, for H hour must be kept a secret until the last minute.

July 1st

Grey weather. Big clouds rolling very low over the hills. At ten o'clock the group captain commanding the station called all the squadron leaders together to brief them on the attack, which was set for twelve o'clock. It is the heavy bombing of the two aerodromes at Abbeville. More than five hundred planes were to take part in it. The bad weather has disappointed all hopes. No one has taken off.

July 4th

Three days of mist and rain. Which has not prevented three other squadrons installing themselves here. That brings the number of squadrons on the Tangmere aerodromes to eighteen. The mess is packed. Tents have sprung up almost everywhere to accommodate all these people.

We have stopped training flights so as to have a good effective strength of planes ready. This morning a note came round to paint broad white bands round the noses of our planes to make them visible at a great distance! The Boche will not miss us now, but the Tommies will not fire at us.

Sir Anthony Eden and his wife and Sir Archibald Sinclair and his wife have been to visit us. The whole thing is like the presentation to the ladies of strange animals, the French pilots who will be off tomorrow to get bloody noses. We later invited the great ones to take a *porto* in our little mess and admire our artists' ingenious decorations and caricatures (full marks on this occasion to Fournier and Lambert). Lady Sinclair invited me to go and see her in London more often. As he left me, the Minister very kindly whispered in my ear, 'And good luck on the operation, Mouchotte!'

July 7th

A day of mourning here. This morning, squadrons taking off from the Tangmere aerodromes woke us with their heavy drone. 'Something's going on without us,' we thought. Ah, yes, something was going on indeed: the anticipated offensive has been postponed! All the squadrons which were to form the shock units with us are going back to their bases, leaving our aerodromes stupidly empty.

After today, one of the unhappiest for a long time, everyone feels bitter and bad-tempered. Dupérier, disgusted, has gone to London for three days.

July 8th

The group captain called me urgently to his office this morning. He first questioned me about our pilots' reactions to the operation being postponed.

He seemed very anxious to know to what we attributed the English G.H.Q.'s decision; when I told him that we were all convinced that the bad weather alone was responsible for the contretemps he seemed relieved.

It is evident that he feared we might have had some apprehension as to the British preparations or the plan of campaign. I could have been funny with him by insinuating that as great haste in tactical decisions has never been an English characteristic, we were sure that when they did attempt something it would be with all the trumps in their hand. I simply said to him that we were sure the thing was only postponed and that the next moon would see the other squadrons landing again at Tangmere.

'That is so,' he said, 'the importance of the operation that was going to be carried out may have been concealed from you, but it was nothing less than an attempt at invading the continent. A very calm sea and a cloudless sky are indispensable conditions. But don't give up hope; it will be soon.

I saw soldiers weeping with disappointment yesterday when the news was announced on the Isle of Wight. Do you know which troops were entrusted with the first assault? British and French Canadians. Since the French Armistice they have been complaining because they were not fighting. Many of the latter wanted to go back to Canada, saying that from the moment France was out of the war there was nothing for them to do but go home. It took a lot of diplomacy to teach them that on the contrary their part was only just beginning, since they would have the sacred task of liberating her. They've been biting their nails off to the wrist with impatience ever since. If you had only seen them yesterday!'

The Duchess of Gloucester, official godmother of the squadron, paid us a visit today. Never has a visit from an English minister or the Premier caused such care and even disquiet among the station commanders than this visit of a member of the Royal Family. I heard the news with very little enthusiasm, noticing yet again the annoying coincidence of Dupérier's absence, which leaves me with all the consequences and responsibilities of such receptions. I asked Group Captain Appleton some questions about the customs and protocol of such occasions: should I kiss Her Highness's hand? Or ought I to bow, or was a pirouette necessary? His reply rather embarrassed me: 'Do what you would in France on such an occasion.'

At 3.30 precisely I saw in the distance a whole procession of black cars making the round of the aerodrome, five minutes later a splendid black limousine stopped before the door of our dispersal. Other cars drew up behind it, numerous officers, among them Group Captain Appleton, pouring from them. A small, smiling woman, in the uniform of Air Commodore of the

W.A.A.F., stepped out of her car, acknowledged my salute impeccably and came forward, still smiling, to shake hands. Her face has great sweetness. She is still ravishing.

We went slowly towards dispersal; inside, all the officers of 340 awaited us, at attention. As we walked, I gave her the excuses of our commandant, urgently called (pious untruth) to London. Then they were all presented. A horrible thing happened to me: a frightful lapse of memory with one officer, made me incapable of remembering his name. And I had lived with him for six months. It did not matter; I didn't hesitate, I gave some name at random. Ouf! Nobody noticed, and the obstacle was overcome. Her Royal Highness seemed very interested in the mural decorations, maps, trophies, etc. I escorted her back to her car, which was to take her back to our little mess, where we were giving her tea. We had to be quick then; four officers following me, we jumped into my car and got there by devious ways before the official ones arrived. The same ceremonial. This time I was seated on the Duchess's right. Brilliantly assisted by the group captain we kept up a sublimely banal conversation....

I should have loved to cry *'Vive la République'* to the beautiful ladies, instead of all those remarks on the possibility of a change in the weather with the next phase of the moon, etc. ...

July 12th

The aerodrome and the squadron have been preparing for a visit from General de Gaulle for some days past. He arrived yesterday morning, half an hour late – very properly. 'You must excuse the General,' Colonel Coustey said to me, 'I bumped into the back of his car on the way. Our brakes weren't working.

After that alarm, whenever the brakes went on, he turned round and looked most uncomfortable.' We had broken a brand-new flag and everyone was in full uniform.

'Well, Mouchotte, everything all right? Still happy?'

The sailors executed an operatic 'order arms'. They were practising it all day yesterday. But I felt it was up to me to relax the atmosphere and while the Great Charles continued his inspection I stepped forward and, wanting to perform my little part with *brio*, turned round and shouted in a stentorian voice, 'Pilots! Attention for the Commandment!' The immediate result of which was to let loose the finest burst of general laughter I have ever heard. The annals of the squadron were enriched with a new word ... which our

Great Charles did not even have the pleasure of hearing. Splendid blow-out, speeches, toasts to the King and to France.

The General expressed a very legitimate desire to 'wash his hands' and I made as much haste in showing him the door as he did in pushing it open. Inspection of the lines and men's rooms, etc. Touching farewells. Our great man disappeared in a cloud of dust. Our historic day is over.

July 13th

While I was brooding over bitter thoughts of the second anniversary of my arrival in England, Dupérier came to tell me that tomorrow he is taking me to be decorated with the Croix de Guerre by General de Gaulle in London. On a glorious morning, in the great courtyard of Wellington Barracks, overlooking Buckingham Palace, I received from the hands of the Great Charles a magnificent Croix de Guerre with the silver Star and two bronze Palms. The crowd had been at the railings for a long time when the General's splendid Packard entered, greeted by thousands of cries of '*Vive de Gaulle! ... Vive la France!*'

The *Marseillaise* struck up at once. The General reviewed the troops and saluted the flags; at last, shot by a dozen newsreel and press photographers, he came and stood between the two flags with his back to the crowd. His great silhouette dominated them. He began by decorating a junior naval officer, whose heroic conduct had saved his submarine, with the Cross of the Liberation. Then came our turn. We were called. I followed Dupérier and we took up our position out in front between the two flags.

The drums.

I was terribly affected. I felt I was dreaming. After pinning the Cross on me, de Gaulle gave me a long handshake.

'All my congratulations, Mouchotte. Believe me, I am particularly happy to shake your hand here and on such an occasion, in front of everybody.'

The drums again.

I returned to my place, much embarrassed by the applause which burst out.

The General took the salute as the troops marched past. The naval commandos were very much remarked, for their impeccable turn-out and also for their wicked look. They wore khaki battle-dress and a sailor's flat cap with red pom-pom. Some carried a machine gun on their shoulders. They really did look tough. They got lots of applause. The W.A.A.F.s also enjoyed a great success. Unfortunately, they were led by a fat girl who marched in front of them, her head thrown back ridiculously and her posterior very noticeable and well behind her.

The other girls marched past perfectly, an English stamp on their bearing, and, oddly enough, they had a good deal of majesty. We broke up without taking part in the march, which was to be to Marshal Foch's statue, at which General de Gaulle was to lay a wreath. We were invited to cocktails at the Grosvenor Hotel.

July 15th

The whole squadron took off on a mass rhubarb. I did not want to miss such a rare occasion, so I went up at the head of my flight this morning. After twenty-five minutes' flying just above the crests of the waves, we saw the cliffs of Saint-Valéry-en-Caux at last. Not a single enemy ship.

As usual, my heart began to beat a crazy dance and I felt the curious sensation in the stomach. The white wall of the cliffs approached rapidly; we had gone straight in to within 50 metres of their base, and all pulled the noses of our planes towards the sky, making an almost vertical ascent. Dupérier's and Fayolle's flights were to follow the coast south, then after between three and five kilometres they were to fly parallel with me, along and above the coast. Though Dupérier's and Fayolle's flights found no targets to fire at, and though the latter succeeded only in shooting a superb Boche rider off his horse, my flight and I were not idle.

Once over the coast, I had hardly straightened out to go down to ground level again when some 200 metres ahead I saw a queer kind of apparatus in a field, which I recognized as a radiolocation post with its swivelling framework on top of it. I was already over it and could only give it one short burst, without seeing any apparent signs of destruction, when I felt a violent blow beneath my plane, accompanied by a dull sound, like the blow of a huge fist on a table of crockery.

'No doubt about it, I'm hit,' but I was surprised to find I felt no excitement on that account. Just before I crossed the coast, I was almost physically ill with nerves: now, in the midst of danger, immense calm tripled my strength and gave an incredible precision to my actions. There was a great determination, a complete absence of fear, though the awareness of danger makes one behave as if by its own will the unconscious mechanism dominates and puts to sleep the reasoning animal. Two or three tests with the stick and the rudder bar proved I was not fatally damaged.

Then I forgot all that. The fields flew past. Hundreds of cows. A few peasants; some waved their hats, handkerchiefs and arms in lively fashion. Others lay flat on the ground for fear of being noticed and machine-gunned. A group of poor old women fled, terrified of my plane; I was horrified to see one of them tumble to the ground. I swear if I had had the slightest chance of landing, I would have done so to pick her up and tell her how ashamed I was. I have a huge pity for these invaded, wretched folk. But most of them were waving me greetings and I am sure they saw my arm waving back.

A second radiolocation station attracted my attention. It looked more important than the other. I attacked it with cannon fire and a great sheaf of sparks escaped at once. As I turned round, I saw my pilots following my example and attacking in their turn. Good, the Boche had got his, but he spat back and tracer came up from all over and passed under our noses.

A valley! It was so strange, that plunge into such a peaceful-looking valley. Little roofs, amid the green of the trees, and quiet smoke.

I found myself at the other end, very surprised at not having been more knocked about by the defence. I exercised myself once more on a little machine-gun nest. The gleam of a gun barrel in the sun had caught my eye. So very little would have been enough to save those Fritzes' lives. Fate.

At last came the order to leave the coast. A few more turns and I passed over Etretat. I could not make up my mind to return, disappointed at going back with some shells still to fire. Then an opportunity presented itself. Far off I could see a small wooden building which could be nothing but a gun emplacement. Off we went! Both hands on the stick, to aim better, I flew at the level of the daisies.

The red dot just on the middle of the cabin, I was about to press the centre button and let fly with all my guns when I saw, 20 metres away to starboard, five superb Germans in uniform making off at full speed and, oh! ingenuous ones, all together. What an opportunity! A few degrees to starboard. Gannon and machine guns, I gave them all I had. A great cloud of dust, then emptiness and the sea below.

I plunged my plane down, flung it up, making it turn madly while bullets ricocheted starboard and port of me in the water, tracer outstripping me, a most unpleasant feeling. Finally, a delicious feeling of well-being possessed me. It was over, I was still alive. Is it the quest for that satisfaction that makes me fond of this kind of sport? It was only ten or fifteen minutes later that I remembered I had been hit. Was I wounded? Apparently not.

When I turned round, I saw the thing, the frightful thing. My tail had been completely gutted by a shell. It was a miracle my controls had functioned. For the love of Heaven, fly straight and no shocks! I was appalled when I thought back to my giddy capers as I left the coast. Fortunately, my elevators seemed not to have been hit. I saw them later – another two centimetres would have done it. What a lovely somersault I should have performed!

Fayolle has noted in his report that having crossed the coast at the same point this morning, he fired on and destroyed an enemy gun, whose barrel was idly pointing to the sky and whose crew were lying all over the place, apparently lifeless.

July 18th

We are going to Ipswich for a shoot. Eight days' rest ordered for the squadron.

July 19th

Obviously, the rest is not for me. The commandant is going to London for the eight days and I am taking his place.

July 26th

A memorable party yesterday evening in the great mansion that serves as mess for the squadron. We shall remember Ipswich.

This morning I learned that as soon as we return to Tangmere we are to leave it for another station in 2 Group. I told the squadron; everyone seems in great consternation.

July 29th

We flew to Westhampnett on Sunday, where we learned our future station: Hornchurch. God, how far it will be from France. Packed our bags for the tenth time, then flew to Hornchurch, where we found greater comfort and more plentiful food (just as well – I was pining away at Tangmere). Its position, north of the Thames estuary, means that the station is wrapped in mist in the morning. The balloons being three miles from here, we shall have to get to know the lie of the land pretty thoroughly.

July 30th

Two sweeps today, both quite deep, into France: Saint-Omer, the first, went off without bother. The second seemed a bit dangerous as the ceiling was 5,000 feet and there was no protection from altitude. Dupérier not being here, I led the squadron. The inevitable happened.

Once we were well over French territory, we were attacked by a large enemy force. More than forty F.W. 190s dropped out of the sun to port behind the squadron; we lost five planes. Then they fell on me, and there was a free-for-all scrap at barely 1,200 metres. Although I flung myself about wildly, I did not get any of them in my sights. The turning mass of aircraft hypnotized me a little.

I was probably wrong to look over my shoulder so often, thinking of protection against attacks from the rear, but the battle was far too unequal, and it was better to think of saving our skins than to risk a massacre to satisfy the offensive spirit. In any case, we finally succeeded in getting out of the infernal torment and regaining the sea by hopping over the tree-tops. Two were missing tonight: Sous-Lieutenant Lambert, Adjutant Debec; excellent pilots.

It will be long before I forget the sight of planes bursting into flame, others crashing on the ground and turning into great balls of fire. I shall always remember the man who baled out from a plane blazing like a torch, whose parachute was suddenly consumed by the bite of a stupid little flame invisible to me when the pilot jumped.

August 1st

Another busy day. In the morning we escorted eight Hurricane bombers over Yvetot, nearly 250 kilometres from our aerodrome. We circled the town for at least five minutes before deciding what to do. At that moment a goods train had the unfortunate idea of entering the station. It did not take long: one bomb and the locomotive went up. Then we went into the attack.

I was the first to attack the distillery. I saw my shells pierce the roof, and a Hurricane which followed me dropped its bomb just as my number two was attacking. His plane was a bit shaken but he escaped with a fright.

The general attack was then let loose. There was not much left of the distillery and the station, which are next door to one another. The men employed there certainly had time to take cover, on account of the incessant noise we were making 300 metres above the town. We expected the Boche any minute; it was incomprehensible that we saw none coming for us.

In the afternoon, close escort of six Bostons over Flessingue on the island of Walcheren in Holland. Extremely hot ack-ack barrage, particularly accurate. The gunners at Le Havre have never shown as much skill as their colleagues in windmill-land. Even so, the bombing itself was still first class and the docks were hit hard.

From my 12,000 feet I even saw the bridge of one of the basins get a direct hit. The formation disengaged to starboard and had to stand up to the furious ack-ack fire at Blankenberghe. One shell burst right behind me, between my number two and me, i.e., less than twenty-five metres from us. The cockpit of one Spitfire was full of the smoke it had flown through. Another of St. Teresa's miracles.

Immediately after that some flak burst right in the midst of the Boston formation. I saw one wing jump 200 metres in the air, while an engine dropped like a stone. The plane leapt curiously, skyward, then began its tragic tail-spin. Poor lads! Unfortunately, a second Boston had also been hit. Its port engine was smoking and the four other bombers were leaving it dangerously far behind. The Boche fighters might turn up and there were 150 kilometres of sea to cross. I decided to stay behind it with my section as escort. It was not going very fast and we had to fly in S's to keep with it.

As I passed quite close, I saw the engine had been stopped; then I saw the horrid sight of a treacherous little flame still licking the rear of the engine. If only they could get back to England! With his plane flying crab-wise on one engine, the pilot did not realize that he was flying due north instead of about 310 to make Martlesham. Then I found I had no radio contact. It disheartened me. Impossible to make my pilots understand the fatal error. Fortunately, we had no Fritz behind us. After half an hour the fire was bigger. Showers of sparks flew from it; black fragments broke away. The grey smoke became dense and black. The situation was becoming critical. Was the pilot going to have his plane blow up? We were barely at 1,500 feet. I was afraid the wing would soon break off. He must take a decision, and quickly, but how could he be told without radio?

Only five minutes later, with huge flames escaping, the pilot throttled back his single engine and ditched in the sea. Two of the crew succeeded in saving themselves. I went down to their level; they did not seem to be wounded. I had time to see a third, motionless, his head in the water and a wide pool of blood round him.

We made for England; we had hardly any petrol left. A quarter of an hour got us to Martlesham where we immediately alerted the rescue service. A few minutes later six Spitfires took off and fast motor-boats made for the scene of the drama. Our two pilots were saved.

August 4th

I have just seen my films, the results of our mass rhubarb of July 15th. You could see the two radiolocation stations my shells hit. Great sparks and some smoke were escaping from them. But what intrigued me no end was the building near which I killed my five Boche; on the film it was huge, obviously much bigger than I remembered. It looked quite a fortress, small but formidable – Lord, how brave I was!

August 8th

Shall we make the invasion one day? The Russians are in retreat, the Caucasus partly invaded. The Americans are speeding up the manufacture of war material and sending more and more troops to England. ... The latter gives a week's holiday to factory workers. Isn't the English week enough for them?

August 18th

At last! The attack! Tomorrow, at dawn, the first phase of the biggest Allied offensive of the war opens. How will it develop? On how many different fronts? I still do not know.

As far as we are concerned, we have just got details of the operation which is to take place in the Dieppe sector, the outline of which seems to be an attack on the town with a withdrawal of the troops engaged at 11 a.m. Destruction of all military objectives and installations, including the aerodrome, which, if I understand it correctly, will not be a very healthy spot for a picnic.

We are to take off before dawn, arrive over the port five minutes before the ships are alongside and stay there until we have to come back for lack of petrol. We are thus to give them cover. Immediately on landing we are to fill up, reload, if necessary, and take off again at once throughout the morning. Hundreds of planes of all kinds with various missions will be in on the party. What a free fight there is going to be! Good luck, René my boy, and to bed.

Chapter 16

Dieppe

August 20th, 1942

It was, indeed, a memorable *corrida:* 95 British planes shot down to more than 100 German ones. The French squadron lost two planes but one of the pilots is safe.

Took off at 4.30 a.m. in the dark. Arrived over Dieppe at 5,000 feet. The battle was already raging on the ground. Luminous threads of machine-gun bullets passed to and from the coast. It was hard to keep one's attention from being distracted by the impressive spectacle; we realized its grandeur the more as the daylight increased.

Shortly after our arrival, screens of smoke rose the whole length of the coast and thus we could interest ourselves only in our own business – the care of the ships whose security from air attack depended on us. Fifteen squadrons were patrolling the sector with us, disposed at 30,000 feet, while planes of other types shared different tasks. The Boche nevertheless succeeded in boldly slipping into our midst and there was a queer struggle.

The sun had barely risen and planes could only be recognized by their silhouette at close quarters. One thing we saw better than ever was the lines of tracer. I got myself attacked twice by another section of Spitfires. On another occasion, a Focke-Wulf passed quite close to me without opening fire, obviously taking me for a comrade. I should have found it most disagreeable to be shot down by a Spitfire. The whirl of planes and the little luminous threads in the darkness that kept passing under one's nose from nowhere were rather bewildering. And I had not had occasion to open fire. … Soon afterwards, when hosts of Spitfires came from the north to relieve us, we received the order to withdraw.

An hour and three-quarters later we were back. The day had fully broken and should have let us see a little of the battle. No! The smoke from fires and explosions, and that which had been made to cover the troops' landing, covered the whole scene. Only the motor launches, the invasion barges, the ships and the destroyers were visible.

149

We took off again at 8.30 and I had the bad luck to have mechanical trouble. Could not retract my undercarriage. I decided to break formation. I was furious. I could not land, either, my wheels being neither in nor out. It was only after much effort and violent blows of my fist on the lever that I succeeded in retracting it. I had wasted ten minutes, which it was useless to try and make up. To land while my flight was fighting without me never came into my head. I decided to go on my own, but judged it best to gain altitude and be ready to dive like a stone over Dieppe at the first Boche I saw.

At 23,000 feet I happened to notice a heavy formation of twenty-four unfamiliar-looking bombers, a little higher up, coming from the north. I thought at once that they might be Boche, manoeuvring to surprise the English who were busy elsewhere. The opportunity was too good to miss. Climbing madly to get the sun behind me and the bombers in front, I already imagined myself diving on one in the rear. Alas, when I got closer, I recognized American Flying Fortresses. O.K. I would escort them. It would be the devil if they were not intercepted by some Boche. We went as far as Abbeville, to my great surprise. I learned later that they only dropped 75 tons of bombs on the aerodrome – a featherweight! Nothing!

Still no sign of Focke-Wulfs. In the sky there were just twenty-four giant bombers and, ironically, me, a small insect pretending to be protecting them. At last, I parted company with them and made for Dieppe. For five minutes the ether had been ringing with shouts, warnings, notice of attacks, etc. ...

The French accent predominated. My mouth was dry with resentment at having lost too much time. I was about to dive and get into the battle. Too late. I heard the order to make a half-turn and land.

Horribly vexed, I lost interest in everything, forgetting my dangerously isolated position. I was deeply mortified, furious with myself. As I reflect on this, analysing my sense of shame, I hate myself for letting myself be distracted by that ridiculous Abbeville operation while my comrades were shooting it out lower down. I think it was jealousy that inspired my rage and I certainly felt miserably relieved on landing when I learned everyone had come back with an empty bag. How vile we are sometimes.

A vague stain on the sea, between two clouds, suddenly attracted my attention. More to rouse myself out of my stupid apathy than out of curiosity, I went into a dive towards the spot. Three times I lost it and three times I had to use the sun's reflection to find the bit of sea between the clouds again. ...

It was a vague patch of oil. No dinghy, the pilot's individual rescue boat. Only when I was at sea level did I spot a head emerging. Unluckily my radio was not working after the rapid descent. For twenty-five minutes I ran a shuttle service between a faster motor-launch which I had the luck to find ten miles away and the unfortunate fellow. At a distance of 500 metres the boat still did not seem to be able to locate him. I succeeded in putting her on to him in the end. When I landed at Hornchurch I had only three gallons of petrol left. De Labouchère has shot down a Dornier 217. Someone else has damaged an F.W. 190. Two 217s damaged as well. Darbins is missing. Someone saw him crash.

My story was enjoyed by the squadron, but I was bad tempered all day. A fourth sortie, to cover the re-embarkation, did not give me a chance to open fire, either. In the evening I was dead with fatigue.

Fayolle is posted missing. De Labouchère and I are the only two survivors of the happy crowd of the early days. I am remembering a farewell cocktail party at Group Captain Appleton's. Shortly before we broke up, he took me into his garden.

'In view of your service record and your experience in the R.A.F., Fighter Command have decided to give you the command of an English squadron. Do you accept?'

I was a thousand miles from expecting any such proposal, most flattering not only to me but also to the Free French forces. I should be the first Frenchman, and one of the few foreigners, to command a British unit. The prospect of leading my own squadron into battle over France filled me with delirious happiness.

'It will be a small proof,' he added, 'of our esteem for you and of our gratitude to you for the magnificent job you've been doing for nearly two years.'

But when I asked him where I should be posted to, he told me a squadron of Hurricane bombers. What a cold shower that was! I should have to fight in heavy planes without great speed, bomb enemy targets in low-altitude dives and not even have the chance of being able to fight back if attacked by German fighters. Thankless work, out-of-date machines, relinquishment of all my satisfaction in being a fighter pilot! I told him without hesitation that I did not feel the slightest inclination for such work. To be good leader you have to know inside out the work you give your subordinates. I had not the experience, and I had not the bomber spirit.

I confess he seemed rather disappointed by my refusal.

'There isn't a Spitfire squadron available at the moment,' he said at last, 'but we'll give you the next one that wants a squadron leader.'

A month later the group captain at Hornchurch called Fayolle into his office and made him the same proposal, for the same squadron. Fayolle accepted and was promoted commandant. On his first operational flight, eight took off and three came back. Fayolle was among those missing, with Wymmersch and du Fretay, one of our younger brethren, a valiant Breton who took off under the Boche's very nose from his mother's house in his little sports plane, to come and fight at our side.

A small operation round Le Touquet. Nothing remarkable, except one of the heaviest barrages I have ever seen. I was literally surrounded with big black flak which chased me all over and gave me a shaking every time my plane went into the puffs that kept appearing suddenly in front of me.

At one moment the cockpit was full of brown smoke. What a disagreeable smell! Despite myself, I remembered a wise warning posted on the wall of our dispersal in 615 at Northolt: 'When you are unlucky enough to be singled out by an ill-disposed gunner in the enemy ack-ack and he is chasing you hard with his shells, zig-zag: but above all arrange matters so that you are always in the zag when he fires at you in the zig, or in the zig when he fires in the zag. ...'

August 21st

The way the operation at Dieppe went has shown beyond all possible doubt that the Germans were expecting us. Their espionage had told them what was coming off. This was discovered too late, but it is one of the most impressive bits of espionage of the war. I was told about it quite incidentally and have promised to keep the secret. An advertisement appeared in some of the most important daily papers on August 5th, 13th and 17th.

The Dieppe operation was on the 19th. By turning the illustration clockwise through ninety degrees, the branch the woman is holding bears a curious resemblance to the north coast of France, from Cap Gris-Nez to Dieppe, which is on the shears. There is other important information hidden there too, apparently. The four buttons are the four batteries attacked first. The shading on the coat similarly conceals strategic details.

That is how information vitally important in the carrying on of the war reaches Germany under everyone's very eyes.

August 22nd

Some time ago we received a gift of 10,000 cigarettes, addressed to the French Squadron by some vague committee representing an American city. It was acknowledged by such an enthusiastic letter that we have just received

30,000 cigarettes and also a gift of 1,000 dollars to be shared among us. If we send more dithyrambic thanks still and a proportionate response is made, the French Squadron has decided to retire to a castle in Scotland.

August 25th

Suddenly, as if there were a panic, an order has come for all pilots to be vaccinated and inoculated. We have had two days of it. I am ill, my left arm is like a pumpkin. But I shall not get diphtheria, small-pox or typhoid. Do they by any chance intend to send us to the Middle East?

I have just seen one of the French commandos who took part in the Dieppe expedition. He wore khaki battledress and a French sailor's beret with 'Commando français' on it. He told us a number of stories. He seemed very keen and thought of nothing but doing it again. Like his comrades, he refused to wear the regulation English tin hat, being most anxious to show the French in France, not to mention the Boche, that the famous red pom-pom was the sign of the brave.

One of these pom-poms was miraculously shot off by a bullet. He told us that one good woman, in her joy at seeing the fighting French, had absolutely insisted on giving one of them a bag of eggs. The poor devil dared not refuse and went on fighting with his grenades on one side and the eggs on the other. Another found time, it seems, to visit the Mayor. After a short conversation, he said, 'Perfect. Now I know what you're worth. Here's your reward.' And he concluded by thrusting his bayonet through him. But the finest story is the one about the French-Canadian tanks. Their orders were to return to the beach at 11 a.m., blow up their tanks and re-embark.

The difficulty at eleven o'clock was that they could not be got to obey. 'There they were and there they were staying; two years they had waited for the hour of landing in France and they weren't going to turn back now. Too bad, they would go on alone. The others only had to leave without them.' It is hard to imagine those few tanks, isolated in a hostile country, making for Paris along the beautiful roads of France. Who will tell us of those few brave men's heroic end?

Chapter 17

Squadron Leader

September 1st, 1942

I am living in a great mansion tonight, part of which has been converted into a mess. My room is regal, one of the most handsome ones. I have a car and my own plane, and everyone calls me 'Sir' with outward signs of the greatest respect. I have an office to myself, a telephone, secretaries and a unit of about one hundred men attentive to my slightest order.

Finally, I have twenty-eight excellent pilots, all keen to follow their leader – me, since 11 a.m. yesterday – into battle. I have in fact been promoted to the rank of squadron leader by the English and they have given me the command of a British Spitfire squadron. It is doing me great honour to give me such a post. I have also had the good luck to be awarded the Distinguished Flying Cross, my ambition throughout the war, this decoration being one of the finest an R.A.F. pilot can have; wearing it on my breast – I, a foreigner – fills me with terrific pride. Very few among the French have had my luck; I know of five.

My squadron is 65, the East India Squadron, composed for the most part of Englishmen, with three Canadians, an Australian, a New Zealander and an American. I have succeeded Squadron Leader MacMullen, an ace with twenty victories, D.F.C. and two bars. He is taking me to Biggin Hill, our sector, where he will introduce me to the group captain. I hear the same thing everywhere – 65 Squadron, which has been entrusted to me, is one of the best and the best-thought-of in the Group. I really am thrilled that it should have been given to me.

September 5th

I have already made four sweeps with my young men. They follow perfectly, indeed, and it is a pleasure to be their leader. I am getting telegrams of congratulation on my D.F.C. and my promotion, but in spite of all this I mustn't relax; all that matters is the job, which needs luck, luck to meet the Boche and to be in a good position to attack him; with our inferiority in planes, we mustn't expect the impossible.

September 6th

I have just had some shocking bad news from Dupérier on the phone: the entire 'Yellow' section, the one I was leading latterly at 340 Squadron, was wiped out this morning over the Somme by fifty F.W. 190s which dropped on them from above without them having a chance to react. My two best friends, de Labouchère and Dubourgel, are among those missing.

I shall never forget my poor François, always so gay and keen in battle. If I had stayed another week with the French Squadron I should have taken up 'Yellow' section in his place. Would a different manoeuvre have enabled me to avert the catastrophe? One of the mysteries of fate.

I have just flown to Hornchurch. They are all rather cast down by what has befallen them. I remember young Dubourgel coming to see me here at Gravesend two days after my departure and begging me to do the impossible so that he could come with me. …

September 7th

The air marshal commanding 2 Group paid a visit to the squadron and very kindly congratulated me on my D.F.C. and promotion to squadron leader. He expressed his regret at the loss of Fayolle and de Labouchère.

September 11th

Oh, my little mother, did you suspect for one moment that the Frenchman of the 'Ile de France' Squadron of whom they spoke on the radio this evening, who has just been appointed to the command of an English unit, is your own son?

It is clear that 'Commandant M-' stirs no feeling in you, for your son is working obscurely in a headquarters office in London. In any case, isn't it better thus? You will await his return with so much more patience and confidence. How that return, that return, haunts my dreams, but what a sacrifice yours will have been.

September 15th

The wing commander of the Biggin Hill sector has just told me it is possible we may get Spitfire IXs, with qualities of speed and altitude far superior to the present Spitfire's. We shall thus be the fourth squadron to be given them. We shall be able to fight on equal terms with the F.W. 190s and be superior to them at 20,000 feet and over. Let us hope this promise isn't a disappointment.

September 18th

And what a disappointment! The crowning irony is that 340 Squadron has pinched them from under my very nose. I went in my Spitfire to call on them yesterday and they got the news while we were at lunch. They are wild with delight.

To complete my disappointment, I hear from official sources that my squadron is being sent north to be rested, on the grounds that it has been in 2 Group for a year. That is the end. We are in Britain for winter sports and wooing the ladies of Glasgow and Edinburgh! I am going to Fighter Command this afternoon fully determined to try and get the squadron posted to Malta.

The procession of journalists goes on at the 'Ile de France' Squadron. There were Americans there yesterday during my visit, from the *Sun* and the *Tribune*, I think … I thought I should pass unnoticed in my English uniform but everyone stupidly pointed me out from a distance to the vultures and they fell on me, notebook and pencil in hand.

'Commanding an English squadron? D.F.C.? How did you like the Dieppe expedition? How long have you been here?', etc.

September 20th

This is it. The Station Commander took me aside after dinner. Before he opened his mouth, I could tell from the look of him that he had bad news for me; what the news was, I guessed only too well. We are being sent north, to Drem, where we were with the French Squadron last year. It really is a hard blow for me. My idea of a posting to Malta either has not been considered or I raised it too late.

Moral: I am going to spend another six months in the north, while 340 has just got Spitfire IXs and will continue its prowess in France. I really am unlucky. And I foresee another thing: when I return to 2 Group, Dupérier will probably be promoted to wing commander. They will send for me to take over the French Squadron. As it will then have been a year in 2 Group, we shall be sent north. And then? Another six months in Scotland! In that case, I shall leave the Air Force.

September 26th

Uneventful journey. I had a lot of luck with my navigation, for I arrived straight over Drem aerodrome. Nothing has changed here, but the faces are nearly all different. Temperature noticeably cooler than in London; the nights are beginning to be icy. Tomorrow I am going to pay a call on Wing Commander Guinness at Turnhouse. I shall take the opportunity to spend the afternoon in Edinburgh.

October 1st

Wrapped up in all imaginable precautions, news has arrived of a move to the south tomorrow morning. According to the order, it is an 'exercise' in the rapid concentration of squadrons in 2 Group. I have no great belief in the exercise in question. I think it is neither more nor less than an operation of the Dieppe kind.

It was far from easy to organize the move of the squadron in a few hours. My adjutant, who deals with administrative matters, was on sick leave, so I had to do it all myself for the second time. The problem was complicated on this occasion by the mystery surrounding it. In fact, only the Station Commander and I know the destination. Eighteen pilots will take off at 8.30 a.m. tomorrow, following me blindly.

Those who left tonight by train will unseal the envelope in London that tells them where to go. I feel there will be sport in the south this week. Unfortunately, on account of our move to Scotland on September 26th, they have withdrawn our good planes and given us heavy old iron.

October 2nd

For the second time I took off with my whole squadron behind me, eighteen planes. Despite a discouraging weather report, I decided to move. The first part of the trip, from the north to Catterick, meant flying over mountains. The signal received specified that on no occasion must our altitude exceed 200 metres, so that the German listening posts will nò pick up the large-scale movements of squadrons. My boys and I were only too delighted to have the opportunity to do some hedge-hopping (a sport severely forbidden) for us to miss the chance today, especially as the signal ordered it.

Thus, it was practically by leap-frogging over trees, skating down and skimming up mountain slopes, that we covered the 700 kilometres between Drem and Lympne. After Newcastle, unfortunately, a thick fog on the ground tortured my sense of responsibility. In addition to the fog, the light went to such an extent that visibility was cut down to a few hundred metres. I had gradually gone too deep into the murk to think for a moment of turning back. I could see only a few planes, sticking close to me, outlined through a veil. How many were following behind?

We passed over an aerodrome. Impossible to try landing. Some would succeed, others would get lost circling the aerodrome or be in danger of colliding. The situation was really critical and I prayed Heaven that no hill or other obstacle would force us up at all, for we should be lost at once in the dense cloud. My sole hope was that the cloud would lift once we were over the Newcastle depression. But my torment went on for twenty minutes, with vague lifts gradually increasing the visibility by a few hundred metres; soon afterwards the murk became just as dense.

Suddenly it turned grey, then bright orange. A mile further on we came out of the inferno under an immaculately blue sky, visibility unlimited. We light-heartedly resumed our amusement of hedge-hopping, myself the more because I had the pleasant surprise of counting my full tally of sheep, magnificently in order astern. Without seeing their leader, they had followed one another, showing good discipline and a great spirit of trust. And I had some small gratification of my vanity in having followed my course correctly and arrived bang over my destination, Lympne.

But the days went by. No announcement of a great event troubled the family atmosphere of the delightful little mess at Lympne. It was formerly the home of a millionaire. Dining-room, drawing-room, hall, bathrooms, everything in marble. The style is Egyptian and the decoration sumptuous. The garden is in rather a complicated *de luxe* style, all the trees trimmed into the most varied shapes. Ornamental pools, fountains, kitchen gardens with unlimited produce, statues, temples, cunningly concealed nooks; this hillside garden, with its lovely view of the sea, would be an ideal paradise for newlyweds.

Weather execrable, sea rough. No landing possible.

October 6th

At the wheel of the luxurious American car which is mine while I am here, I spend my many days of leisure at Folkestone, a town overcrowded with troops. I have telephoned Group but they do not know anything. Our orders are to spend our days as we like.

I went up in my Spit one day when the mist seemed less thick and landed at Biggin Hill, where Dupérier and his 340 Squadron are; he was most surprised to see me. He does not know anything either. My account of the trip from Scotland to Lympne with my eighteen planes at tree-top height really amused him. He seemed very excited, as I am, deducing that a very important operation is on the way.

His pilots are about to get Spitfire IXs, only a matter of days ... apparently. We both went to see the group captain. He 'knows nothing', naturally, except that there is going to be an operation; we are only held up by the time-factor. But what mystery! I hope the Germans are not warned this time as they were about Dieppe.

October 7th

At last, I have been summoned to Northolt. The weather is fine, the forecast good, only a lot of wind. As soon as I took off, my first concern was to fly over the sea. Hell! It was running very high. I don't fancy myself in my dinghy in such weather. The motor-launches would never be able to fish me out.

There was a meeting of all the squadron leaders of the squadrons involved, also some wing commanders and group captains. The A.O.C., Leigh Mallory, presided.

All the top brass of Fighter Command was in that small room round the green table. A heavy, anxious silence. The A.O.C. began by telling us that a show as important as Dieppe, but which would certainly have been more successful, was to have taken place but that it had been cancelled on account of the weather. The fact that it was put off until next year prevented him giving details of it. An exercise in co-operation with the Navy, supplemented by a Flying Fortress raid on Lille, would take up all tomorrow morning.

The technical details followed. I was so disappointed. So, this is all the effort the Allied Forces can produce to set against the vast Russian fighting on a 2,000-kilometre front! I no longer believe in the opening of a second front in Europe next year. A succession of raids of the Dieppe kind will give us the consciences of men who have done their duty. But must we not do more than our duty sometimes and take risks to win through? A considered boldness is better than a fearful caution. We must not think of losses, however heavy they may be. Our potential of honour and of pilots is ten times superior to the Germans'.

We must remember what the ten months' waiting in the phoney war cost France, when she was busy with nothing more constructive than organizing concert parties for the armies in the Maginot Line. Here the artistes come from America to amuse 'the brave soldiers' (Great Britain is riddled with all these Y.M.C.A.s). Concert parties, charities by the thousand, each presided over by half a dozen lords, avid to display their names and titles on notepaper and prepare the way for social advancement or reward after the war. This mass of useless folk is mobilizing an army that encumbers the mechanism and is rusting the soldiers' keenness bit by bit. Some seem to have understood and are beginning to rouse their neighbours out of their lethargy by brandishing the standard of the fashionable idea, 'The Second Front'.

October 8th

This morning's operation, as far as we were concerned, took place at 28,000 feet, between Calais and Graveline. A hundred heavy bombers were to bomb factories and marshalling yards at Lille. The monsters crossed the French coast dead on time, with clockwork precision, grouped in light formations of six. Nothing but four-engined planes beneath us, going past as majestically as if on parade. Protected as they are with their machine guns, six heavy ones, and by the armada of fighters about them, it would have been a bold enemy who ventured to attack them.

October 10th
Return to Drem.

November 30th
A lot has happened in the theatre of war between October 10th and November 30th, 1942, but my life at Drem has been troubled only by violent and recurrent desires to throw my hand in and offer my resignation as squadron leader. The spirit prevailing among those who command the station at Drem is characteristic of 13 Group, and it has got it a sorry and unenviable reputation. Administration is all in all here and turns the tiniest regulation into a rut.

The sergeants are dead keen on meeting the whims of their superiors; they turn advice into compulsion, rules into tyranny. The pilot is made for the station and not the station for the pilot. People who throughout the war have never heard a shot fired in anger, and who will claim to have won it, make two of my sergeant-pilots sleep in a tent with the temperature 10° below zero without even a rug or groundsheet because a little dust was found under their beds!

These same pilots, in a month, will be under fire, getting themselves killed for these gentry's tranquillity and well-being! What a change from 2 Group, where everything was for the pilots' comfort.

The same is true of training. It is framed on a rigid scheme in which the pilot's character and qualities and present-day tactics pull no weight. An inflexible programme, taking no account of individual freedom. A puerile and ingenuous struggle at each month's end to send a satisfactory report off to Group, the good drawing up of which gets the station people the approval of their venerated chief, the A.O.C.

The latter has been to Drem for the third time. His visit, always invested with the solemnity of that of someone of importance, was to give me my D.F.C. officially.

Great spring-cleaning on the station; for days past people had been pondering over special orders and having rehearsals of the review that was to be held. Fortunately for him, the principal person involved was in London, on leave. Much to the authorities' concern, I only came back the morning of the ceremony. The troops marched without any accidents, and, never having learned to march to their special step, I applied myself gravely to moving my legs forward, the toes shaving the ground, while my arms swung almost to the horizontal.

Alone, in front of the troops, my French uniform gleaming with gold, my mind was hypnotized by my medal keeping step and bumping happily against my pocket-button, making a really artistic tinkling sound. I was unable to see the effect of my parade, good discipline forbidding me to turn my head. There was a cocktail party in the afternoon, during which Air Vice-Marshal Andrews was good enough not to make a speech, thus enabling me to forget the one I had taken so much trouble to prepare.

While I was in London, I dashed over to Biggin Hill to see my comrades of 340 Squadron. A bond of feeling draws me to them. How good it is to hear French spoken. You have to be an exile to learn to love your own country. I was so happy to see all those excellent chaps again. Nothing has changed, apart from a few new faces. They have their Spitfire IXs. *My* Spitfire IXs, I should say, stolen from under my very nose. They are tickled pink with them. They are doing well. One story after another. In a month they have run up a bigger score than in six months of 'my time'. Moynet has two F.W. 190s that ran into one another with fright, Boudier has two, Dupérier two, young Massart[4] a probable, etc. And I, the veteran, after the moment of pleasure in knowing that the French have the biggest percentage for the month and are as capable as their British comrades, after the rush of happiness that made me want to embrace these comrades of yesterday, I, the oldest pilot of Fighting France – I was filled with shameful fury with

---

4. Olivier Massart escaped from France in 1940 with de Labouchère to come and join the R.A.F. He took command of the 'Ile de France' Squadron in 1944.

myself and my lack of luck, and of bestial jealousy of these fortunate ones who have a chance to fight every day!

Summarizing what can be called my exploits, I can be really proud and go clinking my medals in drawing-rooms. What wouldn't I give to be what I used to be, a modest number four of a section, rather than what I am, lost in the Scotch mist. Really, I shall never be satisfied! It is true, though, that I have never asked to change; neither time nor events will ever make me forget the imperishable hours with 340 Squadron. To get back my place in combat is my most ardent desire, and pray God I may fill it honourably and well. If I am not to survive this war, let me at least have the satisfaction of falling in battle under the enemy's fire. What could be more stupid, after braving death a thousand times on operations, than to die a victim of some mechanical trouble in one's plane.

One of my flight commanders, among the best pilots of my squadron, killed himself at Drem yesterday in tragic and mysterious circumstances. As he was returning to the aerodrome and was about to make his last circle of the landing-ground, his speed still about 350 m.p.h., his plane suddenly exploded and a hail of metal, broken parts and wings fell on the field. His parachute opened, goodness knows how, for (having jumped into my car) I had the horror, when I got to the spot, to find that he was dead and appallingly mutilated.

I listened to his heart; it was no longer beating. His small, very young face, so full of hope, the eyes which had always shone with such ardour, his fine curly hair were all unrecognizable, soiled with earth and blood. I learned later that he had his spinal column broken. Death instantaneous, parachute opened by accident, cause unknown. I went to see the engine, some miles away. It had not exploded. Nor had the oxygen bottle burst. Flight Lieutenant Hewlett was engaged to be married. I am expecting a new flight commander; no interruption, the war goes on.

At Biggin Hill I also shook hands, not without some emotion, with my two good old mechanics, Simon and Varney. They seemed very pleased. I had brought them 1,000 cigarettes from Scotland. They would like to see me back in the squadron. The second-named is a Tahitian and to my great delight he presented me with two shell necklaces made in Tahiti, very lovely, orange and white; unless looked at very closely one would swear that they were wild flowers really growing. I am taking great care of them.

I was glad to see young Bouguen, to whom I used to give a lot of advice when 340 was formed. I sensed a keen pilot in the beginner, whose qualities only needed developing. I have watched and praised most of his offensive missions and combats with special interest as they were carried out under my leadership. Young Sergeant Bouguen has now become a sous-lieutenant, very proud of his badges of rank, which he has well deserved. He implored me, almost with tears in his eyes, to take him back with me to my squadron. I did not conceal from him that he disappoints me.

How can a lad of his mettle, alive with such ardour, ask to leave the squadron in which almost any day combat may give him the eagerly awaited opportunity to distinguish himself? The squadron where all his friends are, where he flies the most modern aircraft, and the country where the cold is not as intense as it is in Scotland? It is a problem to me. I suspect him of having reasons he is concealing from me. His official one is that he does not enjoy 340 now so many of his friends are missing and that he would like to be with me again, even in Scotland. His despair seems sincere; I promised him I would speak to Dupérier about it, though I didn't like taking such a step. I had hoped to get results by pleading his fatigue. I failed. I was all the more surprised when Guignard, finding me on my own, made the same request to me. In the evening I was dining in London with Moynet and his wife and he asked me the same thing! It's a conspiracy! I am not trying to find what it all means.

November 8th, memorable day. Scene: a small studio, rented in London for my leave. Actors: me first, in bed, sleeping the sleep of the just, at 9 a.m. Enter the batman, who, bringing me my breakfast, my papers and his Britannic phlegm, says, 'Good morning, sir. Lovely day, sir.' He draws the curtains, goes out in silence, taking his phlegm with him.

Every day, whether it is raining or whether a glorious sun is shedding its light on Nature, he wakes me with his 'Good morning, sir. Lovely day, sir.' Considering the pleasant warmth of my bed, I decided the hour was too early for me to rise. An hour later I shot up bolt-upright on my pillow: 'The Americans have invaded North Africa at six points!'

I had just noticed the newspaper headlines. I shall never forget the huge joy that filled me, the thousand prospects I could see for the Allies, the consequences for Vichy, for the Fleet, for Tripoli, threatened on two sides. What attitude would the French Army take up in North Africa? Darlan, now in Algiers, would be a prisoner. I should leave England at last and perhaps form a French squadron in Tunis? My decision was made: go to Headquarters and knock on all the doors. My cold breakfast did not even get a glance. I found Headquarters in a fever. Part of it is going to Algiers. De Gaulle had lunch with Churchill yesterday, etc., etc.

I went to pay my respects to General Valin, with appallingly ulterior motives. He had not seen me since I took over the British squadron and therefore asked me no end of questions. In the end I told him of my keen desire not to stay in England if the Fighting French forces were moved to North Africa.

I knew my arguments would not influence the General's decisions much but I was far from ignorant of his fondness for discussions of this kind and I wanted him to understand my eagerness to leave England as soon as possible.

'You have a better chance of my selecting you,' he told me, 'being on your own in a British unit, rather than your comrades in the French Squadron, who will probably be staying a little longer.' That was all I wanted to know. I could have embraced him. He seemed to be in a very good humour and presented me with a signed portrait of himself. We finished our talk at the bar over a *porto*. After lunch I continued my tour at Colonel Coustey's and Commandant Bouderie's, begging them not to forget me if there was anything interesting in the air. The following evening, I returned to Drem with a lighter heart. The liberation is approaching: North Africa is part of our poor wounded France. We shall be at home there, fighting on our own soil.

To be able to speak French freely without being regarded as a curiosity by those about you. To feel and think French, to get worked up without scruples, without fear of upsetting a coldly dignified atmosphere. ... Some days I find it hard in my English squadron to play my part imperturbably. Sometimes I feel stifled, oppressed – the difference between the English and us.

A month has passed since my leave in London. I have taken up again the task of forming my squadron, a task comparable with that of the child in Scripture who tries to put the sea into a hole with his little pitcher. My squadron is continually being renewed and my efforts always have to go back to the beginning again. At this rate I shall never be able to get back to the south.

Each letter I receive from comrades in 340 brings new evidence of successes, while the crowd in Group at Newcastle have as much flying spirit as certain bureaucrats in the French Air Ministry. I read a passage from my last letter from Schloesing, who is now commanding 340, Dupérier being on the point of departure for a tour of inspection in Canada: 'Yesterday we had a great trip over France, almost as far as Mantes, 50 kilometres from Paris, which we saw quite clearly, with the Tour Eiffel etc. ... It's wonderful, the Spit IXs are the real thing. ...' I feel like going back to civilian life as a baker's man.

December 23rd

Yesterday, December 22nd, 1942, at 10.30 p.m., I was in bed and had just opened a book when a cipher message arrived. Only after reading it twice did I persuade myself I was not dreaming and that what I was reading was real, written before my very eyes: '65 Squadron has been selected for training in landing Spitfires on aircraft-carriers.'

Thus, there is every possibility that we shall soon be on a lovely voyage in the Mediterranean, aboard a luxurious British aircraft carrier.

Chapter 18

Aircraft Carriers

December 24th, 1942

Yesterday I started some training on landing between white strips. Not very easy in a Spitfire. I went first. You have to keep your eyes open, because it means making a three-point landing, on a given spot, at minimum speed. The nose of the Spit being very long and visibility in front nil, it must be done crabwise if it is to come off. Moral: yesterday evening I already had one plane crumpled up.

Darlan has been assassinated. That may speed our departure from England.

December 29th

I have chosen sixteen pilots to go and train on an aircraft carrier. For some days past an officer from the Royal Navy has been lecturing us on aircraft carriers, signals, etc. During training he posts himself three or four metres from the white strips, representing the deck of the ship on the landing-ground, and signals us our position, speed and altitude by means of two yellow discs like table-tennis bats, which he holds in each hand.

This 'batsman' is an important person on board ship; the pilot must obey him blindly for he is himself a former pilot, highly experienced, and he has the responsibility for landings on the flight deck. If he signals that the plane's approach is bad, whatever the man approaching in it thinks he must start his engine again and circle once more. Bitterly cold. The snow put in an appearance today; my office, with its seven windows, is a glacier. If we make a muck of our landings and take a forced bath here in Scotland, they will haul us out stiff from the water with stalactites under our noses.

December 31st

Last day of this cursed year. Let us hope 1943 will bring us victory! Could France stand another winter?

The second stage of our training in landing on aircraft carriers began today. We left Drem this morning, my boys in a nice little Holland transport plane, me in a Spit. Our new station, Arbroath, 80 miles north of Drem, belongs entirely to the Royal Navy. What a difference after the R.A.F.! Cleanliness, discipline, mess like a grand hotel, trained waiters, very good food, comfort, etc.

From time to time, as in a ship, there are sharp strokes on a bell, the sound of which is multiplied around the camp by invisible loudspeakers. My 'cabin', as they call it, is extremely comfortable. As Commanding Officer, I am treated with great consideration. We began training this afternoon. I had to perform first. Bad luck. There wasn't a breath of wind, and never did the accursed Spit seem so heavy and so fast in landing. What a delicate business it is to bring it in, losing speed, exactly at the minimum, to hold it and put it down, wheels and tail-skid, on that tiny space.

After my own experiment, I spent the afternoon watching my colts training. The beating of the heart it produces, watching them from such close quarters! I would a hundred times rather be in the plane myself. One has the impression it cannot stay in the air any longer, so slight is the speed, and that it will crash. But no, the undercarriage stands it. The Spit is stout. Several of them opened the throttle without being able to land and circled again. I confess I was a little scared. Will the experiment on aircraft carriers be satisfactory for some of them? The slightest accident would be catastrophic.

Yesterday evening, at midnight, the officers of the Navy celebrated the New Year. After drinking much more than usual, which, to the English, means drinking on 'an occasion' (I think they find 365 occasions in the year, and when by chance they find no occasion, they drink to the lack of one) we were served with a well-laced punch. Then came the traditional song, 'Auld Lang Syne', sung while forming a great circle round the room, arms across and hands clasped, the whole embellished by a gentle inclination of the body from right to left and vice versa. The atmosphere was soon 'there'.

Before dinner I had the honour of being introduced to Rear-Admiral Boyd, on a visit to the station. He said to me, 'I hope your pilots won't have too much trouble landing on the aircraft carrier. I think you realize how incredibly lucky you are – no pilot of the R.A.F. has been so favoured before. I wish you good luck and lots of Boche to shoot down in the operation that is coming off.' Afterwards we talked about Darlan, who has disappeared from the political scene, much to our satisfaction.

This is it. This 'experiment' is no other than our future participation in some kind of combined operation of the Dieppe type, somewhere between Norway and Bordeaux. As Dieppe proved, a fighter umbrella is necessary. The Royal Navy pilots having no experience of fighter work, especially in giving air cover, the R.A.F.'s participation becomes indispensable. But all the trained squadrons are in the south, on Spitfire IXs, and will probably be destined for some diversion. I therefore conclude that as I have 'done' Dieppe myself, plus sixty or so sweeps, with my squadron nearly trained, all the necessary conditions for this special choice are fulfilled. Naturally, I know nothing official and all this is probably the result of bold hypothesis. In that case, I do not see what use this training is.

The training at Arbroath has not gone particularly well. Whether because the wind was not strong enough, or because it wasn't in the exact direction of the runway (a concrete track for landing) or because the task was too much for some of my young pilots, accidents have been numerous, each time putting a plane out of action and twice making one definitely useless. My heart sank with apprehension, fearing that this succession of mishaps might drive the authorities into giving up the idea of transferring us to aircraft carriers.

Finally, they put us on 'arrester wires'. This means a strip on the ground, representing the dimension of a ship's deck, fitted with hydraulic brakes similar to those of aircraft carriers. Four cables across the deck, spaced five or six metres apart, stretched twenty centimetres above the deck. Each Spitfire has a stout hook underneath, a little in front of the tailwheel. Once released by the pilot, the hook is lowered under the plane, so that it touches the ground lightly, before the wheels, at the moment of landing. The machine is then stopped in about twenty metres. The cable, which is very strong, resists all the time. Very often the hook breaks, as we realized only too well.

The Spitfire is a modern fighter aircraft which was never meant for such work. Until last year no one would have dreamed of making one land on an aircraft carrier. It took a pilot in distress who tried it successfully one day for the idea to be born and to be carried out. It is none the less true that the manoeuvre is a very delicate one for a plane with a minimum landing speed of about 150-160 kilometres an hour. Even at the extreme minimum of 120 kilometres an hour, the speed must become nil in 20 metres. The pilot gets quite a shock but it is not violent if his speed is right. Obviously, aboard an aircraft carrier this speed is further reduced by the contrary speed of the wind and by that, too, of the ship. In any case, our experience at Arbroath has not been very satisfactory. I myself had the luck not to do any damage. I should have cut a sorry figure if I had, as squadron leader!

After each accident, I expected we should be recalled to Drem. Then Flight Lieutenant Kitchen, unluckily landing too fast and not quite against the wind, broke his hook and went on to crash his plane 100 metres further on. A brand-new plane, delivered a bare quarter of an hour before, and it was my flight commander who smashed it! Really, I was getting seriously annoyed. I also sensed a certain wavering, not to say discouragement, among my pilots. The task seemed too difficult. I took pleasure in contrasting the spirit and ardour which would have prevailed among the pilots of my French squadron, if they had been given such an opportunity. Here, except for my Poles, I was disappointed by nonchalance and placid acceptance of the inevitable. Fighting, for most of them, is not an end which contains their conception of duty; it is a planned eventuality, which many would gladly dispense with, were not the passionate love of sport involved in it.

And I think the Royal Navy must have found our experiment extremely costly. Do its leaders hesitate to return us to the protection of the R.A.F. or have they perhaps decided that on the whole the lack of wind on Arbroath aerodrome makes training there more difficult? I myself, whenever the opportunity has presented itself, have insisted on the uselessness and costliness of this training, and on the fact that it would be a hundred times more useful to send us straight to a ship. One fine morning they brought me the news that although everyone had not finished, we were to go aboard the *Argus*, on the west coast of Scotland. We, apparently, had priority over all other training.

January 4th, 1943

We embarked on H.M.S. *Argus* at 9.30 in a thick fog, which made the ships look curiously like cinema studios. A fast motor-launch took us away and at once everything was drowned in dirty darkness. Our voyage had already lasted a quarter of an hour. No light to be seen. Huge black masses rose before us, the engine raced in reverse. Blindly we turned round. Unsuspected voices answered the hail. A violent shock sent the launch over on one side; we had just collided with a buoy. The prospect of taking a bath in the middle of the night, in the freezing fog, had nothing very attractive about it, but we got off with a fright.

We were soon against a gigantic black side, from the top of which a searchlight was sweeping the sea. A small door and we entered the monster's belly. A good dinner, then the reception in the wardroom bar. The Royal

Navy for the first time received and adopted a squadron of the R.A.F. We had to drink and drink again. The Navy gave us a charming welcome and seemed delighted to talk to us about the ship; they were asked innumerable questions.

It was the first time I had set foot on an aircraft carrier, and the next morning, when I ventured to explore, I was dumbfounded by its vastness. An enormous hangar, which took up most of the length of the vessel and all its width, gave an impressive idea of its size. Unfortunately, when I reached the flight deck, I saw it with my pilot's eyes and could not help but find it appallingly short and narrow. We should have to perform miracles to take off and land. At 10 a.m. we were already at sea. The officer in charge of flying had called us together to give us final instructions. I was making the first flights. A Spitfire, hoisted from the hangar on an enormous platform-lift, was pushed to the end of the flight deck. Only the chocks stopped it slipping back on the slope which forms the end of the deck.

As I climbed on the wing, I cast a glance beneath me, to see the wake set up by the ship's propellers 20 metres below. One thing comforted me, a good 35-knot wind, which made my task much less difficult. It would be saying a good deal to say I was quite free from apprehension; I noticed that I was warming up my engine with more than usual care. Then everything happened quickly, without thought. The little flags dipped, two men flat on their bellies under my wings took away the chocks, two others hung on to the wingtips. My brakes on, I opened the throttle; released the brakes; tail in the air, I taxi'd along the deck. No time to think, I was at the other end already, then in the air.

Several minutes later, after setting the pitch of the propeller, retracting the undercarriage and making my first turn to port, at above 500-600 metres, I realized the horror of my situation. A minute aircraft carrier was sailing there below me, as small as half a matchstick, and on it, in a few instants, I was going to have to land myself and my Spitfire. It was so good in the air that I hadn't the least desire to go down. My approach, as I lost altitude, looked more and more difficult and the deck hardly seemed to have changed in size. I had to touch down with my wheels immediately behind the bulge of the deck. If I succeeded in placing myself well in the centre, the cables would do the rest, provided my speed were correct. Therein lay the difficulty.

My task was to circle twice, as if about to land, but to open the throttle at the last moment without touching the deck with my wheels. The third time, thank God, I landed without damage; the cables stopped me loyally.

I made four complete landings, after which I almost regretted not being able to go on. I was very pleased, the task in the end had proved easier than I had imagined. Unfortunately, all my pilots did not have my luck and we had some small (not serious) accidents to regret. The result of all this was, according to the officers, that our 'experiment' was a success, so much so that the Captain decided to keep the ship at sea to make some more landings. Life on board is so agreeable that nobody found fault with that.

My cabin is very large, and I have certainly had beds in the R.A.F. less comfortable than this one. As for the food, nothing, or almost nothing, is rationed and its quality is perfect. I learned that as far as *Argus* is concerned the Admiralty has given us priority over other training. I should like to know what is at the back of their minds and whether an 'exciting' operation is in view or not.

Chapter 19

Mouchotte Forms 'Alsace'[5]

January 9th, 1943

I certainly did not expect a surprise like this on my return to Drem. I am leaving 65 Squadron ... *my* squadron, over which I have taken so much trouble!

The task of forming and training such a unit, teaching it up-to-date methods of combat, giving it singleness, indeed, a *soul*, is arduous and delicate work, demanding unwearying assiduity of the squadron leader. Knowing my pilots individually, leading them by the hand, in short stages, helping them, encouraging them, above all giving them zest for their work: that is what I devoted myself to with all my heart, all the more passionately because I knew the value of the reward I should get from a well-formed unit when I once went into battle at their head in the south. And today, on the eve of being recalled to 2 Group and reaping the reward of my efforts, they take my job away.

A British squadron leader is coming to replace me while I, good soul, am condemned to start right from scratch again and spend another four months in Scotland. I am being entrusted with the formation of a second French squadron, 341, which will be comprised of elements from Syria and Libya or from pilots on their own in English units. I leave for London with the blessing of the A.O.C. 13 Group, who for his part is dead keen on keeping me in 65.

January 11th

I went straight from the train to Headquarters. Congratulations, which I didn't know what to do with, rather irritated me. Then they flattered me

---

5. A squadron under this name had already been formed on February 5th, 1942, in the Nile Delta; it was disbanded when operations ceased on that front. Its moving spirits were Commandant Tulane, killed in Russia in command of 'Normandie', and Commandant Pouliquen, with Captains Littolf (killed) and Ezanno as flight commanders. The latter had the honour of afterwards commanding a Typhoon squadron (198 Squadron) in the R.A.F.

a lot. My selection had brought forth nothing but approval, I was the only one to have had great experience and, above all, such knowledge of R.A.F. ways. I had no right to refuse; besides, there was no question of that. But if so, why make me waste five months in Scotland with that British squadron instead of letting me go on fighting with 340? I felt it would be better to bury these questions in our gentry's dusty dossiers adorned with the titles of Politics, Propaganda, Honours, etc. ... The whole Headquarters was busy today with the new-born 341, on which they were already basing great hopes.

Every office initiated me in its mysterious depths: the genius of red tape. So, I shall have to feed each one of these with a mighty correspondence, reviews, reports, lists, proposals, weekly, monthly, bi-annual states, etc. ... This time my ground staff is 100 per cent British, which will facilitate things in one way and complicate them in another, for I shall have no one to correspond for me with French Headquarters. In no time at all I shall be a past master in the art of keeping my head above water.

'Well, Commandant, so you're forming the new fighter group in Scotland?' As if they couldn't just call it a squadron! Isn't it identical in all respects with English squadrons and doesn't it form an integral part of the R.A.F.

No, for our Headquarters in London, the group will consist of two squadrons, each represented by one of my flights. I saw Dupérier. He was to have left last week on a publicity tour and inspection of training units in America. His voyage has been postponed.

'I'm waiting for the Boche submarines to come back,' he confided to me, 'apparently, they went away to re-victual. One is game or one is not.' General Valin noticed my disappointment at leaving my British squadron.

'Mouchotte, you're going to command a magnificent unit. Nearly all your pilots are experienced and many have already been noticed for their exploits. As for you, no one hesitated for a second in choosing you. In the face of such unanimity it is your duty to accept.' It could not have been said more clearly that they had found no one else. ...

Now difficulties began. One of the two squadron leaders did not suit me. Too young, too little experience. I went to Fighter Command, the British fighters' holy of holies. I made my conditions: he or I. I had nothing to lose. I knew I had to put up a fight for I had learned that the pilot in question was no other than cousin to an air vice-marshal and that they were taking care of him in high places. Strong opposition was put up, but I stood firm; if they gave me the post, I was ready to assume its responsibilities. The success of

173

the squadron depended only on me. Let me choose the elements, especially the squadron leaders. Seeing that I did not give in to any of their arguments, they thought they would corner me by asking me point blank for another name in his place.

'Martel!'

Martel, with whom I did my military service in France in 1936, whom I met again as an instructor at Etampes and Salon, and who had succeeded in escaping from France with my old pal Dick Farman barely six months ago. He had just left the English training unit – one of the cleverest pilots in France.

'No operations, no experience, doesn't speak perfect English – that's what you're suggesting?'

I explained that Martel (alias de Montet) had proved himself and would be capable of teaching many a squadron leader how to fly. Talked to them about the man, the leader and his capacity for assimilation. It took time, at the end of which I had the satisfaction of realizing that I had won the day.

Colonel Corniglion-Molinier is to be our immediate and beloved chief. Nine victories in the last war, five in this. He seems very keen and impatient to see my group in action. He even wants to come and train with me to take part in some raids over France with us (there are no more children!). He seems first class, very inclined to adopt all my suggestions. As for Colonel Coustey, he does not beat about the bush, and he plunged me straight in, instead of into an administrative waste-paper basket.

Visits, meetings, conferences, luncheons, the four days in London were pretty full and I went back to Drem with my mind full of golden resolutions, somewhat reassured about my fate. If I was condemned to spend another three or four months in Scotland, I had the near-certainty of forming a squadron exceptional in the quality of its pilots. Martel is my colt and I am going to make him work. He asks no less, of course. But from the R.A.F.'s point of view he is starting from scratch: in two months I shall have to make him find out all there is to know about the organization of a flight and the combat tactics a British flight commander learns in over two years' experience. I have guaranteed him and am convinced he will not let me down.

I have been at Turnhouse since January 18th. I have seven pilots but no planes. When I read the papers and think of the Russian advance threatening Rostov and Kharkov, the British Eighth Army's entry into Tripoli, the Allied successes on the Tunisian front, etc., the idea that the war may end while I am here brings me out in a cold sweat. I have been to see the air marshal commanding 13 Group for the sole purpose of asking a great favour. The idea that my old 65 Squadron might soon be taking part in combined operations on board an aircraft carrier without me, their squadron leader, is unthinkable in view of the training I did with my pilots. I therefore asked him to intercede with Fighter Command and the Admiralty and get them to see that our training should not be discounted.

By a slight breach of the regulations, I could lead my old squadron into battle, though I am not now their C.O., if there were a Commando raid and 65 took part from an aircraft carrier. He was a good sport and promised that he himself would send off an application at once. Not only was he not surprised at my cheek in bothering him about such a personal matter, but he seemed delighted and gave me a long hand-shake when I left him. So now I have to wait, hoping hard. I have since learned from Flight Lieutenant Day, who met him in the Group offices before joining 341, that he has a great esteem for me. And when Day told him he was very glad to be coming to 341 under my command, he said Day couldn't be sure of having me as squadron leader because he knew I had gone to London with the sole purpose of remaining with 65. 'Mouchotte took a lot of trouble over training his British squadron and I think he did very well to form a really well-knit unit, so I've decided not to put any obstacles in his way and to give him a completely free hand. He can make up his own mind and I will always back him up.'

February 22nd
Our 340 Squadron, which was at Turnhouse last year, left a shocking reputation behind it which even the exploits of the last few months have not altogether wiped out. Its pilots' aggressive spirit plus their contempt for everything not concerned with flying (even station discipline), their open contempt for certain rules, their unconcealed indifference to reprimand and their tendency to keep themselves to themselves, caused them to incur more and more criticism, and then the scorn of the majority of the officers when luck went against them: they smashed five planes in as many days.

A year has gone by and now another French squadron has been posted to Turnhouse. So, all noses are turned up and tongues are wagging. There has been the inevitable exaggeration; people who had never seen us expected some kind of barbarous animals. It was very unpleasant to sense them murmuring behind our backs and it could have done us no end of harm. I did not want my 341 to suffer for its predecessors' stupidities and mistakes.

I therefore called my pilots together, and then my ground crews, to explain the situation to them. I pointed out that our speedy departure to the south depended not only on good training but equally upon all the silly little things that make a squadron's good name.

A month has passed. From the very first, my pilots have mixed well, doing their best to be as polite as they are friendly. Some of the English who were against us at first have been glad to see the good spirit prevailing in 341. I told them not to upset certain people who are sensitive on these points by aerobatics or formation-flying low over the aerodrome, but I did not in any way prevent them giving proof of their skill. For a squadron in formation, everyone has been struck with my pilots' quality.

On my side, I have been very diplomatic, patient and common-sensical, as opposed to banging my fist on the table. The fact that I have commanded a British squadron has opened an incredible number of doors to me. I do not know whether it is the air vice-marshal's friendliness that is making things so easy for me, but a month has sufficed to wipe out not only all last year's bad impressions but also to build up a golden reputation which is full of possibilities for me and leads me to expect that the squadron will have a most brilliant future.

Indeed, I am not dissatisfied with the results obtained; during the first two weeks, with 50 per cent of my planes here, I put in more flying hours than any other squadron in the Group at full strength. Out of seventeen pilots (instead of the thirty I should have had) I can certify that twelve are already of excellent quality.

March 16th

I have so much to do that I haven't even time to write down here the main outline of my days. Here, in a few words, is the past fortnight's news.

Intensive training of the squadron, maximum effort. I have been delighted to see it brought up to strength by the pilots I asked for. They seem to have a good idea of the spirit prevailing here and there is ideal harmony. I made no bones about getting rid of three doubtful ones, one for technical reasons, another for reasons of morale, the third for both. I have been back to Fighter Command and to the Air Ministry in London. I was the first to be surprised by 341 Squadron's good name. I took advantage of it to put in applications and try to get good planes for our posting to the south. ... Problematical.

The moment I got back to Turnhouse I was grieved by the loss of my very dear comrade de Mézillis, killed in a flying accident. Jacques is a great loss to us all. He was such an example of courage; he wanted to fly and fight again, despite the amputation of his left arm.

Poor old Jacques; we will avenge you. I cannot remember having grieved so much over the loss of a friend since old Bouquillard's death in aerial combat in 1940.

Chapter 20

'Alsace' in Action

March 17th, 1943

The incredible signal came yesterday evening: we are moving south to relieve and replace old 340 at Biggin Hill. We are beating all records: we began flying on February 1st and we go on operations on March 18th. My boys are wild with delight.

Martel and Farman, who came to England together after crossing Spain as far as Portugal on foot, simply cannot contain themselves. I have managed to get young Lafont, a friend since the first days in England. He was sick for a long time, then went to Libya, where he distinguished himself – brilliantly. Once he returned, he never stopped trying to get back to me. He is always spoiling for a fight. Boudier and Bouguen, veterans from 340, are here too, one as a flight commander, the other for health reasons, but really, I think, for sentimental reasons, as he has been under me since he first went on operations. Also, veterans of the first 'Alsace' Squadron, among the best: Raoul Duval, Chevalier, Bruno Bourges, to mention no others.

These young pilots, meticulously selected from British units, have at last come to 341, though there was an uphill fight to get them. The phone calls I've made over them! I even threatened to throw my hand in if I did not obtain satisfaction. I do not know how many officials I've given my two famous lists to, the golden list of the pilots I wanted and the black list of the ones I wouldn't have at any price, being ready, as I swore, either to let them take my place or to send them back to London. And what a result! Here I am at the head of a squadron I can boast about, with some chance of it being the most famous in all Fighter Command.

Wait till they see us on the job. I mean to go very carefully for the first month, to give my whole mob a quiet initiation and perfect the new kind of formation I have invented. No breach of discipline in the air will be tolerated; no individual attack allowed without my order. We shall not try at first to shoot down the Boche but to learn our business, improve our

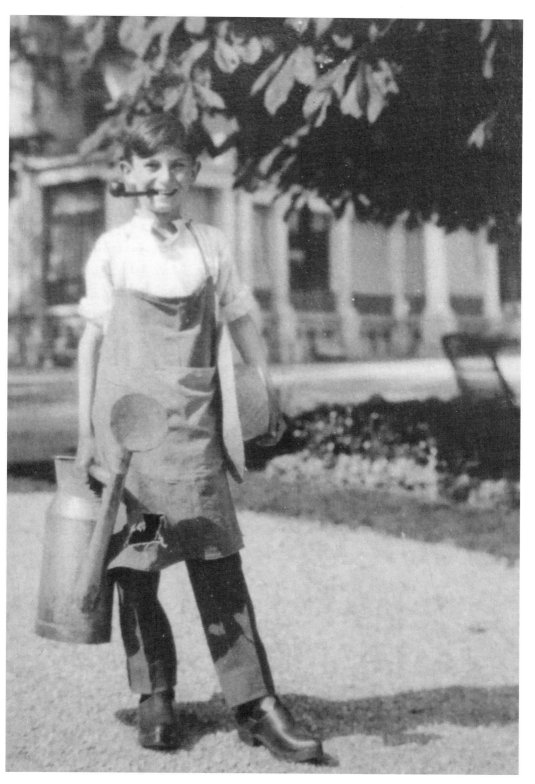

René in the garden of their home in St. Mandé. (Courtesy of the Mouchotte Family)

Left: A cartoon of
René Mouchotte.
(Courtesy of the
Mouchotte Family)

Below: René
Mouchotte in the
cockpit of one of his
aircraft. (Courtesy
of the Mouchotte
Family)

A portrait of René Mouchotte. (Courtesy of the Mouchotte Family)

Commandant Mouchotte with his Free French Spitfire pilots at Biggin Hill after the Station's historic 1,000th aerial victory'.

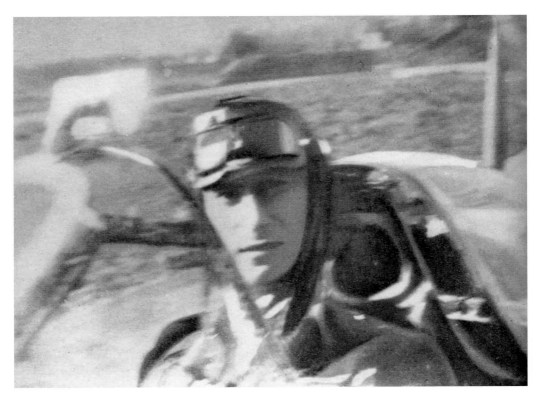

René Mouchotte, pictured just before his last flight.

Right: Oberleutnant Waldemar 'Waldi' Radener, the Fw 190 pilot of 6/JG26 who shot down Commandant Mouchotte over the Channel off Dunkirk. Radener survived the war with thirty-seven combat victories and was decorated with both the coveted Deutches Kreuz (German Cross) in Gold and the Ritterkreuz (Knight's Cross). Having joined the post-war Bundesluftwaffe, he was killed in a flying accident during 1957, aged thirty-six.

Below: The target on that fateful day, 27 August 1943, when the Biggin Hill Wing escorted American bombers to attack the formidable Blockhaus Éperlecques, near St Omer. The raid on this V-2 rocket site was a great success, rendering it inoperable – but René failed to return.

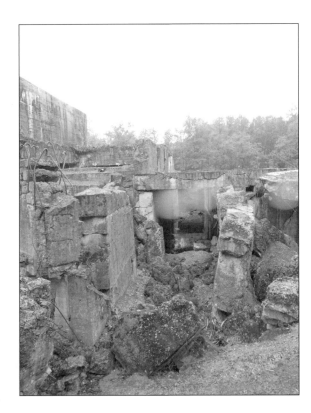

Left: Damage to the Blockhaus Éperlecques.

Below: A plaque commemorating René Mouchotte at Éperlecques (note the incorrect birth date).

F.A.F.L.

PRO PATRIA
2-8-1914 – 27-8-1943
COMMANDANT RENÉ MOUCHOTTE
COMMANDANT LE G.C.1 "ALSACE"
MORT EN COMBAT AÉRIEN AU DESSUS DE NOUS

Above left: René Mouchotte in RAF uniform. (Courtesy of the Mouchotte Family)

Above right: René at an airfield in the UK. (Courtesy of the Mouchotte Family)

A shot of René Mouchotte
from the family archive.
(Courtesy of the Mouchotte
Family)

Above left: A portrait of René in his Free French uniform. (Courtesy of the Mouchotte Family)

Above right: A cartoon depicting René Mouchotte. (Courtesy of the Mouchotte Family)

Signed by René – Biggin Hill's 1,000th victory. (Courtesy of the Mouchotte Family)

René Mouchotte, General de Gaulle and Colonel Valin.

René Mouchotte's funeral with full military honours at Les Invalides, Paris. Colonel Valin is carrying the French hero's medals.

Above: General de Gaulle, unknown, René and Colonel Valin.

Left: Jacqueline Quentin Mouchotte, receiving her brother's medals, including the coveted Battle of Britain Clasp to the 1939-45 Star, with Jan Leeming.

René's aunt showing his newly awarded medals, which were presented by Sir (Lord) Peter Ricketts at the British Ambassador's Residence in Paris.

A proud Mouchotte family at the British Ambassador's Residence in Paris.

Commandant Mouchotte's French Air Force pilot's qualification badge.

Casaux air base.

A modern French Air Force fighter jet commemorating Commandant Mouchotte.

Jan Leeming at Westende beach, Belgium, on which René Mouchotte's body washed ashore.

The RAF HQ on Gibraltar which has been re-named 'Mouchotte Buildings'.

Jan Leeming with the plaque at RAF HQ Gibraltar.

Colonel John Powell, who recommended that the RAF HQ be renamed and in honour of René Mouchotte.

HUNDREDS of
WELCOMING FISHING
BOATS off
LE TRÉPORT—

A page from René Mouchotte's Pilot's Flying Log Book. Also a talented artist, what might he have gone on to achieve, had he survived?

The personal inscription in the 2009 French edition of 'Mes Carnets': 'To Jan Leeming, these diaries were written during the Battle of Britain, J Quentin Mouchotte' (The sister of René, grateful for and admiring the work accomplished by Jan Leeming so that his memory may live on).

form, make it perfect as that of a fine, well-oiled machine. We shall let the enemy come and sniff at us, merely showing him our strong teeth; they will keep him at a distance. The day of the offensive which is fast approaching will find us a young force, terribly armed with a science of warfare and discipline. We shall put our whole soul into this holy war of liberation and the octopus shall perish, even if it costs us our lives. ...

April 18th

A month at Biggin Hill now. 341 Squadron has begun its sweeps over France at a faster rhythm. We have moved into the still warm beds of 340, who have gone up to rest at Turnhouse. They certainly needed it, poor devils. The veterans were terribly worn, and deserve not only physical and mental rest but also health-giving peace of mind. They had a lot of success latterly but they paid dearly for it, losing more pilots than they shot down Boches. Happily, a fortnight after being shot down, their C.O., Schloesing, sent news of himself from Switzerland; a fortnight later their next C.O. was shot down in his turn. ...

Group Captain Malan and Wing Commander Deer got some of the Biggin Hill people together and asked me to explain the principles of my formation to them. They had a few criticisms to make, but I must admit that on the whole they seemed to like it for its manoeuvrability and its rational use of each unit, giving the maximum of security. The weak point, they say, is that I have to count on the blind discipline of each of my pilots for it to be successful. ...

Today, which brings us up to twenty sweeps, I can affirm the complete triumph of my theories. Never, the wing commander is saying to anyone who cares to listen, has a squadron kept formation so well and shown so much flexibility in manoeuvre.

As far as operations go, we have resumed our flying over our poor France. The young members of my squadron who went off 'to the war' with their hearts racing said, 'So that was all,' when they came back.

The sky seemed pretty empty for the first fortnight. We tried to set traps for the Boche to attract him to us and make him fight. The radio often announced a squadron of the enemy at one point but when we went after them, they disappeared at once. We despaired of ever seeing them, and one day I said to General Valin, 'We shall soon have to land on aerodromes in France and give the Germans a boot in the backside to make them get into their planes and fight.' I was taken up on this imprudent remark. The very next day a shower of 200 Boche fell on a mere twenty-four of us. They tackled it like beginners.

We took 'evasive action'. They dropped out of the sky on us like stones, miraculously passing through us while we went round like circus horses … for the most part, they hardly ever followed up their attacks. When the last of them had vanished and was undistinguishable from the sea, we regained formation and confirmed, with relief, that no one was missing.

The operations which followed taught us that the enemy's effective strength has tripled since last year and that he accepts battle only when he is sure of numerical and tactical superiority. Whereas we, unlike last year, rarely take off in numbers greater than twenty-four.

The operation immediately after that one was unfortunately less favourable to us. Fate would not have it that 'Alsace' should register a victory in the first battle. In consequence of a mistake on Flying Control's part, we found ourselves in a whirlwind mass of Spitfires and F.W. 190s or Me. 109s coming from above and below. All my pilots stayed prudently close to me but one and he got himself shot down before we could even try to help him. Poor Raoul Duval! Ardent, enthusiastic, he made us all share his good humour. Béraud, one of the best, did not come back either, victim of engine trouble.

Powerless, we watched him leave us quietly, long after the battle, heading his plane for the south. He vanished from our eyes, soon lost against the carpet of fields on which he meant to land if some over-curious Boche did not put an end to his schemes. A mysterious disappearance, which the future may perhaps explain. …

Duval was engaged to be married and lived in peace-time in the same Le Havre region over which he was shot down in flames. Béraud was married and not a little proud of a delightful little girl of four, whose photograph he loved to display.

These two first losses of the squadron, cruel and unjust as they are, far from discouraging us, have stimulated us all the more.

Operations resumed tomorrow. Nothing to report. The Boche gets to hell out of it. Impossible to engage him when he has the advantage of either altitude or numbers.

May 17th

To retrace this last week's events and describe them in all their detail with the colour, the realty, that made them so 'exciting' for us all would take time I haven't got and moreover would need literary talents I am far from possessing.

So, I will sketch them quickly, mentioning that as the fine weather continued, we went on making sweeps on an average of one or two a day. Furthermore, those who order them and give them to us to do seem to be getting bolder and bolder. Never have we flown so far with so little petrol; the prospect of prolonged aerial combat leaves us with the further prospect of a dip in the North Sea. ...

One day we went to Antwerp, escorting some American bombers; the day after, to Courtrai; then to Méaulte, near Albert; yesterday, from Cornwall, we went on a visit to Brittany, over the pretty town of Morlaix. How much water, water, there is to cross!

Thanks to the generosity of our godmother, Mme Ida Rubinstein, I organized an enormous ball on the occasion of our squadron's baptism. It took up a lot of my time, especially on account of wartime difficulties in getting gin, whisky, etc., and providing a suitable buffet to satisfy 350 people's hunger and thirst. Its scene was the ballroom of one of the finest London hotels and I proposed to invite some celebrated people – the Air Minister, his wife and his daughter Catherine, the head of Fighter Command, the air marshal commanding 2 Group, General de Gaulle, etc.

Other invitations were sent to his personal staff-officers, General Valin, General d'Astier de la Vigerie, General Bouscat (Giraud's representative), a dozen officers from the diplomatic mission, nearly all the officers from General and Air Headquarters, some of the personalities from the Comité National Français, and the rest I forget. Before the ball, the announcement made a tremendous stir, for London no longer sees balls on such a scale and in such style. But it was exactly what I needed to 'launch' the 'Alsace' Squadron in London society ... (victories being conspicuous by their absence!). I dreaded to add up all the figures circulating in my head, I was so afraid Of being thunderstruck by the terrifying total. Poor dear godmother!

The Biggin Hill station, where we are, has the highest total of enemy aircraft destroyed by squadrons from its aerodrome. There is competition between the Fighter Command stations, and Biggin Hill was winning with 995. It had long been anticipated that the day when Biggin Hill got its 1,000th Boche would see some choice parties and celebrations. A sweepstake had been on the go for over a month. Whoever so desired could buy a ticket which might correspond, after the draw, to the name of some pilot on the station. The ticket bearing the name of the pilot who shot down the 1,000th plane would win a very large sum of money. It was also understood that the pilot himself would get £300, a good round sum, enough to make those least greedy for gain think twice. ...

On the 10th, a pilot of 611 Squadron, which flies with us, shot down the 996th Boche. People began to get excited. On May 14th we were over Belgium – Courtrai – and we were engaged by F.W. 190s. I attacked two of them, but being unable to get nearer to them than 350 metres, in a vertical dive, in spite of the terrifying speed of 540 m.p.h., I thought it better to save my ammunition and return to my squadron.

During this time, Martel, after another engagement, suddenly found himself on his own and climbed back like lightning towards what he thought were three Spitfires until he saw the black crosses under them. He opened fire and saw one of them explode and disintegrate in the air. The two others thought it best to make off. … Well done, Christian! The squadron's first victory, which brought Biggin Hill's total to 997. … Pilot society was getting noisily excited.

Our party was this evening, May 15th. No sweep in the morning. At two o'clock we were hoping that nothing would disturb us and prevent us from bathing, scenting ourselves and getting ready.

No luck! Take-off at four o'clock for a small and apparently inoffensive operation. … We all got ready with a bad grace. We took off. First, we had to fly at sea level until the French coast was in sight, then do a breath-taking climb, so uncomfortable that your feet were almost in the air. You had the feeling that if the engine stopped you would fall, tail first. The radio announced the Boche, lots of Boche. We checked the sight contacts and made sure instinctively that the button was in the firing position. …

Le Havre slid past to port, here was Trouville, 22,000 feet below. And, all at once, battle. Shouts over the radio, the other squadron was attacking. I noticed one parachute already. I gave the order to turn, intending to help them by getting the sun behind me and thus drop more easily on the offered prey.

Hardly had I begun to turn to starboard when a nice little job slid under my starboard wing. I turned on my back without even trying to identify it. I went at terrific speed, giving the plane all it had. As I dived after my National Socialist, for I could see his black crosses shining now, I gave rapid orders over the radio so that my faithful troops would cover my attack. The other plane went on diving vertically. … 'Too bad, I'm having a go.' Yesterday's experience had been too mortifying. I got the nose gently into position and opened up.

The great distance between us gave me little hope. But I was somewhat startled by what I saw: there was a violent explosion in the fuselage of the Focke-Wulf, followed by a huge flame. The plane rose in the air, then burst into bits, seeming to disintegrate in the air. It is a miracle I got through without damage. The return to the aerodrome would have made all the gossiping *concierges* of Paris pale with envy. Never was the radio so loud with useless chatter. We were all exultant, for Squadron Leader Charles, of 611 Squadron, had shot two of them down, thus bringing to 1,000 the total of planes shot down by Biggin Hill. After we landed there was a great problem as to which of us, Charles and I, had got the third Boche....

I immediately said I had seen the parachute of Charles's first victim, about two or three minutes before I shot mine down. Charles had shot his down consecutively, one after the other. I remembered having said, immediately after firing, 'Hello, boys, I've got one too!' The Operations Room then confirmed that mine was the third.

But the wonderful coincidence in all this was that our party was this very night. What a gift for the baptism of our squadron! It was a magnificent ball, the kind of thing we hardly ever see nowadays. Lots of top brass, generals, etc., and vast numbers of pretty women. The open windows at the beginning of the evening overlooked the park and the mild temperature of the end of a splendid spring day allowed elegant ladies to show off their toilette to the curious. In addition to a British orchestra (obtained by a miracle) I had a French accordeon band. It was wildly successful. The cocktails also gave satisfaction.

I, as was 'understood', had to do the honours, and my success of a few hours before, in addition to the fact that it was the celebrated '1,000th' at Biggin Hill, meant that I had to shake twice as many hands; my sweet modesty was put to the test. The writer Joseph Kessel was there: he plans to spend a few days with us; Germaine Sablon would not give us the pleasure of hearing her. A famous producer, some well-known English film stars, politicians, Giraud's military mission, journalists, etc. ... A French radio announcer told me he meant to speak of the '1,000th' that same night on the radio, at 2 a.m. ... In short, everyone seemed to be enjoying themselves and getting on well together.

One thing gave me great pleasure, which Pompéi told me: the Conseil de l'Ordre de la Libération has just admitted me as a Companion. I am terribly proud of getting this decoration, so sparingly awarded. This is for my family, who will read this in time to come, if I am no longer here: Pompéi added, 'If they had been as severe two years ago as they are today, I certainly should not have received it. Let me tell you that when they had been through Commandant X's file they rejected him, but, my dear fellow, I had the pleasure of seeing unanimity over you.'

May 16th

We are resuming our sweeps, no pity for our sleepless night. Rapid take-off, landing an hour and a quarter later at the extreme west point of Cornwall. After lunch we took off to escort some bombers over Morlaix. Four and a half hours' flying after only three hours' sleep last night.

May 17th

Caen again. Last year I damaged an Me. 109 at Caen; the day before yesterday the F.W. 190 was at Caen again. Today I shot down an Me. 109 at Caen.

It was midday, 23,000 feet. There was the usual radio news of Boche all round. Lower down, at about 12,000 feet, the twelve Boston bombers, in two groups of six, were flying in close formation, crossing the coast in a dive directly at their target. Starboard and port, rising towards us, five or six squadrons of Spitfires were escorting them like sheepdogs. Then, with brutal suddenness, battle. ... Some turns, and after passing above us, the Boche escaped without any chance of being pursued. ...

A few minutes later, when I had succeeded in re-forming my Spitfires, I spotted four suspicious planes astern. I took them for Spitfires at first, on account of their manner of flying being exactly like that of our formations. Nevertheless, I gave the order to attack and swung my plane. It was well and truly a group of Fritzes, protected, I noticed much later, by a much greater umbrella of their colleagues.

An exciting battle began, during which I began by choosing my victim. But just as I was letting him have my first burst, unfortunately deflected to one side, my attention was caught by cries of 'Hello, number one Red, hello, number one Red, I've a Messerschmitt on my tail.' Turning my head to try and spot the poor unfortunate was enough for my prey to get away for good. But I had the luck to pick out my poor sick bird straight away. Still followed by my faithful number two, I turned over and dived above a queer succession of planes composed of two Spitfires turning desperately, pursued at equal distances by a Messerschmitt and two Focke-Wulfs.

I went for the former while the other two, seeing me, turned over and vanished. The Boche, finding himself attacked in his turn, abandoned his pursuit and fled as best he could with me on his tail. I learned after I landed that the two F.W.s came up behind to try and help their leader, and but for my number two's presence of mind in facing them and making them scatter they would have set about me while I was so busy getting the Fritz in my sights ... and would probably have shot me down.

I began by giving my fugitive a visiting card from about 250 metres, without seeing any other result than a sudden slackening of his speed; I was obliged to throttle back my engine quickly so as not to overrun him. He was getting so unnaturally large that I thought I was going to crash into him. The film gives an astonishing impression of it, so close was the distance at which it was taken. Unfortunately, only one of my cannons was working, with the result that each time I fired my plane swung to starboard. Little accuracy. The ground was getting dangerously near, for we were in a nosedive. I soon had to think about pulling out to avoid feeling the hardness of French soil. I relinquished my prey regretfully, trailing a thin thread of black smoke behind him.

Following him with my eyes, I saw him crash in a ball of fire. That devil of a Fritz did not expect to finish the war so soon. To harden my heart, I thought of the wretched convoys of defenceless French peasants machine-gunned on our roads when they were fleeing the savages' bombing and unheroic advance. If, tonight, I say a more heartfelt prayer than usual, it is for all our unhappy fellow-countrymen who fall each day beneath their blows, and it is to implore Heaven to leave me enough life as a fighter pilot to avenge, to avenge over and over again, the whole martyred, starved generation of French youth which is longing to fight and all those, too, who suffer in France, chained like slaves.

What awaited me on landing made me pay dearly for the feeling of pride which had momentarily taken possession of me. The news of this further success had reached Biggin Hill before our return. Thirty reporters, who had come on the occasion of the 1,000th plane, were waiting for me, bold and well-armed.... Strategic retreat to my office, where I learned that 'Alsace' had distinguished itself brilliantly: Boudier and Bouguen each had a Boche too. A loss to regret, unfortunately – young Sergeant Bourges, whom a witness saw baling out. Three for one. ...

I escaped to lunch. I was called to the phone. I scented the enemy and had them say I wasn't there. Unable to find me, the camp loudhailer tore its lungs out calling me twice. No way out, it had to be faced. I went to the Intelligence Room where the reporters, sucking their pencils, were waiting for their victim. Two ravishing young women were among the fiercest of them.

On the way-out photographers on the watch shot us pitilessly. I was accompanied by Malan, Deer and Charles. At last, naively, I thought it was over and was off back to the mess when Malan took me by the arm: 'René, it's the price of success. It's the cinema's turn now, and I'm very much afraid you'll have to say a few words. ...' That was the limit! All this for one poor Boche who had the bad luck to be in my sights.

For nearly an hour we had to play the film star, say stupid things and repeat them interminably, for each time something went wrong. I had to shake Charles's hand theatrically at least ten times while saying, 'Yes, let's share it (the 1,000th). I think that would be fair.'

Then it was the B.B.C.'s turn. Once more we had to improvise and recount our brief battles and finally repeat the comedy of 'We're going to share the 1,000th sportingly.' Then we simulated and lived over the battle and the famous return, talking from our planes, as if our conversation of the other day had really been recorded at the time, etc. ... That went on until tea, when we were set free again.

The following days I received numerous telegrams of congratulation, some really moving. One of them, addressed to 'Monsieur le Commandant René', said, 'Our most cordial congratulations on your magnificent exploit. Love. Austin family.'

Also got a very lovely telegram from Lady Sinclair: 'All my congratulations to you personally and to our magnificent Squadron. My husband and I thank you from the bottom of our hearts for this new proof of France's fighting spirit. Long live "Alsace". Marigold Sinclair.'

It is incredible how keen the English are on autographs. I noticed this when I had to answer many letters from unknown people sending my photograph, found in a paper, to be signed.

North Africa is free at last. ... Thousands of prisoners and an enormous amount of booty. Tunis delirious. Will Tunisia be the springboard for a forthcoming landing on the Continent?

Dupérier is back from America, where he has been on a tour visiting American factories and flying schools. I am taking him into my squadron to fly on some operations again.

The parties, fêtes and dinners in celebration of the famous 1,000th follow one another. The last party was here in the mess; about midnight the draw of the sweepstake took place, after which Air Marshal Saunders gave Charles and me each a cheque for £90.

We are continuing our sweeps regularly. Nothing very exciting to report, except that I look at France with fierce determination to return there soon as a conqueror. I have more than once wondered how many French lives the landing will cost. But the Boche will pay dearly for his attempt to enslave the world.

I have already led the wing ten times and I have confided to Wing Commander Deer my ambition to command it the day we land for the first time on the other side. To my great contentment he promised me this, which will give me the honour of being the first Frenchman to lead the first squadron to set foot on our poor soil.

I have just been testing a new plane of a very recent type, which our squadron may be among the first to get. Its performance is stupefying: by my watch it climbed to 6,500 metres in 4 minutes 30 seconds. And I think it can do better. The angle of ascent is such that in the pilot's seat the legs are as high as the head (I was going to say higher). The same sensation when beginning a loop. To see the ground, you have to look behind you. The diving speed is clearly superior to that of our Spitfire IXa and in trying a nose-dive from 18,000 feet I touched 560 m.p.h. without pushing the plane. I had to pull out, my ears were giving me an unbearable sharp pain.

The famous ball given in London by Biggin Hill in honour of the 1,000th plane shot down has just been given in the biggest hotel, Grosvenor House. By general consent this was 'the most gigantic reception of the war.' It cost a mere £2,500! If German prisoners could have been brought to the buffet, they would not have believed their eyes. Hundreds of ducks, chickens, lobsters, perfectly prepared, were offered to the gourmandise of some 2,000 guests. Gorgeous side-dishes, beer, cocktails, champagne, all generously served. Vickers, the maker of the Spitfire, paid the evening's expenses.

The legendary Windmill Girls, in on all the Biggin Hill parties (for some mysterious reason), gave one of their little numbers. Numerous aviation celebrities crowded among the guests. Besides top brass, like Leigh Mallory, Saunders, etc., there were Jimmy Rankin, Malan, Screwball McMullen, Johnny Walker and Appleton. The photographers have had another go at me, obviously stupid!

Chapter 21

The Supreme Sacrifice

July 9th, 1943

The sweeps go on. Boche quiet. It has been noticed at Fighter Command that when the enemy gathers from the radio that Biggin Hill is coming into a sector they give their fighters the order to withdraw. Not encouraging, making war under these conditions. I hope we are going to adopt new tactics. …

Great news. Today, June 15th, I have had a telegram according to which we are getting the new Spitfires of the IXb type. That is the new plane I tested a few days ago. We are the first and only ones in Fighter Command to be issued with them. The Focke-Wulfs will only have to face them. They won't understand in the least, this latest Spitfire looking exactly like the older one. …

The acquisition of these very recent planes for my squadron coincides curiously with a recent conversation with Wing Commander Deer. Latterly, at Fighter Command, he was told that those in high places are extremely satisfied with my squadron. …

The day before yesterday I led the wing over Rouen. Didn't even see the Boche's tail. The bombing was rather a washout. One stick fell in the Seine, another on the bank, just by the works, without scoring a hit, a third got lost in the country and must have hit a few isolated houses. …

Today I went on my 105th sweep, representing 148 hours on offensive operations over occupied country. I have also flown on 178 defensive operations, representing about 250 hours in the air. Nice things one collects in a war. …

My pilots are gradually being formed in my methods of combat. From time to time they have to be brought to heel a little. Combats are rare, which gives the new pilots a chance to get used to flying over France. We often go with the Flying Fortresses, which venture into France in lots of 80, 120 and even 240. They always return with impressive figures of Boche shot down, which makes us say ironically that in reality it is the Americans who are protecting us.

It is not unusual for them to declare a figure of fifty to sixty F.W. 190s shot down while we fighters have only seen a dozen and shot down one or two. Our orders are not to go too close for they often fire on us: one victim more to record. As there are seven of them on board, that makes seven victories, to be multiplied by the number of bombers which might also have been able to open fire, etc.

The Boche often stupefies us with his bizarre tactics, only attacking when he is sure of getting someone without danger to himself. When our strength is too great or we are too well protected, they stay above us and escort us amicably as far as we are going. Magnificent weather. We are in the middle of a heavy programme. One or two sweeps a day. Often three. *I go on them all*, of course, but *am deadly tired*. What can I do? Impossible to stop. I cannot leave my squadron. And yet it is more than necessary for me to be in the attack on the day of the invasion. They are talking about that blessed invasion. The Allies are in Sicily. Mussolini's scale has been turned. The massive attack by the R.A.F. on German cities, the Russian advance, all the premonitory signs are growing more numerous. Recently they have even fitted a mechanism under our wings to drop two small bombs. We shall soon have seen everything! Our new Spitfires are turning out to be fantastic.

This is certainly the best fighter aircraft in the world. I feel quite comfortable among the Fritzes. Each time we meet them we feel ourselves much superior. So do they, too, for they refuse battle and fly off fearfully. Impossible to chase them; we have to go on protecting the bombers. A change for me, after fighting for almost three years in planes inferior to the Germans'. My Spitfire is the best, too, and I take jealous care of it, no one having the right to fly it but me.

The bombing of aerodromes in France, Belgium and Holland goes on to a steady rhythm. Isn't this the pounding before the invasion? Caen, Saint-Omer, Merville, Tricqueville, Abbeville, Courtrai, Rotterdam, even Amsterdam. How much water, how much water to cross for such distances. ... We feel we are braver and braver.

The wing commander has taken twelve days' leave. I am leading the wing in his place. Hum! I have now passed out as tactician in charge. I am gradually getting more confidence and my orders are becoming calculated. Special operation only yesterday, on which I had to lead two wings at once. Everything went off well. No Boche, no combat.

189

On July 27th we had a success which beats all those of Fighter Command since the battle of Dieppe. I was leading the wing near Lisieux when the radio announced about sixty Boche. I was manoeuvring in the sun and gaining altitude when, without warning, we found ourselves engaged in a gigantic combat. For the first time the enemy seemed to be accepting battle. Spitfires and F.W. 190s whirled. In the ensuing confusion I managed to slip in a few orders, but shortly afterwards each section found itself on its own and could only act independently.

What a lovely machine, the Focke-Wulf, seen at close quarters, especially from above, I couldn't help thinking. Too busy manoeuvring to help one of my sections, I could only give one of them a short burst. Did I get him? I don't know. As there is a doubt, I would rather not claim. Someone behind me clearly saw an F.W. going down in a tail-spin with heavy black smoke, but was that the one? My horror of being thought a fraud made me keep quiet when we landed. But what joy to know that we got five of them without one of us being hit. One of my young men, Closterman, who should go far, got two of them himself.

The other squadron in the wing got four, which makes nine altogether, perhaps more, without loss. A considerable success, which will further exalt our 'Alsace'. I received telegrams of congratulation, one of them from Churchill as follows: 'Please give my warmest congratulations to Squadrons 485 and 341 of Biggin Hill for their performance yesterday. Nine for nought is an excellent result.'

And the sweeps go on, at a terrible pace. I am at the record figure of 140. *I feel a pitiless weariness from them.* It is useless for me to go to bed at 9.30 each night; I feel my nerves wearing out, my temper deteriorating. The smallest effort gets me out of breath; I have a crying need of rest, were it even for forty-eight hours. I have not taken a week's leave for two years. Always at readiness to fly or stuck in the office on administrative work! Anyway, where can I go?

These last days I have tried to hold myself back, fearfully anticipating the hard period of fighting ahead, for which I shall need all my strength and fitness. I have therefore cancelled all offensive work, confining myself to going nowhere but to the office. But this three days' relaxation has softened my nerves and my will. I am still as tired. Tomorrow morning, I am flying again.

Epilogue

Searching for René

by Jan Leeming

My quest for René Mouchotte began at Capel-le-Ferne near Folkestone in Kent, site of the iconic Battle of Britain Memorial. The memorial was opened in 1993 by Her Majesty, the late Queen Mother. It was a very windy day, and the helicopter pilot suggested they 'Turn back'; Her Majesty reportedly responded, 'Our boys never turned back. We will carry on' – which rather set the scene for subsequent events.

In 2005, HRH Prince Michael of Kent unveiled the Sir Christopher Foxley-Norris Memorial Wall, in honour of the late Air Chief Marshal Sir Christopher Foxley-Norris, one of The Few himself and a long-serving Chairman of the exalted Battle of Britain Fighter Association, membership of which is exclusively restricted to The Few. The wall is inscribed with just under 3,000 names of the RAF aircrew known to have fought in the Battle of Britain, between 10 July and 31 October 1940; no ranks or decorations are included on the wall, and names are in alphabetical order.

In July 2007, I received, out of the blue, an invitation to the annual Battle of Britain Memorial Day at the Memorial, organised by the Battle of Britain Memorial Trust, which is also responsible for maintenance and management of this special site. Though I had no idea what a great occasion this is – one which rightly commemorates The Few and their achievement in saving Britain from invasion – I attended.

On the day, there were twenty-five of The Few present, laying wreaths around the Memorial, a statue of a pilot seated and gazing across the Channel, where so many aerial combats occurred. The statue is surrounded by the badges of all the RAF Fighter Command squadrons and appended units which took part in the battle; it is also at the centre of a huge three-bladed propeller marked out on the ground.

On the luncheon table was more information about the Memorial and some sponsorship forms. I like to 'pay my way' and as an invited guest thought the least that I could do was pay to sponsor a name. Not long afterwards, I received a note from Janet Tootal, the wife of the Battle of

191

Britain Memorial Trust's hard-working Honorary Secretary, Group Captain Patrick Tootal, asking which name I would like to sponsor.

To my knowledge at that time, none of my own family members were in the RAF (although I later discovered two distant Atkins family relations are commemorated on the Runnymede Memorial to missing British and Commonwealth aircrew), so having French heritage I asked for a French name. There are thirteen Free French names on the Wall and I could have been allocated any of them. Randomly but fortuitously, as things turned out, I was allocated the name of René Mouchotte – and, naturally, after a professional lifetime of interviewing and researching, I was eager to find out more about this total stranger.

Was I in for a surprise? Up came René's name on a Google search and the fact that he had written diaries during the war and that these were published soon after. René, I discovered, was killed in action on 27 August 1943. Flying a Spitfire, he was lost during a raid on the huge concrete bunker being constructed at Éperlecques in the Pas-de-Calais, from which it was proposed to launch deadly V-2 rockets at the UK.

René's mother only learned the truth of his death at the time of the Liberation. She had previously continued to hope that he had somehow remained alive, despite still being officially posted missing in action. She gave her son's diaries, sketches, photographs, press cuttings, medals, citations and his pilot's flying logbook to family friend André Dezarrois, with the words, 'Here is all I have left of him. Will you read it? Will you publish it?'

Dezarrois hesitated, asking 'Have we the *right* to publish?'; Mouchotte had not, after all, written his personal diaries with publication in mind. Recently returned from Germany's prisons and torture camps, the great French Resistance leader Colonel Heurtaux gave Dezarrois his answer: 'The diaries are not *literature* – they contain love of country, the heart of a fighter pilot, a leader's soul. The sons of France need the nourishment they have to give'.

Consequently, the diaries were published in France in 1949. An English translation did not appear until 1956.

I just *had* to have a copy and duly found one on the internet, expecting it to be a book more for men, with a 'gung-ho' attitude to war. What I found was a sensitive story of a man wedded to duty, determined to fight on after his beloved France had capitulated to the Germans. He writes of his French comrades being killed and watching, helpless, as his best friend keeled over and disappeared into the sea while on a convoy protection patrol.

He, Charles Guérin, was blinded by the effect of a glycol leak, the vapour enveloping his aircraft (there were many glycol leaks – later found to be sabotage).

René wrote, too, with considerable humour and much humility over his accomplishments – and always there is a huge display of love for his mother, family and homeland. I have read *Mes Carnets*, as the original French edition was entitled, seven times – and on every occasion have been moved to tears.

I am a romantic, pure and simple, and had decided I would source a copy of the original diaries in French. Finding a copy in an antiquarian bibliotheque in Belgium, I sent off the very reasonable sum of 10 Euros plus postage and soon received a copy with, would you believe, a little calling card stuck inside the cover to a Monsieur and Madame Griser, thanking them and sending her best wishes from 'Madame O. Mouchotte'. Perhaps she had visited and given them a copy of the diaries as a gift? What are the chances of that happening and that particular book ending up in my possession? I did not realise then, though, that I was 'on a mission' and the more delving I did, the more I discovered, and the more deeply moved I became, throughout the years ahead.

I am honoured to have been invited to the Battle of Britain Memorial Day every year since 2007. In 2008, after the ceremony and laying of wreaths by the surviving Few, air attachés from Commonwealth countries and various civic dignitaries, families and friends walk to the Foxley-Norris Wall and we lay our tributes. As I was placing mine, a gentleman asked, 'What is your association with the Battle of Britain?'

I replied that I was researching the story of René Mouchotte and eventually hoped to have a television documentary made. The gentleman introduced himself as Wing Commander Tom Neil – one of The Few, a wartime fighter ace and an author. Tom told me that together with his lovely wife Eileen, he had served with René at Biggin Hill. Eileen told me René was a very reserved and intense man. This was incredible! I could not believe that I was actually talking to people who had personally known my hero, as he had now become. That link created a friendship between the Neils and myself which lasted until their deaths.

I regularly wrote on my website about my search for and appealing for any information on René. In March 2011, I was contacted by one Mark Chapman who told me that his father had worked with René while a member of ground crew. We met for coffee, and I learned a great deal more about the man I felt I was beginning to know, albeit posthumously.

Mark's father had written a very interesting but unpublished work on his years of service and in which he described René as a great man to work for; strict but fair, exceedingly generous and who encouraged and befriended everyone on his team, regardless of rank, role or status. Mark also showed me a lapel badge given to his father by René from the Aero Club Jean Mermoz, of which René was a member (many years later the Mouchotte family gave me another of these little badges once belonging to René, which I naturally treasure).

In early May 2011, I went with a friend to Biggin Hill, one of our most famous wartime fighter stations, where René had served, in addition to various other airfields across the country. I saw Mess menus for special dinners signed by René, his name carved on the Reredos in the Chapel of Remembrance, and – most poignantly – his name inscribed in the Book of Remembrance which is opened every Sunday and shows the names of those who died for their country.

After visiting the Chapel, we crossed the main road to a housing estate which had previously accommodated military personnel, but since been sold off by the Ministry of Defence for private use – or most of it had been. As I crouched to take a photo of 'Mouchotte Close', a man jogged by and demanded to know what I was doing on MoD property.

I blurted out my explanation, that I was researching René Mouchotte. His attitude immediately changed, and he, Colonel John Powell, invited my companion and me into his home for a cup of tea. His poor wife was hanging out the washing when she was suddenly having to make tea for two total strangers. It transpired that a small part of the area had been retained by the military and service families were housed there when their men folk were posted overseas on active service. Apparently, *The Mouchotte Diaries* were given to any newcomers to Mouchotte Close. John and his wife, Claire, and I remained in touch over developments in the story, and then he was posted to Gibraltar.

Also that same month, friends in Paris invited me to stay. I adore France, and Paris in particular, so was keen to take up the invitation and to spend time trying to find more about René. By this time, I knew that when René was killed on 27 August 1943, his last words were 'I am alone with the bombers!' Radio contact with him was lost, although back at base all were hoping that he might have baled out of his Spitfire and there was a chance he could be picked up in the Channel. Hope, sadly, eventually died. Grown men were moved to tears.

A week later, his body washed up on Westende Plage in Belgium on 3 September 1943. In fact, during the course of the Second World War, the currents carried the remains of over ninety poor souls – soldiers, sailors and airmen – onto that same beach. At the time, however, René's body was not identified correctly, because his identity disc read 'R. Martin'. Why was this?

The Free French, of which René was one of the first, were condemned to death by the Germans if caught. In his diaries, René speaks humorously of what might happen if he were shot down and captured, adding that although no German would take him for an Englishman, they might, just might, think he was French Canadian. Consequently, and indeed sensibly, he assumed the identity of an RCAF man who had returned to Canada – one R. Martin. The families of Free French servicemen and women were also liable to be persecuted by the Germans, so this was another vitally important reason for concealing true identities.

René was buried in Middelkerke Cemetery and later moved to the Commonwealth War Graves Commission section, where he remained until 1949.

Back to my French sojourn in May 2011 … By this time, I knew that after an extensive search by Flight Lieutenant R.N. Archer, in liaison with (what was then) the Imperial War Graves Commission, the body in Middelkerke Cemetery had been correctly identified as that of Commandant René Mouchotte (one piece of clothing, his vest, actually had his real name printed on it) and his remains had been taken back to France. He was then given a full military funeral at Les Invalides in Paris and interred in the Mouchotte family tomb in Père Lachaise Cemetery, on the north-east side of the city.

So, off to Père Lachaise I went, armed with a map and a reference number. It was not too difficult to find the Mouchotte tomb on the corner of Avenue de la Chapelle. It was in very good condition and looked well cared for. In the centre, above the altar, was a photo of René and a memorial plaque. I have mentioned being a romantic, and suddenly had an idea: people have placed messages in bottles and thrown them in to the sea, so why could I not leave a message in the tomb? My French is far from flawless, however, and as I had no writing materials, I returned to my friends, wrote a letter in English, which they translated, and went back to the cemetery. The letter was placed down the side of the tomb near the door. And then I waited.

Spurred on by knowing where René Mouchotte was buried, I then decided to go to Belgium and to Dunkerque. In September 2011, a friend asked if I would like to go over to France on a wine-buying daytrip. The ferry was inexpensive and a decade ago it was worth the trip, except that we usually spent what we saved on the wine by having a lovely meal before returning. Asking if we could extend the trip up the coast, my friend readily agreed.

During my research I had ascertained there were various memorials to René all over France and knew there was one just north of Calais at the Aérogare Blériot, Dunkerque, which was on the way to Middlekerke in Belgium. Incidentally, it was from there that Blériot had set off to fly across the Channel on 25 July 1909.

When we arrived, I went into the small airport building just to make sure it was in order for me to take photos of the Memorial. The entrance hall was being decorated and was devoid of any pictures or flight paraphernalia. The manager, hearing of my interest in René Mouchotte, went into a back room and returned with a large infographic including the stories of both Blériot and Mouchotte, explaining that it would be put back up when the re-decoration was finished. I took a photograph of it and the memorial. When I visited again some years later, it was disappointing that the infographic remained not displayed but still hidden away in the back office. It was then given to me. I had it framed and it now has pride of place in my home.

My friend and I continued our journey to Middelkerke town hall where I knew a small memorial to René had been unveiled after the war in 1955. Again, not wanting to offend anyone and always mindful of rules, I enquired in the kiosk as to whether I could take photographs. The gentleman rose from his seat and came out – I thought he was going to evict us! But no, he told us to follow him and took us to a back office where he introduced us to a young man called Simon Vosters.

It transpired that Simon was the very new and enthusiastic Archivist of the town and, miracle of miracles, had just been dealing with the Mouchotte files, documenting the inauguration of the memorial. René's mother, sister and her children had attended. In addition to the memorial, the Mayor presented Madame Mouchotte with a beautiful enamelled plaque representing the memorial. The ceremony was documented in numerous black and white photos which Simon kindly let me copy. Then he took us to Middelkerke Cemetery and showed us the small part which is reserved as the Commonwealth War Graves plot and in which René's body had lain at rest for several years. I could not have been more grateful for all the help received and returned home with renewed confidence.

In October 2011, my oldest friend, Sue, who lives near Leeds, rang to let me know there had been an item on the local news about the French at York Minster and a flypast. Again, turning to the internet I learned there had been a dedication and unveiling of a plaque in York Minster to the French bomber crews stationed at RAF Elvington during the Second World War.

Apparently, when the French 'Bomber Boys' were sent to Elvington, all 2,500 of them, the WAAF were moved out. Too much temptation with the French boys in their glamorous uniforms and all their gold braid! Joking aside, they did a superb job and the attrition rate for their crews was incredibly high.

Researching Elvington, I saw it was still very much as it had been in wartime, with all the Nissen huts and turning 'pans' for the bombers. Now it is the Yorkshire Air Museum, with a very impressive collection of aircraft and aviation artefacts, run by Director Ian Reed. We began correspondence, which was to have a happy outcome.

Then, in November 2011, I received an email from Colonel Hubert de Lisle – son-in-law of René's sister, Jacqueline Quentin Mouchotte, who was still alive and soon to celebrate her 101st birthday. My letter was found when the family visited the tomb on 31 October 2011 – All Souls' Day – when tradition dictates that Catholics visit the graves of their dear departed.

Although born in France, Hubert had spent most of his adult life in England and had been a Guards officer, so had seen me often on television, reading the BBC News in the 1980s, and appreciated that, as he said, I was 'bona fide'. He invited me to meet Jacqueline, who apparently had received many approaches over the years with the promise of honouring her brother, none of which had come to fruition – much to her's and the family's disappointment.

The following month, December 2011, I hired a cameraman and set off for Paris on the Eurostar to visit Jacqueline the day after her 101st birthday. Hubert and his wife, Marie Dominique, took us to lunch in a traditional bistro where we indulged in typical French fare – steak and frites. I had sent a list of questions in advance to Hubert, so that he could prepare Jacqueline for our interview. My French is far from fluent, but I felt that if I kept to the script we would both know what we were doing. I understood most of Jacqueline's answers and when we both floundered, Hubert was there to help.

Jacqueline related the sad story of how René's mother learned of his death. Many French arranged to have a tin of sardines sent monthly to their families (don't ask me how they did it) to tell them they were still alive. Madame Mouchotte was receiving her sardines, but she had a bad dream, a premonition, in which she saw René floundering in a stormy sea.

The family were Catholic and had gone to Mass, leaving Madame Mouchotte at home. At point a telegram arrived addressed to Mme

Quentin Mouchotte, which was meant for Jacqueline. In that missive – and all alone – René's mother learned of his death in action during 1943. The news was compounded by the fact that for all these years she had thought him safely working for de Gaulle in an office in London, René having kept his true role from her.

The family, like many in France during the war, listened to BBC radio reports. Though these actually mentioned René, they did so only by the letter 'M'. René's mother, therefore, had remained in ignorance of his demise until that fateful telegram arrived. Jacqueline spoke so fondly of the brother she had not seen since he went off to war, remembering him as always laughing and kind.

Being in Paris I had taken advantage of my French friends' hospitality and was staying with them for a couple of nights. Then I received an email from Ian Reed, whom I had not met but corresponded with. He asked if I was still in Paris and, if so, would I like to accompany him to the funeral of Henry Lafont (Henry spent much time in the UK after the war and changed the spelling of his first name, originally Henri, because there was a French traitor with the same name as his, from which he naturally wanted to distance himself).

'Young Lafont', as René called him, had been one of the six French airmen on the stolen Caudron Goéland which left Oran and flew to Gibraltar. The journey was hazardous, and the reader will doubtless note from the diaries that the aircraft had difficulty taking off, with sabotaged propellers locked in coarse pitch. All René had to guide him on that journey, in fact, was a map torn out of a geography book – but he made it and landed safely in Gibraltar, where, a few days later, he and his comrades boarded the armed trawler *Président Houduce* bound for the UK.

I was due to catch the six o'clock Eurostar that day, so there was time to attend the funeral. Ian and I met at the Lodge Entrance to Les Invalides where we were able to deposit our luggage. On arriving at the Chapel (now the National Cathedral of the French Military), with typical old-fashioned British modesty we positioned ourselves at the back, only to be met by an official and led to the front – just one row behind the Lafont family.

It was a Catholic service, after which the coffin was carried to the huge forecourt for a musical tribute and a gun salute. We found ourselves lined up behind a little placard reading 'Great Britain'. Ian had been asked to attend by the British Air Attaché, who was unable to do so at such short notice. So, we were there together, representing our country. Ian also noticed that of all the medals decorating the coffin, the British awards were absent. After the ceremony we were introduced to a grandson of Maréchal Foch, to the

French Air Attaché and other dignitaries, and went off for an interesting lunch.

Ian was booked on the same Eurostar home, and I admit that I 'ear bashed' him about René for the whole journey. Ian had undertaken a great amount of research about the Free French bomber crews based at Elvington, but not heard of René Mouchotte, a fighter pilot – he certainly did during that journey. When I alighted at Ashford, I left him with my book of notes.

Ian Reed is very knowledgeable about the Battle of Britain and after his work to get a plaque to the Elvington bomber crews erected in York Minster, he had some valuable contacts in the RAF. He realised that none of the thirteen Free French who took part in the Battle of Britain had received their DFCs or coveted Battle of Britain Clasp to the 1939-45 Star, awarded only to The Few. I suppose those who survived had returned to France post-war, where there were other more important issues – like locating the remains of those killed in action – so no medals had been awarded.

Ian, therefore, set about remedying this omission. He duly got the medals for the Mouchotte and Lafont families. Jacqueline Quentin Mouchotte, however, was very ill at Christmas 2011, and nearly died. Her son-in-law, Hubert de Lisle, believes she clung to life in order to receive the medals due to her brother.

In June 2011, Ian and I went to Paris and presented the medals to Jacqueline. We showed her film clips of her brother at the prize-giving for Biggin Hill's 1,000th aerial victory, which René had shared with Squadron Leader Jack Charles, as well as his presence – smiling and happy – at the Grosvenor House Hotel ball in London celebrating the event. She wept and thanked us for bringing her brother back to her after seventy years. Sadly, Jacqueline died just weeks later.

Over a year later, in July 2012, thanks to Ian Reed's connections, there was an official presentation of René's medals to his family in the British Ambassador's Residence in Paris. We were honoured to be joined by Sir (now Lord) Peter Ricketts, then the British Ambassador, and the Chief of the Air Staff, Sir Stephen Dalton, who presented the medals – a DFC and the Battle of Britain Clasp. Also included in this occasion were the family of Henry Lafont, who also received his British medals.

A few days later, when Sir Stephen Dalton attended the Battle of Britain Memorial Service at Capel, he mentioned Mouchotte and Lafont in his speech. I felt very proud of my part in sharing the story.

Moving on to September 2012, as previously mentioned there are thirteen Free French names on the Sir Christopher Foxley-Norris Wall.

After the presentation of medals to the families of Mouchotte and Lafont, the other eleven families naturally wanted their loved ones' medals. They too were presented at the British Ambassador's Residence in Paris, but with not quite such fanfare as we had received earlier in the year. Nonetheless, those families also received those medals due, which is the important fact.

Over the years, I never gave up trying to get a broadcaster interested in the Mouchotte story, which also has other interesting aspects to it. René's paternal great grandfather, Jean-Pierre Duvelleroy, for example, founded a fan making business in Paris in 1827, which became famous world-wide – Jean Pierre being known as the 'King of Fans and Fan of Kings'. Madame Mouchotte sold the business to a M. Maignan who continued with the making of fans until the 1950s, when the business lapsed. M. Maignan preserved fans, drawings, tools, materials and furnishings kept since the foundation of the House of Duvelleroy in 1827, and passed them to his grandson in 1981. In 2010, two young Parisian women bought the collection and resurrected the Duvelleroy fan business.

My project, however, was turned down by BBC 2, BBC 4 and Yesterday, the latter having decided that René 'wasn't famous enough' – demonstrating a complete ignorance of the actual facts and context of this Free French Spitfire hero. I got bounced around between Biography Channel, who declared the subject to be military; the Military Channel told me it was history; History said it was for a Biography Channel. I also approached a few independent production companies. It is all so difficult these days.

When I was younger and there were only three broadcasting channels, BBC 1, BBC 2 and ITV, if you had an idea for a programme, you sent it to the Commissioning Editor. If that exalted person thought the idea 'had legs', it would be passed down to producers, and if any felt it had an appeal, they would take the idea and run with it.

Conversely, today we have a veritable plethora of hundreds of channels, and one is no longer allowed to directly approach commissioning editors. You have to do it through a production company, of which there are hundreds all doing their own thing. It also means that you really need to make a 'pilot' programme (no pun intended) outlining your idea. Unfortunately, I had neither the resources nor contacts to do this.

It is true – it's not 'What you Know, but Who you Know'. I was fortunate to meet a retired BBC director at a drinks party. I monopolised his time with my story of René and fortunately it struck home. He, James Murray, knew the Commissioning Editor of BBC South-East. I had already done all the work – research, scripting and paid for some filming. The Commissioning

Editor approved, and a short piece was destined for inclusion in the local BBC programme 'Inside Out' – every region has this outlet focusing on stories of local interest.

Because René was based at Biggin Hill and his name is on the Sir Christopher Foxley-Norris Wall at the Battle of Britain Memorial at Capel-le-Ferne near Folkestone, both in Kent, his story qualified as 'local interest' for the south-east. I was subsequently allocated a delightful film crew. We shot film at Capel, Dunkerque, Westende, Middelkerke and Paris, particularly at Père Lachaise Cemetery where the only recently finished plaque to Jacqueline Quentin Mouchotte had been placed in the family tomb.

Inserts into the *Inside Out* programmes are usually of five minutes duration. However, the lovely producer, Matthew Wheeler, declared he simply could not edit the material below fifteen minutes, adding that what he had 'in the can' would easily have made a half hour. Sometimes *Inside Out* devotes a complete half hour to a subject, but it was not to be. I was, though, extremely grateful to get fifteen minutes after years of trying. I am proud of the fact that the programme, which was aired on 28 January 2013, trebled viewing figures. 'Searching for René' was also shown on BBC South and in a modified version on BBC Yorkshire. It must have been viewed by around a million people – not bad for a project constantly turned down!

For me, one of the most moving pieces in all the filming we did was standing on the beach at dusk at Westende, thinking not only of René's body being carried there by the current, but of the other ninety odd souls, sailors, soldiers and airmen who had washed ashore there. We also stayed overnight in the Hotel Belville – constructed of concrete and now mainly apartments – but during wartime it was the only building left standing at Westende, which had been extensively bombed.

The story, though, still does not end there.

Fast-forward to September 2013. Earlier, I mentioned having remained in touch with Colonel John Powell, who had been posted to Gibraltar. It transpired that the RAF were considering changing the name of the RAF Headquarters there from 'Jaguar Buildings'; John mentioned the Mouchotte story and René's landing at Gibraltar prior to boarding the *Président Houduce* bound for Britain. It was then decided to rename the HQ 'Mouchotte Buildings' – and I was invited for the inauguration which took place on 14 September 2013 (the day before Battle of Britain Day, which is commemorated annually every 15 September and/or on the closest Sunday to that date).

Through another stroke of serendipity I have now written about my Search for René Mouchotte. Dilip Sarkar, a professional historian, prolific author and internationally recognised expert on the Battle of Britain and Spitfire stories, was meeting Trustees of the Battle of Britain Memorial Trust at the RAF Club to begin organizing a major project. One of the Trustees happened to mention my work and the BBC film, which immediately struck a chord as Dilip had recently produced a new biography on that legendary South African Spitfire ace and fighter leader 'Sailor' Malan, under whom René served at Biggin Hill.

We thus communicated by email and found much in common, and arranged a visit to Gloucester, where Dilip now lives. At the time I was planning a 'progress' to visit friends in the West Country – each Christmas sees the Christmas card list get shorter and I wanted to catch up with them before it is too late! I contacted Dilip, arranged the trip and decided to give him one of my two treasured copies of *The Mouchotte Diaries*. My 'sacrifice' was a blessing: Dilip took one look, listened to my story and before I knew it, with just one telephone call to Pen & Sword Commissioning Editor Martin Mace, minutes later had organised the republishing of the diaries with new appendices, my 'search' and previously unshared photographs from the family archive and elsewhere. And now, that vision has become reality, which you, our esteemed reader, hold in your hands.

My 'Searching for René' has been a wonderful journey. Along the way, I have made friends and become a member of the extended RAF family. Hubert and Marie Dominique de L'Isle keep in touch and have been most generous in allowing us to reproduce cherished family photos in this book.

I am very grateful to all who have helped me and given unstintingly of their time. But for them the story may never have been told, and, certainly, the reproduction of the diaries, with extra historical context and the record of my personal journey, would not have come to fruition. Thank you all, and God Bless you René Mouchotte.

In conclusion, we give René the last word, who speaks to us years later through his personal 'Testament':

> If Fate allows me only a brief fighting career, I shall thank Heaven for having been able to give my life for the liberation of France. Let my mother be told that I have always been very happy and thankful that the opportunity has been given me to serve GOD, MY COUNTRY, and THOSE I LOVE, and that, whatever happens, I shall always be near her.

Further words would be superfluous.

Appendices

Appendix I

The Aerial Activity of the Free French Forces

The *Diaries* were prepared for publication early in 1946. They were held up in the press by various difficulties and could not take into account certain evidence which came to light later and which enriches the brief biography of René Mouchotte, sketched in the Introduction, with some new material. It may appropriately be presented in succinct form. For further details the reader is referred to the French edition.

The hope that those near to them would publish the intimate notes left behind by Mouchotte's comrades who were lost like him is gradually being realized. Those who survived are fast contributing to the archives of our air history.

The noble anthology of the dead awaits the care of some reverent hand, but the living have fortunately taught the French (who could not know what was really going on in the world between 1940 and 1946) the truth.

On the particular point which concerns us here, the truth is sufficient in itself and its eloquence is moving. The public is no longer ignorant of it. Those fellow-countrymen of ours who went to join the Royal Air Force after the Armistice and continue the fight in England, whose wings later led what aviation we had left in Africa worthy of the name, were not the pack of adventurers beyond the laws of war, the handful of pirates quite negligible as far as military value was concerned, that Goebbels' and Goering's propaganda and their emissaries' in France represented them to be when it promised them exemplary punishment in front of a firing squad.

Their units were not numerous, but they were organized and powerfully stiffened by the men their peers judged the best, created little by little amid all manner of difficulties by the will of General de Gaulle, under the impetus of his chiefs of staff, first Admiral Muselier, then General Valin assisted by Colonel Pigeaud. They were of increasing help to our Allies, as the latter have long acknowledged, on the Western, Russian and Eastern Fronts.

If French wings did not disappear from the battle for long, we owe it to these men. Their units proudly bore the names of our provinces. It is a delight to repeat them to oneself: *Ile de France, Alsace, Normandie* (Niémen), *Berry*, not forgetting *Les Cigognes* (could Guynemer's Cigognes not be in this crusade?). Names which will live in our air-annals, for we know, alas, the price these magnificent units paid for the losses and damage they inflicted on the enemy. Without enlarging on this, a few figures must be given.

'Ile-de-France' had thirty pilots killed out of the fifty on its strength; thirty-eight were shot down, five were taken prisoner. The *Diaries* tell us of 'Alsace's' losses; they increased after the author's death, in the intensity of the landing and the battle fought from French to German soil. Two men could have completed the story of the leader they grieved for ('Alsace', too, awaits its chronicler) but they, his followers, are also dead: Commandant Schloesing, a consummate aerial tactician, and Captain Martel, that admirable man whom Mouchotte liked so much. More than half 'Alsace's' strength was killed in action.

'Normandie-Niémen' published its own newspaper, edited by its pilots, a most lively and abundantly illustrated document.[1] This unit was sent to Russia in 1942 and went through the whole campaign there until the victory, winning the Soviet Command's admiration. Out of ninety-four pilots, it numbered forty-six killed and thirty-one missing. Its saddest loss was that of the leading spirit of its first days, Commandant Tulasne, a worthy brother in arms of Mouchotte in his conscience and purity of sacrifice, shot down in 1943.

'Berry', the last born (which took the emblem of Fonck's stork, with folded wings, emblem of his famous 103 Squadron), was decimated in the French sky in 1940; Captain Accart was its leader and Marin la Meslée its hero. Re-formed by Captain Accart at the beginning of 1944, in one year of war it had thirteen pilots killed out of an average strength of twenty-five. The living and the dead have related and illustrated the unit's life very picturesquely in *Silence, on vole!*[2]

The pilots who fell in these battles – what soldiers, and what battles! – number well over a hundred, but their sacrifice represents several hundred enemy planes shot down or damaged (the Russian Command officially

---

1. *Histoire de l'Escadrille Normandie-Niémen.* Journal de Marche (22.3.42-20.6.45). Office Français d'édition. Paris, 1946. In-8°, 203 pages, illustré.

2. *Silence, on vole!* Vie d'un groupe d'aviation de chasse français dans la R.A.F. Arthaud, 1946. In-8°, 160 pages, illustré.

attributed 310 to the 'Normandie-Niémen' Squadron alone), thousands of hours in the air on fighter operations, reconnaissance, attack, destruction of shipping, protection of bombers, dive-bombing of ground targets, etc.

Let us still hope that a definitive book will shed all the light our young air-army requires on the hard work and sacrifice of such units.

Some of our airmen made a career of their own in certain R.A.F. units, like Commandant Livry-Level, expert observer and specialist in secret landings in France, who has related his adventures in a book which makes very interesting reading (*Missions dans la R.A.F.*). Pierre Clostermann, too, who ended the war as commander of an English squadron of Tempests somewhere on the German front in May 1945, and Commandant Jules Roy, bomber pilot, who 'worked' on the Ruhr, the 'Happy Valley' (baptized as such by those who came back from those deadly night flights), which inspired him to write a bitter and great book, the most human of them all. Just as Saint Exupéry was our greatest air writer before, alas, being killed in his reconnaissance plane in 1940, Jules Roy's books make him the most significant writer for the period after that year.

Clostermann, the first French fighter pilot of the 1940-45 War (thirty-three victories) needs no introduction. He, too, published his memoirs, *Le Grand Cirque.*[3] They burst upon people rather like a bomb, rousing the wider public from its torpor when it became aware of a name hitherto unknown to it and of deeds of arms in which all Frenchmen can take pride. No book about flying has ever had such a reception. It is dedicated to those who died in the Free French Air Forces and in the R.A.F., but in particular to the memory of Mouchotte and Martel, for Clostermann began as a pilot in 'Alsace'. He has never forgotten that.

Another book of memories of the French Air Forces in England, *La Vieille Equipe*, by Lieutenant-Colonel Bernard Dupérier,[4] which we should consider first because it was the first to recall René Mouchotte's service in

---

3. Pierre Clostermann: *Le Grand Cirque*. Souvenirs d'un pilote de chasse français dans la R.A.F. Flammarion. Paris, 1948. In-8°, 308 pages, illustré. *Cirque* is a translation of the English word 'show', which also means a spectacular entertainment, but in R.A.F. slang means 'performance' or 'mission' (An English edition, *The Big Show*, translated by Oliver Berthoud, was published in 1951 by Messrs Chatto and Windus, by whose kind permission the quotations from that translation have been included here. *Translator*).

4. Lieutenant-Colonel Dupérier: *La Vieille Equipe*. Berger-Levrault. Paris, 1946. In-8°, 198 pages, illustré. *La Vieille Equipe* and the *Diaries* often cover the same ground from late 1941 to late 1942 and it is interesting to compare the two pilots' impressions and reactions. This is especially the case with the Battle of Dieppe (cf. Dupérier, pp. 157-166, Mouchotte, Chapter XVI).

the R.A.F., was published unobtrusively in 1946. An important book on our subject, *La Vieille Equipe* ('the old gang') includes those who arrived in England first and threw themselves into the battle with their R.A.F. comrades in the old Hurricanes: de Scitivaux, Mouchotte, Fayolle, de Labouchère, Bouquillard, Choron, Guérin, Hauchemaille, Waillier, Bourgeois and others, all killed in action except Naval Lieutenant de Scitivaux, leading spirit and first commander of the 'Ile-de-France' Squadron, whom Captain Dupérier succeeded when his comrade in arms fell wounded into the hands of the enemy.

Let us hope that one day a larger edition of this sober, simply-written book, quick with the memory of the dead, will complete the history of the 'Ile-de-France' Squadron; the author of *La Vieille Equipe* closes his story with its 100th sortie over the French coast in November 1942. Commandant Dupérier returned to the battle in 1943 after duty in the United States; Mouchotte took him into his unit at Biggin Hill; he drew up the report on his friend's disappearance and momentarily took command of the squadron the latter had made so famous. He made some notes for his own use on the night of August 27th, 1943, which he gave me, at my request, and which the reader will find below.

He knew Mouchotte only by name when the latter landed with 615 Squadron at Manston Aerodrome to replace 242 Squadron, in which there were four Frenchmen: de Scitivaux, Dupérier, de Labouchère and Mouchotte's friend Fayolle, who had followed his example in escaping from Oran. They were so overjoyed to meet again in the same unit that they decided to stay together. Dupérier confesses, in spite of the fact that he was due for a rest, that he 'intrigued fiercely' to continue the fight with 615, the Churchill Squadron, in which Mouchotte had none but friends. Here, from his notes, is Dupérier's sensitive portrait of him on October 11th, 1942:

'Lieutenant René Mouchotte, fairly tall, slender and dark, with imperturbable calm in his pale face. He is already a veteran of the R.A.F. and was a pilot in the Army Air Force Reserve when war was declared. Mouchotte certainly represents an element of stability and solidity, with a marvellous knowledge of fighter work. He has an experience of the R.A.F. which is priceless to us. Extreme kindness and a heart of gold have won him our English friends' profound esteem.'

The same ideal, the same will to conquer, the same faith in the ultimate defeat of the enemy, inspired the authors of *La Vieille Equipe* and of *Le Grand Cirque*, but the former had already served in 1939 and was matured by experience when he escaped from France in 1941. Clostermann was nineteen when he came to London from distant Brazil, where the example and the friendship of Colonel Valin, whom he knew there, showed him the way.

His destiny led him to Scotland in the winter of 1943 to the unit Mouchotte intended should be first of the French and even of the R.A.F. units. He was won over at once. Let us listen to what he says in *Le Grand Cirque*, a shattering book to anyone who has ever practised the terrible duel in which the destruction of a machine and often the life of a man are the stake. Of course, one sees its faults, but they are immediately forgotten as one is swept away by the passion of a violently stark narrative, laconic with humour and youthful fierceness, full of boldness and fear, massacre and blood!

What enchanted him as soon as he met Mouchotte was to feel the impetus of a leader whose intention was at all costs to make his squadron 'a redoubtable combat formation. The planes were incessantly in the air,' he says jubilantly, 'shooting, combat formation, dog-fight exercises, scramble practice. The British were so amazed at how fast the unit got into shape' that they moved 'Alsace' to Biggin Hill, 'an honour which we did not perhaps entirely realize at the time; Biggin Hill, south of London, was the base with the highest number of victories to its credit and was reserved for the most select squadrons of the R.A.F.' 'Alsace' was already an exceptional unit to the British. Clostermann, too, sketches a rough portrait, a pendant to Dupérier's: 'Commandant Mouchotte was to be in command, a tall, dark, slim man with piercing eyes and a curt voice that snapped and admitted of no argument but was followed by a warming, friendly smile. The kind of man for whom you get yourself killed without discussion, almost with pleasure.'

Clostermann's baptism of fire took place in Mouchotte's slipstream. In the chapter in which he sings his joy in his 'first victories' (two planes shot down during one of the Biggin Hill Wing's sorties when nine were shot down), he admires the calm and mastery of his leader directing the operation and who, says the young pilot, was very sporting in giving his number two a plane which it was said they had really shot down together.

The number two is the pilot who flies wing to wing with his leader. Mouchotte singled out Clostermann for this honour on the operation of August 27th from which he was not to return. Was *Le Grand Cirque* going to give the key to the disappearance which so grieved everyone at Biggin Hill in that late summer of 1943? The shock was all the greater because no one could explain Mouchotte's end, not even his number two, who lost sight of his leader and went after a Focke-Wulf, which he finally shot down. Under the heading, 'Commandant Mouchotte Fails to Return', he explains his actions in the engagement and all he could see of an exceptionally fierce encounter. This testimony is published below.

This chapter is completed by a moving evocation by General Valin and a B.B.C. talk by Colonel Corniglion-Molinier, of the London Headquarters, whom Mouchotte instructed on Spitfires. It is yet another portrait: 'You have already heard of the commanding officer. He is famous, terribly likeable and *French one hundred per cent!*' I had hoped for some personal recollections from Commandant de Scitivaux and from Lady Sinclair, wife of the energetic Air Minister during London's great resistance, Sir Archibald Sinclair. The lady who will always be the admired godmother of the French pilots will not hold it against me if I reproduce a few lines from the exquisite and moving letter she was kind enough to write to me: 'René! what an extraordinary person he was! Our house was open to him and he came when he liked (not as often as we should have wished). With him came the sensitivity that so distinguished him from others! A heroic fighting flame which was all his own was burning him up. And how good he was! I have never seen such filial affection. His death was a great sorrow to us and I am profoundly glad that his body has been recovered and rests today among his own people.'

I will not add to that. Yes, one last thing. On that evening of August 27th, 1943, when night had fallen, the grief-stricken commanders at Biggin Hill – English aces, friends of Mouchotte, and Fighter Command staff-officers who had hurried from London, were in conversation. A French witness has reported their words.

'The French have indeed lost their best pilot,' said one.

'And the Royal Air Force its best friend,' added another. Yes, he was French one hundred per cent!

In concluding these editorial remarks, I should like to repeat my gratitude to all those who have helped me to pay homage to René Mouchotte: his surviving comrades (few, alas!) of the Free French Air Forces, the Royal Air Force, the Burgomaster of Middelkerke, among others. I regretfully had to give up the idea, on account of lack of space, of reproducing certain documents and illustrations, notably of some great English pilots lost in action – Group Captain Appleton, killed on D Day, and others who were dear to their comrade of 615 and 65 Squadrons; he would have liked to see them side by side with the heroes who fell in the combats of 'Ile-de-France' and 'Alsace'.

A.D.

Appendix II

The Award Citations of Commandant René Mouchotte DFC, CdeG

June 25th, 1941

Excellent fighter pilot. Volunteer for all operations. Has, in past months, taken part in more than seventy engagements or convoy escorts.

His moral qualities and professional worth have led to his being appointed Leader of Patrol. Recognized by his senior officers and his comrades as one of the best pilots of his squadron.

September 2nd, 1941

Fighter pilot. Has served in a squadron since November 1940. Full of keenness and audacity. An excellent leader, with the best aggressive spirit. On August 26th, 1941, shot down a Ju. 88.

November 17th, 1941

Excellent fighter pilot who made the qualities of the French pilot felt during his service with the Royal Air Force. He has successfully attacked numerous enemy targets during the summer campaign against enemy shipping.

September 1st, 1942. Distinguished Flying Cross

Capitaine (F/Lt.) René Mouchotte (FAFL 30661) No. 340 (Fighting French) Squadron.

Flight Lieutenant Mouchotte has been engaged on operational flying since September 1940 and has participated in 230 sorties. During these operations, which have included high-altitude sweeps, attacks against enemy shipping and ground targets, Flight Lieutenant Mouchotte has destroyed one enemy aircraft and damaged two others. In addition he has damaged ten enemy vessels, one of which he set on fire. He has displayed great determination and has pressed home his attacks.

THE AWARD CITATIONS

May 8th, 1943

The *Croix de la Libération* is awarded to Commandant René Mouchotte, who is admitted Compagnon de la Libération.

General de Gaulle

June 18th, 1943

A remarkable commander of a fighter squadron, in which he has inspired the highest spirit of duty and keenness.

On May 15th, 1943, shot down an F.W. 190, thus inscribing the 1,000th victory on the roll of the wing to which this squadron belongs.

On May 17th, 1943, shot down an Me. 109F over France.

July 31st, 1943. Citation in French Army of the Air Orders of the 'Alsace' Squadron

In action since April 1943 in Great Britain, on offensive operations in close co-operation with the R.A.F. and U.S.A.F., under the command of Commandant Mouchotte, the 'Alsace' Squadron, with its Flights 'Strasbourg' and 'Mulhouse', commanded by Captains Martel and Boudier, has rapidly proved itself an exceptional unit.

Has won the confidence and admiration of Allied flyers by the courage and mastery its pilots have shown during its eighty sweeps or offensive operations, representing a total of 850 flying missions and 1,650 hours in the air.

In four months has recorded eleven official victories in ten combats, shooting down ten Focke-Wulf 190s and one Messerschmitt 109, and damaging three Focke-Wulf 190s. Distinguished itself particularly over France on July 27th by shooting down five Focke-Wulf 190s and putting several more out of action without itself suffering loss, thus carrying out with absolute success the task of giving aerial cover to an Allied bombing operation which had been entrusted to it.

October 1943. Croix de la Légion d'Honneur and last citation

Commandant René Mouchotte, Commander of the 'Alsace' Squadron: a senior officer of great value, having successively commanded a flight of the 'Ile-de-France' Squadron, 65 Squadron of the R.A.F. and the 'Alsace' Squadron.

Has always, by his heroic conduct, set the finest example to the units he commanded. A magnificent trainer of men, with a perfect sense of discipline and a high conception of duty, he has rapidly made his squadron an incomparable instrument of victory and a model for all the Allied air forces.

Has personally taken part in more than 331 operations, totalling 1,743 flying hours, 408 of which were on offensive missions.

Has to his credit four official and three probable victories, ten ships set on fire or damaged.

Appendix III

The Combat Reports of Commandant René Mouchotte DFC, CdeG

After every successful engagement, the pilot concerned would make out a written report to the Intelligence Officer, who would then use this information to produce, when appropriate. A wider report describing the overall action as experienced by the collective formation.

These reports are now preserved at The National Archives and are available online to download as digital files. Naturally these are a vitally important primary source to historians today in interpreting and reconstructing these aerial battles.

The following are the personal combat reports of Commandant Mouchotte.

16.16 hours, 26 August 1941, whilst flying Hurricanes with 'B' Flight of 615 Squadron at RAF Valley, in North Wales, forty miles north of Pembroke Dock:

> I was Blue 1 ... and ordered to patrol base at 20,000 feet. At 1554 hrs, I was told to patrol Bardsey Island. Ten minutes later was ordered to buster (author's note: to make all haste) and I climbed to 13,000 feet. Shortly afterwards I was told a bandit was approaching at 7,000 feet from the south-east. We were vectored 230° and told bandit flying west. My Blue 2, Sergeant Hamilton, sighted the bandit flying north-west at about 11,000 feet.
>
> We went into line astern and into an up-sun position and then, after a 180 turn right, I went into a steep vertical dive onto the E/A. I opened fire at about 150 yards range, closing to 50 yards, when I had to pull away quickly, to avoid ramming the E/A. I did not definitely see my burst hitting the target, but I was so close that I am confident my bullets went home.

> The E/A turned to port and dived into cloud 1,000 feet below.
> I followed him down but was unable to see him again. We
> were given several other vectors but did not regain contact.
> I then returned to base.

The 'E/A' (Enemy Aircraft) on this occasion was a Ju 88, and undoubtedly a reconnaissance bomber which was credited as 'damaged'.

The next recorded combat success came whilst commanding 341 Squadron and flying Spitfires with the Biggin Hill Wing, at 17.11 hours on 15 May 1943, ten miles south of Caen:

> I was leading 342 FF Squadron, flying due west about ten miles
> south-east of Caen at 23,000 feet, when Control reported some
> Boche immediately below us. The Wing Commander ordered
> 611 Squadron, who were below us, to dive and asked me if
> I could see anything. I replied that I could not and continued
> on the same course for about two minutes, then turning hard to
> starboard with the intention of bouncing any Boche who might
> have been split up by 611 Squadron's attack.
>
> On seeing nothing, I completed the turn onto my original
> course and saw a lone Hun flying level on a westerly course
> about 4,000 feet below. I dived sharply and started firing at 300
> yards, from dead astern and slightly above, continuing firing
> in the dive up to 250 yards, seeing strikes on the cockpit and
> wing roots. At this point the Hun suddenly climbed vertically
> and blew up in mid-air, forcing me to climb rapidly to avoid
> the debris which was flying in all directions. Nothing else
> being seen, I reformed with the Wing and proceeded home.
> From this engagement I claim oneFW190 destroyed.

On this day, JG2 lost three Fw 190s to the Biggin Hill Wing, one to Commandant Mouchotte, and two to Squadron Leader Jack Charles DFC, commanding 611 Squadron. The two pilots jointly shared Biggin Hill's 1,000th aerial victory.

At 10.48 hours on 17 May 1943, Commandant Mouchotte was in action again, ten miles north of Caen:

> I was leading 341 Squadron and had just crossed the French
> coast at Cabourg at 23,000 feet, and was about half-way from

the coast to Caen aerodrome, when an FW190 dived on us from slightly astern, passing just in front of me. I fired a short burst, but without any results as I must have used too much deflection. Shortly afterwards I saw four Me 109s in line astern coming from the south-east, who fired on my Yellow Section, slightly below me; immediately I dived on the leader, ignoring the others who were by now at a disadvantage in relation to my Yellow Section, and he broke away in a dive, turning to port.

I followed and fired from 200 yards dead astern, closing to 100 yards. Here he throttled back, still turning; repeating the same tactics I closed to within 50 yards, still firing, when he took no more evasive action, but dived sharply, crashing into the ground without any trace of smoke or flame. Having followed him down to 1,000 feet, I turned back and re-crossed the coast at Houlgate at treetop height.

This Me 109 was credited as destroyed. The next combat success came on at 11.50 hours on 19 August 1943, over Amiens:

I was leading Blue Section and flying at 18,000 feet, coming back about five minutes after the bombers had bombed the target, when we found some activity below about mid-way between Amiens and Abbeville, and the Wing Leader decided to orbit. During the orbit, I saw a few E/A diving on some Spitfires at about 8,000 feet below and I decided to go down and give them some help.

I then found myself engaged in a dogfight against 25 – 30 E/A, both FW190s and Me 109s. In the dive, a FW190, coming from the left and climbing, made a head-on attack on me and I opened fire from 150 yards to point blank and the E/A had to break below to avoid collision. I was unable to break because my speed was about 400 mph indicated. I saw many cannon shells bursting all over the E/A before losing sight of it underneath the nose of my aircraft. I was unable to observe further results at the time owing to the presence of other E/A, one of which I attacked without result.

My No 2, however, who saw the attack, states that the E/A broke away downwards with an increasing amount of black smoke pouring from it.

After I broke off my second attack, I also saw the FW190 still going down vertically with a lot of black smoke pouring out.

This Fw 190 was credited as damaged. Three days later, at 15.15 hours on 22 August 1943, Commandant Mouchotte scored again, whilst leading 341 Squadron on Ramrod 251, a fighter sweep over Douai:

I was flying as Red 1, leading the Squadron in a dive on twenty-five Me 109s, Blue Section being slightly in front. Part of the enemy formation dived away into cloud, the others turned to face our attack, one Me 109, coming from the left, in front of me about 350 yards away. I fired a very short burst using full deflection and saw two bright bursts, one on the engine, the other on the cockpit. The E/A passed away and disappeared into cloud.

This was credited as damaged. It was the gallant French squadron commander's last combat claim.

Commandant Mouchotte's final combat record stood at two enemy aircraft destroyed, and three damaged.

Appendix IV

RAF Biggin Hill's 1,000th Aerial Victory

by Dilip Sarkar MBE, FRHistS

RAF Biggin Hill, to the south-east of London, was amongst the all-important Sector Stations sited in a defensive ring around the capital, and remains amongst the service's most famous of fighter stations. When the first wing leaders were appointed in the spring of 1941, to command formations of three Spitfire squadrons based at sector stations and collectively known as a 'Wing', Wing Commander Adolph Gysbert 'Sailor' Malan DSO DFC was appointed to Biggin Hill. Malan, a South African, was already a legend in the RAF, having led 74 'Tiger' Squadron with great distinction throughout the Dunkirk and Battle of Britain period. Indeed, few men understood air-fighting and tactics better than he, and so Biggin Hill got the best.

That year, Fighter Command went on the offensive, taking the war across the Channel took the Germans by day. In what was a relentless period of operations, Malan led the Biggin Hill Wing on most operations, and the famous Station's tally of enemy aircraft claimed as destroyed mounted rapidly. By July 1941, however, by which time he was Fighter Command's top-scoring fighter pilot and a household name, Malan was exhausted and rested from operations, going into training for a period of time – before returning to Biggin Hill, on promotion to group captain, as Station Commander on 1 January 1943.

By that year, the air war over north-west Europe had seen significant changes, in particular the appearance on the scene of the US Eighth Air Force, which, the very month 'Sailor' took over Biggin Hill, bombed a target in Germany itself for the first time. The previous year, the new German FW190 fighter had seen off the Spitfire V, until introduction of the Spitfire Mk IX, with which Biggin Hill's squadrons were now equipped, redressed the balance. By day, however, operations continued much the same as they had since early summer 1941, with plentiful bomber escort sorties supplemented by fighter sweeps and nuisance raids. It was an exciting time – because Biggin Hill was fast approaching a landmark: its 1,000th aerial victory…

By 4 May 1943, the score stood at 994, on which day the Wing Leader, Wing Commander Al Deere DSO DFC, led the Biggin Hill Wing escorting B-17 Flying Fortresses bombing Antwerp, personally destroying a 190 and increasing the tally to 995. Under his command were two Spitfire squadrons: 341, commanded by Commandant René Mouchotte, and 611, by Squadron Leader Jack Charles DFC.

To the public, fighter pilots were glamourous knights of the air, whose exploits were widely propagandised and keenly followed. Deere later remembered that with the 1,000th victory approaching, the pressure was on, consequently, with the press 'continuously on our doorstep'. Poor weather, however, was decelerating progress, and ten days later the number was the same. On that day, the Biggin Hill Wing escorted Fortresses bombing Courtrai. En route, according to the 341 Squadron Operations Record Book (ORB), the Wing was 'busily engaged with several Hun formations'. After the Americans had accurately bombed the target, 341, however, was heavily attacked and scattered. Bounced by four Fw 190s, Capitaine Christian Martell shot one down in flames – which was the Free French Squadron's first victory. Over the target, the CO of 611 Squadron, Squadron Leader Jack Charles DFC, destroyed another 190, whilst Sergeant E. Clark of the same unit collided with the Me 109G of 9/JG26's Leutnant Paul Schauder, both pilots baling out. With the score at 998 and the weather now set fair, excitement was at fever-pitch.

According to 341 Squadron's ORB, 15 May 1943 dawned 'an exceptionally fine day with good visibility'. Circus 297 was to be flown, six B-25 Mitchells being briefed to attack the JG2 fighter airfield at Caen-Carpiquet, which would then be pounded by Typhoons; Poix airfield was also to be attacked by Boston bombers. Such an aggressive operation, it was hoped, would provoke a violent reaction from the German fighters, providing an opportunity to advance Biggin Hill's score.

The following was reported by 341 Squadron:

> Twelve Spitfire IX led by Commandant Mouchotte took off at 1621 hrs as a free-lance wing with the object of bouncing Huns, which might be aroused by the bombing of the airfield at Caen. The Squadron crossed the French coast at Trouville.
>
> When about ten miles SE of Caen, 611 Squadron was mixed up in a general dogfight 2,000 feet below. Commandant Mouchotte led 341 Squadron still on a westerly course ready to bounce any stragglers which may have been split up by 611

Squadron fighting below. He had the good luck to bounce a lone FW190, which after a long burst dead-astern, slightly above, exploded in mid-air.

In the dogfight below, 611 Squadron's boss, Squadron Leader Jack Charles, shot down two FW190s, bringing Biggin Hill's tally to 999, Commandant Mouchotte's Hun being the 1,000th. As there is some doubt as to the exact moment of destruction of the CO's FW190, the honour may be shared with 611 Squadron. This is for the Station Commander, Biggin Hill, to decide.

The actual pilots' personal combat reports, however, possibly tell a slightly different story. Commandant Mouchotte, for example, stated that his combat had occurred at 17.11 hours:

> I was leading 342 FF Squadron, flying due west about ten miles south-east of Caen at 23,000 feet, when Control reported some Boche immediately below us. The Wing Commander ordered 611 Squadron, who were below us, to dive and asked me if I could see anything. I replied that I could not and continued on the same course for about two minutes, then turning hard to starboard with the intention of bouncing any Boche who might have been split up by 611 Squadron's attack.
>
> On seeing nothing, I completed the turn onto my original course and saw a lone Hun flying level on a westerly course about 4,000 feet below. I dived sharply and started firing at 300 yards, from dead astern and slightly above, continuing firing in the dive up to 250 yards, seeing strikes on the cockpit and wing roots.
>
> At this point the Hun suddenly climbed vertically and blew up in mid-air, forcing me to climb rapidly to avoid the debris which was flying in all directions. Nothing else being seen, I reformed with the Wing and proceeded home. From this engagement I claim one FW190 destroyed.

If the stated time was correct, Commandant Mouchotte's victory was actually Biggin Hill's 998th.

Both of Squadron Leader Charles's victories were officially timed at 17.15 hours, ten miles south-east of Caen:

I was leading Yellow Section of 611 Squadron. I saw two FW190s at 3 o'clock, starting to dive on the bombers. I crossed over to them, approaching from directly underneath. I opened fire on the second E/A (4-sec. burst) at 250 yards, closing to 50 yards. Bits came off the wings. A strike went the length of the fuselage on the right-hand side. The underneath of the E/A went on fire. I continued overtaking and crossed to 180 yards (5-secs.). ¾ ring deflection. There were strikes on the wings and then an explosion around the cockpit. The E/A slewed to the right and went diving down. I broke left and saw a parachute over where the first combat took place. This is confirmed by Flight Lieutenant Checketts (Yellow 3), who saw the pilot of the first E/A bale out, and the second aircraft dive straight in.

Again, if the time of Squadron Leader Charles's report is correct, his successes represented Biggin Hill's 999th and 1,000th kills. The official word, however, does not always tell the whole, or even an accurate story. In his diary, Commandant Mouchotte recorded how the combats occurred virtually simultaneously, which was evident from radio transmissions and confirmation by Control. Clearly, therefore, things were, as usual, confused between actual events and written records.

According to Wing Commander Al Deere, back at Biggin Hill, in the debrief René Mouchotte 'chivalrously claimed he had seen Jack Charles' two victims go down before his own – which is borne out by the combat report timings – but Charles, a Canadian, generously refused to accept this and insisted that the honour and prize should be shared'.

Group Captain Malan agreed to the honour being shared by the two squadron commanders. As Deere also wrote:

It was a proud moment in the history of all concerned. While Sailor would undoubtedly have dearly loved to have scored the 1,000th victory, there was some solace: he won the £300 sweepstake! The press soon arrived in droves, journalists, cameramen and radio broadcasters all demanding interviews, while letters to the two conquering heroes, requesting signed photographs, arrived in their hundreds.

By coincidence, 341 'Alsace' Squadron had already arranged a party that night at the Hyde Park Hotel, to celebrate their first victory. The occasion now became a somewhat extended affair.

Wing Commander Deere requested that the Biggin Hill Wing be stood down from operations the following day, given that the party was likely to be a 'late affair'. Although this proved impossible, Deere was assured that his Wing would only be used as a 'last resort'.

The party was a great success, but at 10.30 hours next day Deere was leading his Spitfires to Portreath, from where they escorted Venturas bombing Morlaix airfield. The exhausted pilots returned to Biggin Hill late that evening, fortunately having encountered no enemy opposition – with the official celebration of the 1,000th kill yet to come.

The official party was arranged for Wednesday, 9 June 1943. That day, Simon Wardell reported in the *Daily Express*:

> Some of the brightest stars of Fighter Command will gather in London tonight to celebrate the triumph of the Biggin Hill Sector in shooting down 1,000 German planes.
>
> They and their womenfolk will assemble in the Great Room of Grosvenor House, Park Lane, W1, and dancing will go on till 3 am.
>
> At least 1,000 guests are expected on the invitation of Group Captain "Sailor" Malan and the officers of the Sector.
>
> Squadron Leader Charles and "Commandant René [author's note: Mouchotte's identity was concealed, to protect his family still in occupied France], who shared in the destruction of the 1,000[th] plane, will be there. So will Charles's squadron commander [author's note: incorrect: should be Wing Leader], the great New Zealand fighter Alan Deere, who recently added a DSO to his decorations.
>
> At the top table will sit Air Marshals Sir Arthur Harris and Sir Trafford Leigh-Mallory, leaders of Bomber and Fighter Commands.
>
> For days, the preparations have gone on like this: At Biggin Hill. In the messes there and at the other airfields of the Sector – their names are still on the secret list – fighter pilots have talked between sorties of the girls they will bring. Batmen have been getting out their officers' smartest uniforms, polishing buttons until they shone like gold.

At Grosvenor House. A stream of officers and men were hurrying to and fro last night. "It's been more like an air force station than a banqueting office for the last day or two," commented the banqueting manager, Mr A.T. Abbot.

In front of the gallery along one wall of the ballroom, with its silver-sprayed columns and cream distemper – it used to be a skating rink – eleven of the Biggin Hill ground staff were putting up a full-scale model of a Spitfire in flight, measuring 36 feet 10 inches from wing-tip to wing-tip.

It had been brought from Woking's "Wings for Victory Week"; on Thursday it will go on to Richmond. Behind it will be draped light blue ensigns of the RAF, and the Spitfire will seem to be banking out of a cloud as the limelight from the gallery opposite plays on it.

And on the top table will be placed a perfect miniature model of the Spitfire Mark Nine, with its four-bladed airscrew and cannons – just like the plane that destroyed the 1,000[th] raider.

Tonight, the snacks will be provided by the officers, for the hotel management said they would find it impossible to cater for such a huge gathering. They will find the drinks, however.

"I suggested 50 bottles of whisky," said the banqueting manager, "But it appears they want much more than that. The band will be a special RAF band, provided by the officers. The cost of the party will be less than £1 per head".

The ball is fixed to begin at nine – although they doubt whether it will get into full swing before 10 – to allow pilots who have been out on daylight sorties to get to London in time.

The cabaret is to be provided by Vivian Van Damm, who says he is keeping something up his sleeve. And to round off the evening a showpiece measuring sixteen feet across and painted by a Biggin Hill squadron leader will be unveiled.

"The paint is still wet, so you can't see it," the artist told me. "It embodies the names of all our squadrons, and of the wing commanders of Biggin Hill – Jamie Rankin, Dickie Milne and other great pilots. A 'V'-sign and the RAF badge are included in the design. And grouped on either side of the main piece will be four plaques symbolic of the four other sector stations."

But the night-fighters will miss the party. The thousand kills the RAF are celebrating include many shot down by night-fighter squadrons, and their pilots cannot, of course, attend the ball.

Perhaps, as the daylight aces dance below, they will be winging over the Home Counties after the raiders and intruders that sneak across the coast under cover of darkness.

As Basil Cardew reported in the following morning's *Daily Express*, Malan's 'Wizard war-time party' was actually 'a double celebration':

Only a few hours before, his tall, dark-haired wife, Lynda, had a baby daughter in a county hospital in Kent. She is the second Malan child, for Jonathan, their son, is now three years old.

I found Malan celebrating with Hughie "Taffy" Edwards, lanky VC bomber pilot, in a secluded room away from the dancing crowd. "Lynda wanted a girl to complete the family," said Malan. "Both are doing well. So this is the greatest night of my life."

Two RAF bands played throughout the six-hour celebration, and there was a cabaret.

There was an exuberant Wing Commander Al Deere, the cauliflower-eared New Zealand boxer who now leads the Wing at Biggin Hill; broken-nosed Jamie Rankin, who started the station's sweeps against the enemy in 1941; Barkley [author's note: this is incorrect but refers to Tony Bartley] and Sheen, two grand Battle of Britain leaders, and scores of other men who battled against the Luftwaffe.

Squadron Leader Jack Childs [author's note: this is also incorrect and actually refers to Jack Charles] sent a message of good cheer from his bed, where he is recovering from bronchitis. But the French pilot, Commandant René, the other victor, had brought along a dozen more Fighting French fliers in their blue uniforms and gold braid. René's family live in German-dominated Brest, so his other name must be suppressed.

Sergeant-pilots as well as officers had been invited. Many of the fliers who brought their womenfolk had scarcely had time to shed their flying kit and tumble into Sunday uniforms. Several pilots I talked with had been out on patrol in the afternoon, skirmishing with the Luftwaffe.

They held the dance and party in the Great Room of Grosvenor House, Park Lane, W1, and one of the bands that played swing music and languid tunes in sudden contrast had played to the men during the Battle of Britain.

I have heard and seen them playing at the Biggin Hill Mess at lunchtime, while pilots scrambled a quick meal, in those days of 1940 when Hitler was sending 1,000 planes against us.

At almost every table these young fighter pilots of Britain re-lived again their battles in the sky …

On the same day, the *Daily Sketch* also covered the story under the headline 'Air Aces Hold "1,000-V" Party', although this report somewhat conflicted with the *Daily Express* by stating that Jack Charles was not present:

Biggin Hill, Britain's leading Fighter Command station, last night celebrated the shooting down of their 1,000th plane with the biggest wartime party London has seen for four years.

Group Captain "Sailor" Malan DSO DFC, Commanding Officer at Biggin Hill, sent out 1,000 invitations but far more than 1,000 people came. The smartest air force uniforms of the Allies and most glamorous evening frocks in Mayfair stormed the sturdy RAF guard of 20 strong, and all got past.

Sailor Malan went through the evening with a broad grin on his face. "I have a new daughter," he told me. "She was born today at 1 o'clock. That makes the thing perfect. I already have a boy, aged 3, called Jonathan Winston, Mr Churchill is his godfather."

With him were Squadron Leader Charles and Commandant "René", who shared in the destruction of the 1,000th plane.

And while the day pilot aces danced the night away, the night-fighter squadrons of Great Britain kept their faithful vigil in the skies.

At the party's conclusion, the London cabbies of the Beaufort Club insisted on getting the pilots and their guests home for no charge.

The achievement, whosoever was actually responsible for it, was a significant one in the history of this most famous of fighter stations, and the name of 'Commandant René' will, rightly, forever be associated with that day's hectic action.

Appendix V

Radio Broadcasts Relating to Commandant René Mouchotte DFC, CdeG

'Les Français parlent aux Français', B.B.C., London, July 29th, 1943. By Colonel Corniglion-Molinier (extract):

The day before yesterday, all the aircraft of the 'Alsace' fighter squadron returned safely to their base after officially shooting down five Focke-Wulfs and probably four more. The French commander of the fighter squadron, Commandant René, was wing leader, which means he commanded all the aircraft, French and Allied. When the wing was over Normandy, the commander was warned by Flying Control that there were several dozen Focke-Wulfs near Trouville, on their way to attack a Spitfire squadron. He immediately did what was necessary to position his aircraft with the sun behind them and get them up to a higher altitude than the Boche. The manoeuvre succeeded perfectly and I have told you the final result. You will hear the pilots speak for themselves. Here is some information about them.

The Commandant you have often heard about already. He is famous, it was he who obtained the 1,000th victory of his base a few weeks ago. He is young, thin, wiry, terribly likeable and extraordinarily calm and cool, especially for a Frenchman, for French he is, one hundred per cent.

Allow me to say a few words of a personal nature. It was he who acted as my instructor. Yes, instructor to an old pilot of the 1914-18 War and of the years between the wars! But when I had the happiness of finding myself in the free sky over England, before returning to that of my own country, I wanted to pilot that modern mechanical marvel the Spitfire – a marvel so different from our kites that I had to ask Mouchotte to be my instructor.

And when I say he acted as my instructor, I really ought to say as my mother-hen, if I were not afraid of vexing him. It was with him I made a first patrol, with him I learned to practise all the astonishing and difficult tricks of such a complex aircraft. Commandant René was always good-

225

tempered, never irritated, a wonderful example of our race. The day before yesterday, in the battle I mentioned to you, he almost certainly shot down a plane. No one else doubted it, but he did not claim the victory for himself and gave the credit to one of his pilots.

Address given from the Poste National de la Radiodiffusion française in 1946, by Pierre Clostermann (extract):

I first met Commandant Mouchotte at Turnhouse Aerodrome in Scotland in February 1943. He was to be my commanding officer for nine months with the 'Alsace' Squadron.

An ascetic face, dark, phlegmatic, terribly young, but with a commander's authority in his eyes. He was a Parisian.

He had a quite special and innate ability to handle masses of fighter aircraft. I have seen him commanding two squadrons, ten flights, during offensive operations over France, with a brio that earned him the unbounded admiration of the most senior R.A.F. officers.

One of the few survivors of the French Army Air Force, who fought side by side with the R.A.F. in the Battle of Britain, Commandant Mouchotte revived one's pride in being French.

The most famous fighter wing of all the Allied forces, at that time the one at Biggin Hill, was entrusted to him; it comprised a French squadron – 'Alsace' – and a British one.

Without taking the slightest rest, refusing himself leave, flying on a record number of operations, Commandant Mouchotte fought for over three years. Only a spirit with the temper of steel kept him up, but his body failed him. Constant flying at 11,000 and 12,000 metres, as men did then without pressurized planes, was enough to break down the strongest constitution. By August 1943, Commandant Mouchotte – who had just shot down, among others, the 1,000th Boche for Biggin Hill – was no more than a frail envelope sustained by a sublime will to fight.

On August 27th, 'Alsace' took off to escort a powerful formation of Flying Fortresses to bomb Saint-Omer.

Barely half an hour later, we were intercepted by about 200 Focke-Wulf 190s. There was a fierce fight – one against ten. Our squadron was soon scattered amongst a whirlwind of black crosses. I was the Commandant's number two that day, but my engine cut out at the beginning of the fight for several agonizing and vital seconds and we were separated, I was never to see him again.

Appendix VI

The Last Flight of Commandant René Mouchotte DFC, CdeG

by Dilip Sarkar MBE, FRHistS

The story starts, perhaps surprisingly, on 5 November 1939, when a particular parcel was delivered to the British Embassy in Oslo, Norway. Inside was a sensor being developed for use in a new electrical fuse for both shells and bombs – and a seven-page typed report providing detailed information on secret technical research and the development of new, frightening, weapons by Germany.

This package, which became known as the 'Oslo Report', included information on the far-sighted pilotless missiles and rockets being developed at Peenemünde, on the Baltic island of Usedom. The first of these was the V-1, 9,521 of which would, from 13 June 1944, ultimately be hurled at Britain, killing some 6,184 people and injuring 17,981. Unfortunately, British Intelligence largely regarded the information as either unreliable or a deliberate deception by the Germans, and little heed was taken of it.

British scientist Professor R.V. Jones, however, appreciated that the report had been written by someone possessed of great technical and scientific knowledge, and after the war discovered that the report had been compiled and delivered by one Dr Hans Ferdinand Mayer, a mathematician, physicist and Director of the Siemens Research Laboratory. In 1943, in fact, Mayer was arrested by the Gestapo for speaking out against the Nazi regime; he was saved from execution by high-placed friends and survived the war.

By 1943, though, the research and testing at Peenemünde had made much progress – which had Mayer's 'Oslo Report' been acted upon, may not have been the case. As things stood, another new and terrible weapon was soon to lift-off over the Baltic: the *Vergeltungswaffe* 2, or 'Vengeance Weapon 2'. Better-known as the V-2, this fearsome rocket was the world's first long-range guided ballistic missile, intended to pulverise British cities in retaliation for the Allied strategic bombing offensive. The V-2, capable of achieving supersonic speed, became the first man-made object to reach

227

space (on 20 June 1944). It was considered by Hitler to be a *Wunderwaffe* ('Wonder Weapon') – which, potentially, it certainly was.

Although the British intelligence service, MI-6, had largely discounted the 'Oslo Report' in 1939, Dr Mayer had actually clearly signposted the fact that German scientists were exploring and developing some highly advanced weapons, including the pilotless missiles. Between May 1942 and May 1943, however, Allied aerial photographic reconnaissance identified significant activity, which was not yet understood, at Peenemünde. At the same time, the construction of large concrete sites in north-west France was noted, but, although suspected to be in some way connected with Germany's secret weapons, the grave danger involved had still yet to be fully appreciated. Concern, however, was heightened in Britain when reliable information was received from an Austrian resistance group to the effect that this enemy activity revolved around the V-1 and V-2, this information being corroborated by RAF aerial photographic reconnaissance sorties.

Perhaps ironically, though, the first V-2 target was destroyed by chance when, in June 1943, Bomber Command Lancasters targeted and successfully hit the German radar factory in Friedrichshafen's Zeppelin Works – which, unbeknown to the Allies, also accommodated a V-2 production line. Now, convinced of the reality of the V-2, the War Cabinet's Defence Committee (Operations) ordered Operation *Hydra*, a concentrated attack on the Peenemünde site by Bomber Command on the night of 17/18 August 1943.

That night, under the control for the first time of a 'Master Bomber', Group Captain John Searby, 596 Lancaster, Halifax and Stirling 'heavies' pounded the target. The 560 aircraft which found it, dropped 1,800 bombs on three aiming points that had been marked by Pathfinders' flares: the scientists' and workers' living quarters, the research station and rocket factory. Some 180 Germans were killed, along with, sadly, 500-600 foreign forced-labourers, mostly Polish.

Nonetheless, the raid, which cost Bomber Command forty aircraft, was a great success, possibly decelerating the V-2 programme by as much as two months, and, some say, diluted the scale of the eventual V-2 attacks on the UK.

This, though, was just the start. Allied intelligence services were now taking a keen interest in anything remotely suspected of connection to the enemy's 'V' weapons – and, considering the huge constructions works required to build a V-2 launching and storage base, information was constantly being received from the continent.

THE LAST FLIGHT OF RENÉ MOUCHOTTE

In December 1942, Hitler had impressed upon his Minister of Munitions, Albert Speer, a personal preference for permanent, rather than mobile, launching sites, although both methods would actually be used in practice. The BIII-2b bunker was, at the time, and possibly even now, like something from a sci-fi story: a huge concrete bunker with a roof-top rocket launch-pad, whilst the alternative 2a design saw the V-2 transported to an adjacent pad for lift-off. Speer ordered Organisation *Todt*, the Nazi engineering organisation responsible for numerous civil and military projects, to build two V-2 bunkers in north-west France, one near Cherbourg, the other in the Pas-de-Calais. These were imposing structures indeed, and our story concerns the bunker built at Watten, in the Pas-de-Calais' heavily wooded Fôret d'Éperlecques.

The Blockhaus d'Éperlecques, concealed under the ruse of being a powerplant, was built by many thousands of prisoners of war and slave workers between March 1943 and July 1944. Even bigger than the original BIII-2a design, on which the bunker was based, it was well-sited, near the Calais-St Omer railway line, close to local quarries needed to supply materials, and sufficiently inland to be safe from naval bombardment. Most importantly, it was near the infamous aerodrome at St Omer, home to elements of JG26, and the whole area was a hive of German fighter activity. The great bunker's walls were up to seven metres thick, and the working area was six metres underground. Able to store 108 V-2s, it was intended to launch thirty-six rockets at Britain per day – a devastating barrage indeed.

It was impossible, though, to conceal such a huge construction project. By April 1943, British intelligence was receiving reports from agents in France and RAF photographic reconnaissance images of major excavations at the Watten site, although the purpose was still unclear. Other sites were identified in France, but the Watten bunker was most advanced. As a result, the War Cabinet committee responsible for responding to the V-weapon threat, recommended, on 6 August 1943, that the location should be attacked without delay.

The Air Staff was not convinced, however, that the massive bunker was necessarily a V-2 site, suggesting that it could be a special operations building. Nonetheless, advice was sought from Sir Robert McAlpine, Chairman of the well-known construction company, who advised an attack imminently, before the concrete had set. Previous experience in attacking the great German concrete U-Boat bunkers in Brittany certainly proved how robust such buildings were to air attack, and, although Watten's purpose remained unclear, as Lord Cherwell, Churchill's scientific advisor, remarked: 'If it is worth the enemy's while to go to all the trouble building them, it would seem worth ours to destroy them.'

So it was, then, that Operation *Crossbow* began in August 1943, with attacks directed at the Watten and Mimoyecques bunkers. Although still unsure of the bunkers' actual purpose, it was obviously sinister, and the first Operation *Crossbow* mission, directed against Watten, was an important one – those involved would have realised just how very much so had they been aware of the destruction soon to be wrought by the deadly V-2.

By this time, the Allied air offensive included the USAAF's Eighth Air Force, which had been created for the express purpose of flying unescorted daylight precision bombing missions at high altitude, whilst RAF Bomber Command waged war against German cities and factories at night. Huge though the Watten bunker was, it was a comparatively small target from a bombing perspective – requiring an attack by day.

Consequently, the job of flattening the Watten 'Heavy Crossbow' target, on 27 August 1943, was given to the Americans. The resulting plan involved two elements: first, 159 B-17 Flying Fortress 'heavies' from the 91st, 92nd, 303rd, 305th, 306th, 351st, 379th, 381st and 384th Bomb Groups, and second, sixty-five more B-17s from the 94th, 95th, 96th, 100th, 385th, 388th, and 390th. These 224 bombers were split into four waves, spaced so far apart, in line astern, that the whole formation would take over an hour to pass over and attack the target.

The planners hoped that the German fighters based in the Pas-de-Calais would be scrambled by *Jagdfliegerführer* 2 ('*Jafü* 2': Fighter Leader, *Luftflotten* (Air Fleet) 2), in whose area of responsibility the target lay, and exhaust themselves against the first wave, after which they would have to retire and re-arm. That process, it was perceived, would continue until the fourth and final wave arrived, which was also the earliest German reinforcements would be likely to appear on the scene from *Jafü* 3. The bombers were to be escorted by 173 long-range American P-47 Thunderbolt fighters, from the 'Mighty Eighth's' 4th, 56th, 78th and 353rd Fighter Groups, and twenty-three RAF Spitfire squadrons – including those of the Biggin Hill Wing, on this occasion led by Commandant René Mouchotte.

From the spring of 1941 onwards, Fighter Command had been reorganised with each sector station accommodating three Spitfire squadrons in a formation known as a Wing. Overall operational command of these new Wings was the responsibility of the Wing Leader, or more formally the Wing Commander (Flying), an equally new post. According to Air Vice-Marshal Johnnie Johnson, the RAF's official top-scoring fighter pilot in the Second World War, the position was 'every fighter pilots dream, because the job concerned the fighting efficiency of the wing in the air, not administration'.

In August 1943, the 'Wingco' at Biggin Hill was the New Zealand 'ace', Wing Commander Al Deere DSO, DFC, while the Station itself was under the overall command of the legendary South African, Group Captain Adolph Gysbert 'Sailor' Malan DSO, DFC. By this stage of the war, Wings were often reduced to pairs of squadrons, so as to be more tactically flexible, and up and coming squadron commanders identified as potential future Wing Leaders were given the opportunity to lead Wings on occasion, so as to increase experience. No.341 Squadron, which had been formed by Commandant Mouchotte in January 1943, shared Biggin Hill with 485 (New Zealand) Squadron. The latter was commanded by the distinguished 'Kiwi' Squadron Leader Johnny Checketts DFC, who already had nine German fighters destroyed, two probables and six damaged to his credit, but had only been a squadron commander for a month. Commandant Mouchotte, therefore, was the more senior of the two Biggin Hill squadron leaders, and in Wing Commander Deere's absence, was to lead the Wing, comprising 341 and 485 Squadrons, on the Watten raid on 27 August 1943.

Detailed to fly as Commandant Mouchotte's wingman that day was Sergeant Pierre Clostermann, who had made his first combat claim, a damaged Me 109, on 17 June 1943, following this up with two Fw 190s destroyed on 27 July 1943. Nonetheless, Clostermann remained a comparatively inexperienced, new, pilot at the time and, in order to increase the experience of such newcomers, they were often chosen to fly as No.2 to their flight or squadron commanders, whom they could learn from. Of this particular operation, Clostermann would later recall the following:

> It was close that day ... Commandant Mouchotte was beginning to strap himself in. For the first time since I had known him he had put on his uniform tunic over his white pullover. I heard (Lieutenant) Pabiot remark on it as he passed. "Oh!" answered Mouchotte with a laugh, "You never know. I want to look my best when I make my bow".
>
> Six o'clock less two minutes I saw his emaciated figure slip into the cockpit and, before putting on his helmet and oxygen mask, he did a thumbs up and smiled his irresistible, friendly and encouraging smile at me.

Whether or not Commandant Mouchotte had any kind of premonition of death, we will never know, but, even so, he still found the time and energy to encourage his wingman at what was a crucial time – pre-take-off, when nerves were stretched.

At 18.04 hours that evening, Commandant Mouchotte took-off from Biggin Hill in Spitfire Mk IX, MH417, NL-L, leading twelve other Spitfires of 341 Squadron, and eleven of 485, on what was officially Ramrod 8. So secret, in fact, was the target, that the 341 Squadron's Operations Record Book (ORB) recorded it simply as 'a target four miles north of the marshalling yards at St Omer'. The Biggin Hill Wing was detailed to cover the withdrawal of the first wave (box) of sixty B-17s, 'and come to the assistance of the other boxes if required'. This was, for sure, a complex operation involving many aircraft.

Across the Channel, however, the Germans were alerted to the fact that a major operation was brewing, given the volume of radio tests their listening devices had picked up. That this was occurring during the evening indicated a short-range penetration, and Oberst Vieck, commanding Jafü 2, from his operations room at St Pol, rapidly concluded that the target would be somewhere in the Pas-de-Calais. Consequently, at 19.08 hours, Vieck scrambled all three gruppen (each the equivalent of a three squadron-strong Wing) of the locally based JG26. Then, at 19.22 hours, he requested assistance from the Cherbourg-based Jafü 3, which sent I/JG2 up immediately from Beamont and Evreux, whilst the JG26 Geschwadergruppe (Group staff Wing) and II/JG2 struck north-east from Poix and Vitry respectively. Thus, the scene was set for a sharp encounter between the fighters of both sides.

Commandant Mouchotte led the Biggin Hill Wing on a 'slow climb', according to the 341 Squadron ORB. Crossing the Kentish coast over Dungeness, the Spitfire pilots could see the bombers, so the Biggin Hill Wing's Final Intelligence Report on the operation tells us, 'a long way ahead'.

Commandant Mouchotte increased speed, crossing the French coast at 18.26 hours over Berck-sur-Mer at 15,000 feet, with 485 Squadron to port, and 341 on the formation's starboard side. The latter's ORB records that the Biggin Hill Spitfires then climbed to 20,000 feet, 'and made contact with the bombers ten miles to the south, positioning themselves slightly above on the starboard side. The Squadron flew with the bombers to a point five miles north-west of St Pol, where the whole formation turned to port on a direct course for the target.'

Battle, however, had already been joined. Elements of JG26 and II/JG2 were the first German fighters to appear, but they failed to penetrate the escort and reach the bombers. Hauptmann Ebersberger, Staffelkapitän of 8/JG26, claimed a Spitfire destroyed over Arras, but two of his Me 109 pilots were shot down in the clash with Spitfires and baled out; 11/JG26 also lost a fighter with its pilot safe.

Then, II/JG26's Fw 190s, described in the Biggin Hill Wing's Intelligence Report as numbering 'forty-eighty', pounced on the Biggin Hill Wing, out of the sun, from the rear, and halfway between St Pol and St Omer. Commandant Mouchotte turned the Spitfires to meet the attack head-on, after which the confusion of battle, typical given the numbers of aircraft involved, dictated that it was virtually every man for himself. Having executed their usual high-speed diving ambush, the 190 pilots continued attacking mainly from below and astern before breaking downwards, climbing and attacking again. This combat continued until five miles from Mardyck, and for some fifteen to seventeen exhausting minutes.

The Biggin Hill Wing Intelligence Report continues: 'Both squadrons were heavily engaged, and many pilots, including Commandant Mouchotte, found themselves alone.'

This was not an untypical scenario. Once battle was joined, formations split up, and it was often every man for himself, fighting independently, isolated. In theory, the wingman should stay with his leader, but in practice this was far from always possible.

As the Spitfires were first attacked, the comparatively inexperienced Sergeant Clostermann followed his leader, Commandant Mouchotte, into the tightest of vertical turns, opening his throttle wide open; the former had, however, turned too tightly:

> The engine cut for one precious second and I hung there, with my nose in the air, while the first Huns began to flash like thunderbolts between our sections. My engine picked up, with a terrific jerk, but too late; I had lost contact with my section, which I could see 100 yards further up, climbing in a spiral. Couldn't be helped.

The Biggin Hill Wing Intelligence Report states:

> Sergeant Clostermann (Red 2) and Aspirant Buiron (Red 3), 341 Squadron, both attacked FW190s which were firing at

Spitfires below. The former opened fire from dead astern at 250 yards but the enemy aircraft (E/A) was drawing away from him. Strikes were seen on the port wing and fuselage. When about 800 yards away, the E/A turned upside down, emitting smoke.

It continued thus in a shallow dive until crashing in flames near a small wood. The latter attacked a FW190 from the starboard quarter and hit it in the fuselage and in front of the cockpit. The E/A tightened his turn and went into a spin. Asp. Buiron did not follow, but climbed and re-joined the others, who had remained above with the bombers.

During this combat, Clostermann had descended to just 1,000 feet, the battle still raging many thousands of feet above him.

Wisely, out of ammunition, the Frenchman, by now east of the Forêt d'Éperlecques, set course for home. A 'few seconds later', he 'heard, for the last time, Commandant Mouchotte calling'. That final radio transmission, at 18.48 hours, was, simply, 'I am alone with the bombers'.

As Clostermann later wrote, 'What a hell of a fight for a wing leader – particularly the Biggin Hill Wing Leader – to find himself isolated!' But there nothing to be done, and things continued 'going badly' for Clostermann, who managed to join up with Captain Martell's Yellow Section, which was soon attacked by 190s in a running battle across the Channel, beyond Calais.

The context, however, of Commandant's final radio transmission needs understanding. The Biggin Hill Wing's job was to provide close escort to the sixty Flying Fortresses. The German fighters, however, had successfully pounced on and driven off the escorting Spitfires, only Commandant Mouchotte managing to remain with his charges.

With the enemy fighters having engaged and occupied the escorting Spitfires, Commandant Mouchotte knew full-well that the now virtually unprotected bombers were in grave danger, as other German fighters now had a clear run at attacking them. The nature of such aerial fighter combat is very much a case of formations being broken up and the first few seconds or minutes being every man for himself. So violent was the evasive action that was often involved that it was impossible for a wingman to remain with his leader; in this case, Sergeant Clostermann, in his comparative inexperience, had turned too tightly, causing his engine to cut-out, losing speed and power and in that second, the battle, and Commandant Mouchotte, moved on, rapidly. In the confusion, Clostermann, typically, found himself fighting his own battle for survival.

Unfortunately, whilst his own pilots were heavily engaged with the enemy fighters, Commandant Mouchotte's urgent appeal for assistance, according to the Biggin Hill Wing Intelligence Report, went unheeded: 'Our aircraft were greatly outnumbered and *no assistance was received from the (Spitfire) squadrons or (American) Thunderbolts above*'.

Why the top cover Allied fighters did not descend to protect the bombers we will never know, but clearly the B-17s and Commandant Mouchotte were now extremely vulnerable. The Biggin Hill Wing Intelligence Report continues:

> Blue Section 341 Squadron were engaged with about eight FW190s and in the dogfights that ensued, Captain Boudier attacked one of the E/A. After firing three short bursts without result, he came in nearly dead astern. He saw strikes on the port wing and the port undercarriage leg dropped. The E/A then went into a spin and was seen to crash to the ground. Sous-Lieutenant Laurent (Blue 3) fired two short bursts at another FW190 from about 150 yards, and saw cannon strikes on the port wing before it flicked over and dived away. He then attacked another FW190 which was firing at a Spitfire. He fired two bursts from astern, above, at close range, hitting the engine and fuselage. The E/A started to burn and went down in a spin. The pilot, however, had to break away, as he was attacked by four more FW190s and did not see the end of his victim.
>
> 485 Squadron, meantime, had gone below the bombers in an endeavour to prevent the E/A from penetrating. This was, however, almost impossible owing to the large numbers of E/A operating and the fact that they closed to such short range. It was found more advantageous to attack the E/A as they broke away. In the course of carrying out these tactics, Pilot Officer Houlton chased a FW190 in a hectic dive right down to ground-level, and after a lengthy steeple-chase round woods and over an aerodrome, the E/A, in a sudden turn, hit some overhead cables and crashed, exploding and bursting into flames as it hit the ground.
>
> Most of the engagements took place between 12,000 and 7,000 feet'
>
> One of the Fortresses was hit by flak, which was intense and accurate over the target. The crew were seen to bale out.

Oberleutnant Walter Matoni of 5/JG26 also shot down a B-17 of the 351st Bomb Group.

After the action, the Biggin Hill Wing's Spitfires landed back at Manston, Squadron Leader Checketts escorting a damaged B-17, running on only two engines, to put down safely at the same coastal aerodrome. A head count, however, revealed that 341 Squadron had two pilots missing.

Flight Sergeant P. Magrot had last been seen over France being pursued by a Fw 190. As we now know from German records, he was shot down and killed over Merville by Feldwebel Mayer of 6/JG26.

Also missing was Commandant Mouchotte, who, as time ticked inexorably on, was clearly lost. The gallant Frenchman had been shot down just off the French coast, according to American historian Don Caldwell by Leutnant Radener, the Staffelkapitän of 6/JG26.

Indeed, for Pierre Clostermann, this 'was a tragic blow and the world no longer seemed the same … Commandant Mouchotte, Croix de Guerre, Compagnon de la Libération, DFC … For us he had been the pattern of a leader, just, tolerant, bold and calm in battle, the finest type of Frenchman, inspiring respect whatever the circumstances.'

On 3 September 1943, the body of an Allied airman was washed ashore near the Hotel Bellevue at Westend-Plage (Middlekerke) on the Belgian coast. The remains were buried as unidentified in Middlekerke Cemetery, although a tailor's note found in a uniform pocket recorded the name René Mouchotte.

In April 1949, however, the Air Ministry's Casualty Branch concluded that this airman was, in fact, Commandant René Mouchotte, who had not been lost over land, near the target, but actually over the sea, his body being washed up a few days later. Six months later, Commandant Mouchotte's body was exhumed and interred, on 3 November 1949, with full military honours, in his family's vault in Père-Lachaise, Paris. So it was that this hero of France was brought home, at last.

As for the attack on the Watten Bunker on 27 August 1943, it was a complete success: the appended railway station was badly damaged, and the bunker, which was only 35% complete, left a smouldering heap of smashed concrete and fittings. Once the concrete set, repair was impossible, and, so, Watten was abandoned as a V-2 launching site. Unfortunately, and inevitably, hundreds of prisoners of war and slave workers were killed at the site – exactly how many will never be known. This, in fairness, was because although the Allies had timed the attack to coincide with a shift changeover, the Germans changed their timetable unexpectedly and many workers were, therefore, on site. This was, nonetheless, a good start to Operation *Crossbow*, although a long road lay ahead: until all V-1 and V-2 launching sites were ultimately overrun by March 1945, 10,000 V-1s and 1,400 V-2s were launched, causing thousands of deaths.

It is fitting that instead of having been lost on a relatively pointless nuisance raid, as so many RAF fighter pilots were, Commandant René Mouchotte lost his life on what was a vitally important operation. That said, perhaps if heed had been taken of the Oslo Report in 1939, this and many other lives could have been saved.

Official Report of Commandant René Mouchotte as Missing

COMMANDANT MOUCHOTTE, René Gaston Octave Jean
Missing, believed killed, after aerial combat on August 27th, 1943, in the
region of Saint-Omer

Commandant Dupérier to the Commanding General of the Free French
Air Staff in London*

I have the honour to inform you that Commandant Mouchotte and Sergent-Chef Magrot are missing after aerial combat.

On August 27th at 1802 hours, Commandant Mouchotte took off at the head of the wing, comprising two squadrons, one of which was 341, 'Alsace'.

Engaged between Saint-Omer and the coast by an enemy much superior in numbers, the Allied fighters had to stand up to some very fierce fighting. Commandant Mouchotte found himself isolated from the rest of the squadron and the last information of his position is a message at 1848 hours, to the effect that he was to starboard of the bombers he was charged to protect.

---

* Bernard Dupérier was born in Paris, as Baron Bernard de Armella, on 13 June 1909. He joined the Armée de l'Air in 1927; 'Duperier' was his mother's maiden name, which he adopted as his 'nom-de-guerre' in 1941.

　　Dupérier would succeed Commandant Mouchotte in command of 341 'Alsace' Squadron after the latter's death in action, survive the war as an ace with five enemy aircraft destroyed and two shared destroyed, a probable, three and one shared damaged.

　　Bernard Dupérier OBE, DFC, CdeG, Ld'H became a highly accomplished post-war aviator. He passed away in 1995.

　　These notes were written by Dupérier on that fateful day on which Commandant Mouchotte was lost, 27 August 1944.

OFFICIAL REPORT OF COMMANDANT

Sergent-Chef Magrot was seen by Sous-Lieutenant Laurent when he had been fired on and shot down by an F.W. 190 in the region of Saint-Omer.

To set against these infinitely heavy losses, 341 Squadron has recorded to its credit in the same engagement:

2 F.W. 190s destroyed.
1 F.W. 190 probably destroyed.
2 F.W. 190s damaged.

Commandant Dupérier
Commanding 341 Squadron ('Alsace')

Biggin Hill, August 28th, 1943

Appendix VIII

The Finding of René Mouchotte's Body

(*March 10th, 1949*)

The French and British Air Ministries and the U.S. Air Force have each set up specialist services to find the bodies of their flyers killed in action in operational zones. Let us pay homage to the devotion and zeal of the people employed on these sad quests, some of which have been particularly moving, unknown to the general public.

René Mouchotte's fame both in the R.A.F. and the French Air Forces made them put his name among the first on their lists for enquiry and must be said that the British authorities, who held Mouchotte in such high esteem, sought his remains as tenaciously as if he had been one of their own great aces..

Thus, in the spring of 1949, they were able to inform us that the body of an unknown flyer, found on September 3rd, 1943, on the beach at Middelkerke in Belgium, with four gold rings on his sleeve, seemed to them to be that of Mouchotte. It was a surprise and a joy. The two documents I publish below, a letter from the Air Ministry and the Belgian evidence of burial, are worth brief study if only to confirm this finally established fact.

The search on the French side, practically given up, had been wrongly directed from a single piece of data: the crash in the Saint-Omer region, more precisely, between Saint-Omer and the coast. The official report, rendered by the 'Alsace' Squadron the day after he was missing, conveyed this impression and it was generally shared by the survivors of the terrible combat of August 27th, 1943.[1]

The hero's mother and the present writer believed in the crash in the sea (my Introduction to the French edition reflects this feeling). We relied on

---

1. Sergent Magrot, one of his pilots, who fell in the course of the same engagement, was shot down at Merville, in the Dunkerque district, where his body was found.

various deductions but above all upon a premonition: Madame Mouchotte, in a fearful nightmare, saw her son struggling in the waves, swimming, calling for help, sinking and disappearing. The sea kept the body. But it was not so. A week later the current washed it towards the coast and entrusted it to friendly soil.

Thanks are due to the Middelkerke authorities who took cognizance of this in a precise and detailed report. But for that, no later identification would have been possible. But to be congratulated above all is Flight Lieutenant R.N. Archer, R.A.F., in liaison with the Imperial War Graves Commission at Arras, who passed from research to deduction and picked up the trail which led to Middelkerke. Knowing the bonds of friendship between Mouchotte and his family and myself, Flight Lieutenant Archer brought me the file on his researches and let me know his results. I immediately agreed with his opinion and the enquiries I undertook at Middelkerke, before the body was taken to Paris, enabled me to check the exactitude of what he said. Thanks once more to him for his hard work and his persistence. The official report disclosed everything to him: the unknown man in Grave 87 was Mouchotte.

The characteristics in this report are enlightening. Height, girth, hair and age are his. Even the clothes, which supply additional proof – and what proof! If, on account of some premonition, which at least two witnesses have remembered, he had not taken off that morning at the head of the Biggin Hill fighters in his French uniform ('I want to look my best when I make my bow', he said then, smiling, when he got into his plane) his name would not have been discovered.

Reflections on some of the details in the official report

It does not mention either his French pilot's identity disc made of gilt metal (which he took off, for reasons of caution, as we shall see) or his decorations, the ribbons of which he wore. There are also missing items of the 'odd paraphernalia' which, he says, bulged out his pockets each time he went up. He writes at length on this in a valuable entry in the diary for October 21st, 1941. Though some English money was found on him, no reference is made to a certain 'escape-envelope' carried by all pilots. In case of a landing in enemy territory, it might help him to escape more easily and usually contained 20,000 French francs, 5,000 Belgian francs and 1,000 florins. He was also burdened with concentrated food, chemical products, excellent little maps on silk, a compass, etc.

241

It is almost certain that the body washed up on the shore was searched and these articles were stolen by the Germans. The same with his fur-lined boots, which regulations obliged him to wear over his long woollen stockings; he is described as being shoeless, unless the sea pulled them off, as often happens when a body is in the water for long, or, being still conscious after the crash, he threw them away to lighten himself and swim. The last hypothesis adds to our grief. We return to the mother's nightmare. Did he make use of the little dinghy, the pneumatic raft which was within pilots' grasp? Could it have sunk without being seen by the searching motor-launches? But was there a search? Night fell soon afterwards. Two new hypotheses: either he baled out, wounded or not, or he was flung clear of his plane, which sank after ditching. As a result of combat? Or of engine trouble?

The body was intact. No wound is mentioned in the report. A very important point. Is it certain, though? The authorities at Middelkerke, whom I questioned again this year (1955), answered, 'The body was discovered by German sentries; they informed the Kommandantur, who advised the municipality. The Germans waited for the latter's representatives before approaching the body. After a superficial examination, the body was taken to the town morgue. There it was stripped and thoroughly examined. No wound or trace of a wound on the body or the uniform. The witnesses to the finding of the body on the shore are still alive and the report was drawn up from information supplied by the Town Clerk, who was present at the examination of the body. The Germans who were present at the identification on the shore stole the propelling pencil and wrist-watch.' (This was signed by the Burgomaster on August 30th, 1949).

A last, very important point: the question of the identity discs. The valuable note of October 21st, 1941, enlightens us once more. Throughout, the diaries tell us of his haunting preoccupation: his name must remain unknown, must not be disclosed over the radio or in official papers. His first name alone must suffice. Why? Not for himself, Heaven knows. Solely for the woman he loved with such unique filial affection. He alternated between remorse for having abandoned her and fear that the Occupying Power might avenge itself on his mother for his belonging to the Free French Forces.

He disclosed his system in 1942. Then leader of an English squadron, he wore the word 'Canada' on his tunic. He humorously agreed that his accent forbade him to pass as one born in the United Kingdom but, at least, he said, this label allowed him to take off 'light-heartedly as a citizen of Toronto'. He adored Canadians, and when he was commander of a French squadron and had to wear our uniform, it seems he would not have hesitated to borrow the identity card and discs of a Royal Canadian Air Force pilot who had gone home in 1942 and was, like himself, a Roman Catholic. This stratagem would have allowed him to dupe anyone who took him prisoner. The diaries do not say why the name 'Martin' was chosen. No Canadian flyer of that name has been found, but 'L.C. Thompson' is not a fiction. The mystery, it seems, may be easier to solve than that of the fatal crash. Commandant 'René' substituted for the name of the pilot Thompson, who had been demobilized, whose number he had borrowed, that of Martin, a very common name in French Canada, the better to deceive the enemy. Regulations compelled pilots to carry nothing that could give the least information to the enemy. They therefore carefully emptied their pockets before going up. Mouchotte would have been astonished indeed to know that he had not emptied his altogether and that his old adjutant's tunic bore his name in full. A lucky omission, but for which he would not rest in French soil today.[2]

---

2. René Mouchotte's body was repatriated in October 1949 and buried in his family vault in Père-Lachaise, Paris, on November 3rd, after a military ceremony of much grandeur organized by the Air Ministry at the Invalides. His name was cited during another official ceremony in the little town of Saint-Mandé, in the suburbs of Paris, where he was born in 1914. Classes of young officers and of students have been allowed to be baptized by the name of 'Commandant Mouchotte'. Readers of The *Diaries* number some hundreds of thousands.

The charming seaside resort of Middelkerke in Belgium, where the soldier's body was washed up on the beach after falling from the sky, has made him a freeman of the town. It preserves his memory with touching continuity. An avenue is to be called after him, and on April 17th, 1955, when a day of commemoration was organized for the tenth anniversary of his death, an original little monument was unveiled at the beach Casino.

Appendix IX

Death Certificate
Middlekerke Town Hall, Belgium

(*September 3rd, 1943*)

Body washed up on the beach September 3rd, 1943, just before noon, near the Hotel Bellevue, Westende-Plage (Middelkerke).

Surname and Christian name on identity disc attached to safety-belt:

	R. Martin, C.15.561, R.C.A.F. Officer. R.C.
Probably	Air Force Officer.
Girth	Normal.
Height	1m. 80cm.
Age	About 30 years.
Hair	Dark chestnut (no grey hairs).
Teeth	Complete. 1 left molar in lower jaw filled with gold; 2 molars in upper jaw, ditto.
Clothing	Safety-belt.
	Dark blue tunic and slacks.
	White woollen pullover, beneath it blue woollen pullover.
	Light blue shirt with collar attached and black tie.
	Blue woollen stockings (to the knee).
	No shoes or boots.
Objects found on body	Double identity disc, one red and the other green.
	Four rings of gold on the sleeves. Gold shoulder bars.
	Usual R.A.F. wings above left breast pocket.
	White handkerchief.
	Brown leather belt with ordinary fastening.

MIDDLEKERKE TOWN HALL, BELGIUM

> Two safety pouches in safety-belt.
> Wrist-watch, with compass, stopped
>   3.9, Fri., 8hr. 17min.
> Mica pouch, with various contents.
>   Propelling pencil, four colours.
> A round red lighter, gold-striped.
> 1 threepenny piece, 1 pound note.
> Numbers marked on clothing: Slacks,
>   8.6593 – 2P2 F –; Stockings, H 346;
>   Tunic, M. 658.2.

In an inner pocket there was a label with the tailor's name and, written in ink, hard to decipher: *'Adjt. René Mouchotte'*.

Appendix X

The Identification of Commandant Mouchotte's Body

A long correspondence was exchanged between the Air Ministry, the French Air Ministry and the French Air Attaché in London from 1945 to 1949. This is the key letter of the file:

Air Ministry   *April 6th, 1949*

> Our Casualty Branch have now been able to identify the unknown in question as Commander R. Mouchotte. The solution of this problem is due to the enterprise of the Royal Air Force Liaison Officer, Imperial War Graves Commission, Arras, France.
>
> For a long period this officer has been trying to find Commander Mouchotte, even going to the extent of writing to every local newspaper in the north of France and sifting the hundred or more replies.
>
> Recently whilst investigating some outstanding Low Countries' cases he came across a report on the unknown "René Martin" buried in Grave 87, Middelkerke. He called at the Mairie at Middelkerke and was permitted to see the original "Actes de Deces". He examined that referring to Grave 87 and found that the name René Mouchotte had been noted on a tailor's label inside the tunic when the Belgians had exhumed the body during the war.
>
> 'There seems to be no doubt that Commander Mouchotte lies in Grave 87 at Middelkerke and the Imperial War Graves Commission have been asked to register the grave in his name.'
>
> A prior identification of Grave I. 141 in the Carré Allié at Longuenesse-sur-mer proved incorrect, the American Graves

Registration Command having established that the body was that of an American.

The name René Martin could be Commandant Mouchotte's alias, otherwise it is inexplicable. The identity number C 15561 belongs to Pilot Officer L.C. Thompson of the Royal Canadian Air Force, repatriated to Canada in 1942.

It seems clear, from the evidence now before us, that Commandant Mouchotte fell into the sea, not near the objective, in the vicinity of Saint-Omer, and that his body drifted towards the Belgian coast, where it was discovered on September 3rd, 1943.

Appendix XI

In the Margin of a Report

by Commandant Bernard Dupérier

I have just spent a painful hour trying to draw up a report on today's operation over France ... I had just returned to Biggin Hill after a day at Headquarters. Night was falling. The familiar scene of the narrow road reacted with the hour to tell over a whole chaplet of memories set to the monotonous rhythm of flights and combats.

War, like a subtle poison penetrating us through every living fibre, has numbed both body and spirit. Death and fire have lost their constant effect on us, being only associated now with our flying. The rhythm of our losses, though, is still the same. But the cruel game, to be played again each day, had given the veterans a sense of invulnerability. It was always 'the other' who got shot down. And when the companion of so many memories and fights does not come back one day, astonishment competes with grief. The little phalanx nevertheless diminished incessantly and three years' operations had seen the end of nearly all those who had wanted to keep the French cockade high in battle in the sky in June 1940.

There were still two of us at Biggin Hill; I had René Mouchotte there with me, one of the very first of the Free French, who had been my companion in 615 Squadron in 1941. Together then we patrolled the grey immensity of the North Sea and daily faced the inferno let loose by the German guns. Later we trained our juniors to form the 'Ile-de-France' Squadron and led it together to its first battle. Together still we went through Dieppe; a thousand details, a thousand memories henceforth bound us together. How could I not feel some presentiment of the terrible news awaiting me when I came back to the aerodrome? Boudier, Martel and de Saxcé were watching for me and on their downcast faces I read the whole tragedy at once.

Mouchotte was missing. Mouchotte the wise, great, skilful, calm pilot, had not come back. Separated from the companions whom he had in vain sought to rally in the hostile, cold immensity of the twilight sky, alone in the sky of France, he had met the soldier's death. A death he surely looked in the face with that severe, penetrating look he had at serious moments, the pugnacious mouth tautened a little, teeth gritted, lips compressed.

But René Mouchotte, dying for his country, left her in dying the best part of himself. His spirit remained behind and those he trained will make the German pay dearly for his victory. Few men have made themselves loved as he was by the pilots whose fate he held daily in his hands. His loss, tonight, made tears glisten in fighting men's eyes.

Biggin Hill, August 27th, 1943

Appendix XII

A Homage to Commandant René Mouchotte DFC, CdeG
ON HIS RETURN TO FRENCH SOIL
by General Valin,
Former Chief of Staff of the Free French Air Forces,
Inspector General of the French Army Air Force.

The last note of music has just died away in the courtyard of the Air Ministry. The flag has taken its place in the niche where it awaits another parade. The traditional ceremony in honour of Guynemer is over. Once again, the Army Air Force, faithful to his memory, has listened reverently to the magnificent citation of the great ace of the 1914-18 War.

While the words were being measured out, 'legendary hero, lost in the open sky of glory', I thought of those who during the dark days nevertheless maintained the tradition. I visualized them on just such a morning, on the burning sand of the desert, in Libya or the Sahara, amid the luxuriant vegetation of the Equator, or among the birches which alone break the vast monotony of the plain of White Russia.

But above all I recalled a corner of traditional England; set in an old park were buildings to which the Virginia creeper had given the air of some ancient seigneurial domain, rising from an airfield so green that it looked like a golf course. Biggin Hill, a famous war-time aerodrome from 1940 to 1944.

There are Spitfires drawn up there. The 'Alsace' Squadron is on parade and before these few fighting men their leader, as admired by them as he is loved, a tall, handsome, dark young man, is reading Guynemer's citation as the sun begins to pierce the morning mist. It is Mouchotte, one of the best fighter pilots of the Free French Air Forces, who won his aerodrome's 1,000th victory in collaboration with one of his Canadian (it was even a French Canadian) comrades. He had been credited with only four planes shot down. That was because he had spent many months from 1940 until the beginning of 1942 in carrying out the thankless duty of keeping watch over the sea. There were few opportunities in this to meet enemy planes. Attacks on flak ships were part of this mission, extremely dangerous operations which did not, however, prevent him from destroying a good dozen of them.

But Mouchotte's real greatness lies elsewhere. It must be borne in mind that the last war was very different from the one in which our elders brought such brilliant fame to the wings of France. The commander of a wing had charge of part of an enormous machine which grew from year to year and finished by comprising hundreds of fighters, sometimes seven or eight hundred, flying at many levels in the air. And when the order of the formation was broken, transformed into a dog-fight, during the brief instants when the planes with circles mingled with their adversaries with swastikas, the commander must first think of re-grouping his unit. *Now, Mouchotte was a commander*. I was able to judge that for myself. He often came to see me at Headquarters. Nearly every week, taking advantage of his day off, he paid me a visit, either to make recommendations concerning his men or to discuss some question of organization or tactics. As I listened to him, I found myself back at the head of my squadron, a period not too remote, for I began the war at that post. We had both been struck by Kessel's book, *L'Equipage*, and I encouraged him to persist in the method of command which consists of being the commander by example rather than by badges of rank. *He excelled in this, and was certainly the squadron leader best loved by his men.*

I have, alas, seen many units whose commanders had to be replaced because they had fallen beneath the enemy's fire. Never have I seen such sadness as that which descended upon the flights of the 'Alsace' Squadron the day Mouchotte did not come back. It was desolation indeed. They were lost, all of them. Each one realized the huge loss our fighter strength had suffered. His British comrades, among whom he was the most popular of us, were themselves most moved. Never was the mess at Biggin Hill so downcast and sombre as on that night of August 27th, 1943.

We stood by the radio for several days, hoping our friends of the Resistance would send the good news from France that he was safe and sound and already on his way to the Spanish frontier. Alas, nothing came through. Like Guynemer, Mouchotte had disappeared in the open sky of glory.

Six years later, his body has just been found. There will be many of us waiting for him on the day, now at hand, when he returns to sleep his last sleep among his kinsfolk in Paris, the city of his birth, who honours herself as we do in honouring the man who escaped from Oran on June 28th, 1940, in circumstances which arouse our admiration. A magnificent example, too rarely followed. The volunteers were not many, but their ardour in battle made up for their feebleness in numbers.

On this day when flyers, thinking of Guynemer's fate, raise their spirits towards their dead, I have no hesitation in saying this: the man I knew and who had my whole friendship, Commandant 'René', who wrote his private thoughts each night (they will be a revelation to English readers, as they have been to a vast and enthusiastic French public, thanks to the devoted care of his publishers, of his mother, Madame Mouchotte, whom I respectfully salute, and of the editor of the two versions, who has done so much for his friend's memory in making it possible for these exceptional diaries by an outstanding fighter to appear in the bookshops. M. Dezarrois has been able to declare him the Guynemer of the Free French Forces, and he knew both heroes, in the quality of his spirit and the grandeur of his character) Mouchotte will remain one of the purest figures, if not the purest, among the sons of France who fell beside their heroic comrades of the Royal Air Force in those noble combats between 1940 and 1945.

Bibliography

The National Archives

AIR 27/1738   341 Squadron Operations Record Book
AIR 27/1933   485 Squadron Operations Record Book
AIR 50/132/17   Combat reports, Commandant R. Mouchotte, 15 May
                1943, 17 May 1943, 19 August 1943, and 22 August 1943
AIR 50/132/22   Biggin Hill Wing Final Intelligence Report, 27 August 1943
AIR 50/173/2   Combat report, Squadron Leader Jack Charles, 611
                Squadron, 15 May 1943
AIR 50/175/23   Combat report, Commandant R. Mouchotte, 26 August 1941

Published Sources

Bennet, G.H., *The RAF's French Foreign Legion: De Gaulle, the British and the Resurgence of French Air Power 1940-45* (Continuum International Publishing Group, London, 2011).

Caldwell, D., *The JG 26 War Diary: Volume 2, 1943-1945* (Grubb Street, London, 1998).

Clostermann, P., *The Big Show* (Chatto & Winduss, London, 1956).

Collier, B., *The Battle of the V-Weapons*, 1944 (The Elmfield Press, York, 1964).

Cooksley, P., *Flying Bomb* (Charles Scribner's Sons, New York, 1979).

Deere, Air Commodore A.C., *Nine Lives* (Hodder Paperbacks, London, 1969).

Foreman, J., *RAF Fighter Command Victory Claims of World War Two: Part Two, 1 January 1941 – 30 June 1943* (Red Kite, Walton-on-Thames, 2005).

Foxley-Norris, ACM Sir C., *A Lighter Shade of Blue: The Light-hearted Memoirs of an Air Marshal* (Ian Allen Ltd, Shepperton, 1978).

Freeman, R.A., *The Mighty Eighth: A History of the US 8th Army Air Force* (Doubledown and Company Inc, New York, 1970).

Franks, N.L.R., *RAF Fighter Command Losses of the Second World War, Volume 2, Operational Losses: Aircraft and Crews, 1942-1943* (Midland Publishing, Earl Shilton, 1998)

Kennedy, G.P., *Vengeance Weapon 2: The V-2 Guided-Missile* (Smithsonian Institute Press, Washington DC, 1983).

Middlebrook, N., and Everitt, C., *The Bomber Command War Diaries: An Operational Reference Book, 1939-1945*, revised edition, (Midland Publishing, Earl Shilton, 1996).

Overy, R.J., *The Air War 1939-45* (Europa Publications Ltd, London, 1980).

Ramsay, W., *The Blitz Then & Now: Volume 1* (Battle of Britain Prints International, London, 1987).

Ramsay, W, *The Blitz Then & Now: Volume 3* (Battle of Britain Prints International, London, 1990).

Sarkar, D., *'Sailor' Malan: Freedom Fighter* (Air World, Barnsley, 2021).

Shores, C., and Williams, C., *Aces High: A Tribute to the Most Notable Fighter Pilots of the British and Commonwealth Forces* (Grubb Street, London, 1994).

Wynn, K.G., *Men of the Battle of Britain* (Frontline Books, Barnsley, 2015).

Websites

Battle of Britain Memorial: https://www.battleofbritainmemorial.org
Battle of Britain London Monument: http://www.bbm.org.uk
Jan Leeming's documentary can be viewed on YouTube: https://youtu.be/oVNwEZ8KriM

Other Books by Dilip Sarkar

Spitfire Squadron: No 19 Squadron at War, 1939-41

The Invisible Thread: A Spitfire's Tale

Through Peril to the Stars: RAF Fighter Pilots Who Failed to Return, 1939-45

Angriff *Westland: Three Battle of Britain Air Raids Through the Looking Glass*

A Few of the Many: Air War 1939-45, A Kaleidoscope of Memories

Bader's Tangmere Spitfires: The Untold Story, 1941

Bader's Duxford Fighters: The Big Wing Controversy

Missing in Action: Resting in Peace?

Guards VC: Blitzkrieg 1940

Battle of Britain: The Photographic Kaleidoscope, Volumes I-IV

Fighter Pilot: The Photographic Kaleidoscope

Group Captain Sir Douglas Bader: An Inspiration in Photographs

Johnnie Johnson: Spitfire Top Gun, Part I

Johnnie Johnson: Spitfire Top Gun, Part II

Battle of Britain: Last Look Back

Spitfire! Courage & Sacrifice

Spitfire Voices: Heroes Remember

The Battle of Powick Bridge: Ambush a Fore-thought

Duxford 1940: A Battle of Britain Base at War

The Few: The Battle of Britain in the Words of the Pilots

Spitfire Manual 1940

The Sinking of HMS Royal Oak In the Words of the Survivors (re-print of Hearts of Oak)

The Last of the Few: Eighteen Battle of Britain Pilots Tell Their Extraordinary Stories

Hearts of Oak: The Human Tragedy of HMS Royal Oak

Spitfire Voices: Life as a Spitfire Pilot in the Words of the Veterans

How the Spitfire Won the Battle of Britain

Spitfire Ace of Aces: The True Wartime Story of Johnnie Johnson

Douglas Bader

Fighter Ace: The Extraordinary Life of Douglas Bader, Battle of Britain Hero (re-print of above)

Spitfire: The Photographic Biography

Hurricane Manual 1940

River Pike

The Final Few: The Last Surviving Pilots of the Battle of Britain Tell Their Stories

Arnhem 1944: The Human Tragedy of the Bridge Too Far

Spitfire! The Full Story of a Unique Battle of Britain Fighter Squadron

Battle of Britain 1940: The Finest Hour's Human Cost

Letters from The Few: Unique Memories of the Battle of Britain

Johnnie Johnson's 1942 Diary: The War Diary of the Spitfire Ace of Aces

Johnnie Johnson's Great Adventure: The Spitfire Ace of Ace's Last Look Back

Sailor Malan - Freedom Fighter: The Inspirational Story of a Spitfire Ace

Spitfire Ace of Aces – The Album: The Photographs of Johnnie Johnson

The Real Spitfire Pilot

The Real Hurricane Pilot

OTHER BOOKS BY DILIP SARKAR

Bader's Big Wing Controversy: Duxford 1940.

Bader's Spitfire Wing: Tangmere 1941

Spitfire Down

Forgotten Heroes of The Battle of Britain

Arise to Conquer: The Real Hurricane Pilot (introduction, commentary and photographs supplied to a new edition of Wing Commander I.R. Gleed DSO, DFC's wartime memoir).

Faces of The Few

Spitfire Faces

The Battle of Britain on the Big Screen: 'The Finest Hour' Through British Cinema